Classical Scientific Astrology

George Noonan

First Printing: 1984
Current Printing: 2005

ISBN: 0-86690-049-7
LCC Number: 83-71742

Cover Design: Jack Cipolla

Published by:
American Federation of Astrologers, Inc.
6535 South Rural Road
Tempe, Arizona 85283

Printed in the United States of America

Contents

Introduction

Today the study of astrology is scorned by most members of the academy. Beginning with the renaissance in science in the 15th century, this ancient art was relegated to the scrapheap of superstition, along with such auguries as the entrails of a chicken. So prejudiced has the attitude toward astrology become that even the authorship of such works as Ptolemy's *Tetrabiblos* have been questioned: "No astronomer would ever believe in astrology; and Ptolemy was one of the world's greatest astronomers; ergo, he could have never written a book claiming the truth of astrology." But Ptolemy was a serious practitioner of astrology. So also was Kepler and many other of the most famous scientists of the past.

During the golden age of astrology, measuring instruments were crude or non-existent. The first mechanical clocks were not invented until the 14th century, and then they had no minute hand because their accuracy did not warrant one. Mathematics beyond arithmetic and synthetic geometry was only in the developmental stage. In Ptolemy's time, for example, the identity element for addition, zero, had yet to be recognized. Even into the 15th century (and beyond) the science was that of Aristotle. To educated men the theories of Aristotle were just as relevant and viable as those of Einstein's today. But as primitive as they were, this science, measuring instruments and mathematics formed the basis not only of astrology but also of engineering, architecture and other applied arts.

In all ages man has attempted to put his scientific theories to practical use. Classical astrology was an attempt to apply the science of its day to solve questions of a most pressing nature: the future of the national economy, the outcome of a business or military venture, the quality of national leadership, and the like. These same questions are no less important today, and the full force of 20th century science is being applied to determine the answers. But although the theories of Aristotle are no longer taken seriously, the results of the classicists were no less accurate than many of the predictions being made today through the use of the most sophisticated mathematical models. Indeed, considering the data base then extant, classical astrology was at least as "scientific" as the computerized techniques of the latter decades of the 20th century.

This book is an attempt to reconstruct the astrology of the classicists, (i.e., astrology of the period 200 B.C. to A.D. 1600). No claims are made concerning the efficacy of this astrology. The reader who wishes to apply the principles outlined in this text can determine for himself the practical limits of their applicability. In any event it is hoped that the reader will gain an appreciation for what astrology really was, and how and why it was expected to work. If the misconceptions surrounding this ancient art can be laid to rest, perhaps astrology may once again take its place as a valid course of study within the academy.

The main prerequisite to reading this book is the patience to learn an archaic science. Most of the mathematics has been relegated to the Appendix. The body of the text is applied Aristotelian physics and psychology and Ptolemic astronomy. The relevant principles of these sciences are outlined in the text. However, students who wish a fuller understanding of the subject matter are urged to read the works of Aristotle and Ptolemy, especially those that are referenced in the body of this book.

Science, even an ancient science, is impossible without the tools of mathematics. Readers who wish only a description of the nature of astrology will require little or no mathematics, however. But others who may wish to apply astrology will require the mathematics normally obtained through a good secondary school education in the subject. While the mathematics actually used is elementary, a full understanding of the principles of classical astrology presupposes a mathematical sophistication normally equivalent to two years of college (mathematics through the calculus). These latter students should supplement the Appendix with W.M. Smart's *Textbook on Spherical Astronomy* or equivalent.

Readers who have a knowledge of modern astrology are likely to be confused by parts of this book. I have attempted to include the differences between modern and classical astrologies where they occur. But actually any similarity between the two is almost coincidental. Classical astrology was based on the science of its day; and its tools were mathematics and observational astronomy. It is not without reason that Ptolemy uses the terms "mathematician" and "astrologer" synonymously. Much of modern astrology is based on an occult mysticism that uses the terminology of Aristotelianism while perverting the philosopher's meanings of these terms. Most modern astrologers are also deficient in any strong foundation in astronomy and mathematics. Without such a foundation the practice of astrology soon deteriorates to a pseudo-science. Astrologers who can't tell the difference between the planet Jupiter and the star Sirius in the nighttime sky, or who demonstrate their mathematical illiteracy, have done more to confirm the ill repute of astrology than any one other factor.

Serious modern students of astrology are quite conscious of these limitations, of course. In large part it was through their encouragement that this book was written. Portions of this book have been published in various journals directed to professional astrologers. The feedback has been invaluable towards editing the text and making it more meaningful for modern astrologers. In this regard I wish to thank the memberships of the International Society for Astrological Research (ISAR) and the American Federation of Astrologers (AFA). To name all those with whom I have corresponded would fill yet another volume. But without any intent of slighting others, particular mention must be made of Ken Gillman, Charles Jayne and Ruth Oliver for their aid and encouragement in writing this book.

George Noonan
San Diego, California
1982

". . . Let the astrologers stand forth to save you, the stargazers who forecast at each new moon what would happen to you.

"Lo, they are like stubble, fire consumes them;
They cannot save themselves from the flames. . . ."

Isaiah 47:13,14

Chapter I

Historical Perspective

What Astrology Is and Is Not

From before the dawn of recorded history man has ever looked for a way to draw back the curtain that veiled the future. Today, this activity is quite specialized. The ecometrician builds mathematical models to predict the future economy of the nation and large corporations; demographers project population trends even down to the level of small neighborhoods; sociologists tell of our future mores; the operations analyst, the winner of the next world war; the meteorologist, tomorrow's weather, as well as even longer range weather prediction; and the list can go on almost indefinitely. It is left as an exercise for the student to determine the accuracy, or lack thereof, that these disciplines attain.

The first scientific attempts to predict the future were through correlating the positions of heavenly bodies with events on Earth. For example, the ancient Egyptians (c. 3300 B.C.) marked the beginning of their new year with the heliacal rising of the "Dog Star," Sirius. This rising at the summer solstice presaged the flooding of the Nile, an event of major importance for Egyptian agriculture. Due to the precession of the equinoxes, Sirius now rises about August 10; but the star is still considered to have favorable consequences for agriculture. Another example of the correlation of the positions of heavenly bodies with events on Earth is the relative positions of the Earth-Sun-Moon system and the high and low tides. We know today that the tides are caused by the varying gravitational forces on Earth that are a function of the distances of the Sun and Moon from each other and from Earth. However, whether the correlations of the positions of heavenly bodies with events on Earth have a casual relationship (as in the latter example) or are merely a coincidence (as in the case of the rising of Sirius and the flooding of the Nile), the events portended by them are equally valid. Indeed, as will be seen later in this chapter, modern Russian scholarship has uncovered some interesting relationships with the solar cycle that would have most certainly been incorporated into astrological lore had they been known.

The study of the relative positions of heavenly bodies as correlated to events on Earth is called astrology. That the use of astrology is old is attested to in the last paragraph. Just how old is indicated by the conclusions of the orientalist Jules Oppert at the beginning of this century. He asserted that the Babylonian astrologers could not have known certain astronomical facts (which as a matter of fact they did know) if they had not observed the star Sirius from the island of Zylos in the Persian Gulf on Thursday, April 29, 11542 B.C.! But to say that astrology is very ancient is not to imply that it developed full blown as we know it today. Rather the beginnings were crude, and the events predicted would be considered trivial by today's standards.

Early Beginnings

Let us go back into pre-history—back to the beginnings of civilization. Man was only a bit more sophisticated than the animals he hunted for food. He traveled in herds, following the game; and in some instances insects were a major source of his protein. When man finally learned to cultivate grain and domesticate animals for food, he settled down to become "civilized." Writers as late as the 2nd and 3rd centuries A.D. still referred to those who lived by the hunt as uncivilized savages.

Success in agriculture requires knowledge of when to plant and harvest. Very early man knew that spring followed winter, but was unable to distinguish false spring and "Indian Summer" from the real thing. To do this requires a calendar. Any calendar, even a crude one, is a comparatively sophisticated concept. The Moon served as the first instrument for the measurement of time among all ancient peoples, and the first calendar was lunar—based on successive new crescents. But such a calendar is in itself inadequate to the needs of agriculture. It is the Sun, not the Moon, that makes things grow. It is pure conjecture, of course, but observations of the stars sufficient to distinguish the beginnings of the seasons were not completed until several millennia after the inauguration of the first lunar calendar.

The correlations of the positions of the stars with the beginnings of the seasons was probably the first application of astrology. This was also the commencement of the development of the division of the ecliptic into the twelve signs of the zodiac. Just when the first divisions of the zodiac were made is uncertain. Modern scholars are divided on the subject. Some, such as Neugebauer and van der Waerden, stated that there was no zodiac at all until after 700 B.C. However, recognizable horoscopes were found in Egypt dating from the XII Dynasty (c. 2500 B.C.). In that period ivory batons engraved with astronomical signs and figures and signs of the deities of birth show that these were genethliacal horoscopes. In some of these horoscopes some of the signs of the zodiac and most of the planets can be identified, and the end of life is indicated by the head of Anubis, the jackal-god of death. Ruth Oliver, a modern astrologer who has investigated this subject, places the discovery of the solar zodiac in Mesopotamia at around 8000 B.C., with the beginning of the winter solstice (instead of the vernal equinox, as subsequently believed). While this may be a bit early, it is more or less confirmed by the traditions attributed to the Egyptian priest Manetho (3rd century B.C.) in his *Aegyptiaca*. In fragments of this document recorded by Panodorus (fl. c. A.D. 395-408) it is claimed that "εΥρηΥοροσ" ("watchers, or angels") descended to earth in the general cosmic year 1000 (probably c.

5500 B.C.), held converse with men, and taught them that the orbits of the two luminaries, being marked by the 12 signs of the zodiac, are composed of 360 parts. The modern zodiac consists of 12 signs dividing the ecliptic equally. But such a division requires the trisection of a 90-degree angle, and mathematics did not develop to the point where problems such as this could be solved until shortly before the time of Pythagoras.

Regardless of when the zodiac was finally discovered it is probable that certain correlations between the locations of heavenly bodies and events on Earth, such as the seasons and high and low tides, antedate the event by a long time. It is generally recognized that the Chaldeans were the founders of astronomy/astrology. Indeed the words Chaldean and astrologer were synonymous well into the Christian era. The Egyptians probably learned their astrology from the Chaldeans and Babylonians. However, the Egyptians contested this. Diodorus Siculus (c. A.D. 59) writes[1] ". . . and according to them, (the Egyptians), the Chaldaioi of Babylon, who were colonists from Egypt, enjoy the fame they have for their astrologia because they learned that science from the priests of Egypt. . . ."

Naive opinions to the contrary, Hindu astrology and astronomy were borrowed from her Western neighbors. Ying-Yang, or Chinese astrology, developed independently, however, although there is evidence of early (2nd century B.C.) Greek influence through contacts with India.

Tradition assigns the formation of the constellations in China to Tajao, the prime minister of Hwang Ti (c. 2637 B.C.), and makes much of an observation of the Pleiades in 2537 B.C. from an observatory said to have been erected 2608 B.C. However, the proof of the independence of Chinese astronomy/astrology from Western development is found in the names of the constellations. The Sanskrit names for the constellations are identical to their Greek counterpart. Not so the Chinese, which are entirely different. The Chinese zodiac is: Dog (Aries), Cock (Taurus), Ape

[1]Diodorus Siculus, *Library of History*, Book I.

(Gemini), Ram (Cancer), Horse (Leo), Serpent (Virgo), Dragon (Libra), Hare (Scorpio), Tiger (Sagittarius), Ox (Capricorn), Rat (Aquarius), and Boar (Pisces). In China the zodiac was known as the Yellow Way, and progressed clockwise from the Rat (i.e., in the order Rat, Ox, Tiger, etc.). When the Jesuits came to China in the 16th century, the Western zodiac was adopted, and is in use to this day.

The Japanese learned astronomy/astrology from the Chinese. The earliest extant Japanese horoscope is dated A.D. 1112, although there are references to the subject as early as A.D. 700[2]. Hindu astrology is essentially Greek with large doses of their religion. There is speculation that the Aztecs in the Western Hemisphere developed an astrology independent of the rest of the world. It is known that the Aztecs had an advanced calendar. However, their writings were all destroyed by the Spanish and just how developed their astrology or astronomy was is unknown. But it is from Greece that the world has taken its culture. Even Asiatic philosophy and science reflect the Greek influence, beginning with its first contact with it. It is therefore Greek astrology whose history we shall outline.

Greek Astrology

Before the development of the zodiac there were no horoscopes; there was only an omen technique dealing with the sky and star. These earlier omen predictions are nonetheless astrology, however. Couched in the religious symbolism that permeated all divination, these predictions were essentially judicial in character, concerning events that had a major impact on the nation or its king. Eclipses of the Sun and Moon, comets, meteor showers, and major conjunctions of such planets as Jupiter and Saturn constituted the astronomical phenomena upon which predictions were based. We also have seen that the rising and setting of bright stars, such as Sirius, were used at an early date. Star groups, or constellations or

[2]Shigeru Nakayma, *A History of Japanese Astronomy*, Harvard University Press, 1969.

asterisms, were not originally used; but it does seem likely that such constellations as the Bull and the Scorpion, easy to make out, were correlated roughly with the spring and autumn equinoxes long before the zodiac was developed.

It is now necessary to digress a bit in order to distinguish a sign of the zodiac from a constellation. The first division of the zodiac was a quartering based on the equinoxes and solstices. Originally (c. 8000 B.C.) this quartering probably occurred when Aries was at the winter solstice and Cancer was at the vernal equinox. At about 4000 B.C. Taurus was at the vernal equinox. It is certain that by this time man was able to distinguish the seasons by observing the stars. The precession of the equinoxes continually moved the seasons backward in reference to the stars. This "change" in the beginnings of the seasons must have caused a lot of problems to early man in his attempts to use the stars as a means to aid him in his daily life. Shortly after Aries began to indicate the beginning of spring, it became evident that the change in the positions of the stars relative to the seasons was a continuous and natural phenomena. At about the same time the solar-lunar calendar was developed, arithmetic had been invented, and man was able to predict the coming seasons independently of the stellar background. With this knowledge the ecliptic was divided into twelve equal parts starting at zero degrees Aries. As the precession of the equinoxes changed, the relative position of the stars with respect to the beginning of spring, these divisions remained constant. The first day of spring became known as the beginning of Aries, regardless of what was in the sky at the time. The twelve equal parts of the ecliptic referenced from the beginning of spring are called the *signs* of the zodiac.

Now many of the early correlations of stellar phenomena with events on Earth were not related to the positions of the stars at all, but to the position of the Earth in its orbit around the Sun. The changing of seasons is only the most prominent example of this. While early people generally assumed the solar system was geocentric rather than heliocentric, they well recognized the fact that much of what they wanted to know was related to the vernal equinox. This led Claudius Ptolemais (c. A.D. 150) to write[3] ". . . it is reasonable to reckon the beginnings of the signs from the equinoxes and solstices, partly because the (previous) writers make this quite clear, and particularly because from our previous demonstrations we observe that their natures, powers, and familiarities take their cause from the solistical and equinoctial starting places, and from no other source. For is other starting places are assumed, we shall either be compelled no longer to use the natures of the signs for prognostication or, if we use them, to be in error. . . ."

With the development of the signs a solar calendar could be instituted. Previously the calendar was lunar, or sol-lunar, and the year was twelve or thirteen months, depending upon the number of new crescents or new Moons between vernal equinoxes. It was the 12-month, 365-day year that brought about the beginnings of astrology as we know it today. Astrologers now began to use their art for the benefit of individuals. Instead of only predicting events of widespread importance to the nation, such as floods, famines, earthquakes, success at war, and the like, astrologers began to also predict events of importance to individuals. The length of life and the manner of death, marriage, and success in business or politics were the most frequent prognostications. Such applications of astrology were not always accepted, however. The great geographer and historian Strabo (c. A.D. 15) records[4] that in his day ". . . A settlement is put apart for the local philosophers called Chaldeans, who are chiefly devoted to the study of astronomia. Some, not approved by the rest, profess to understand genethliology or casting of nativities. . . ." Ptolemy (or C. Ptolemais), and the later Arabic astrologer al-Biruni (A.D. 973-1048), considered genethliogolical astrology of less validity than judicial. This is not at all surprising when you consider that many of the predictions made by judicial astrology are now incorporated in the sciences of astronomy, meteorology, and physics.

---

[3]Ptolemy, *Tetrabiblos*, i:22.

[4]Strabo, *Geography*, xvi.

Astrology began in Babylonia, and was used extensively in Egypt; but it was not until it fused with Greek mathematics and philosophy that astrology made decisive advances and became a viable scientific discipline. The Greeks discovered astrology rather late. It is not mentioned by Homer, and Heisod (fl. 8th century B.C.?) wrote a didactic "Work and Days" (an advice to farmers) without referring to astrology. It is said that Cleostratos of Tenedos first made the zodiac known to Greece about 500 B.C. from his observations on Mount Ida. However, astrology proper was probably brought to Greece through the Persians and Egyptians. Shortly after the Persian Wars (500-499 B.C.) the astronomer Eudoxus of Cnidus and Aristarchus of Samos wrote tracts warning their countrymen against believing this foreign philosophy.

But the evidence for astrology was too strong. The logical Greeks not only began to study and use astrology, but also attempted to merge it into their philosophy and science. The vehicle for this melding of astrology and science was the works of Aristotle. While Aristotle himself does not consider astrology directly, his disciple Theophrastos, as cited by Proclus, stated that ". . . his Chaldean contemporaries possessed an admirable theory on the subject of the signs of the zodiac. This theory predicted every event, the life and death of every human being. It does not merely foresee general effects, for example good and bad weather. . . ."[5] The amalgamation of Greek science and astrology reached its peak in A.D. 150 with the publication of the *Tetrabiblos* of Claudius Ptolemais (the great Ptolemy of science).

Until the end of the Renaissance, Ptolemy was preeminent in astronomy, geography, and astrology. He was also noted for his work in mechanics, optics, and mathematics. He continued the development of trigonometry begun by Hipparchus (c. 150 B.C.) and computed accurately the diameter of Earth and the distance from Earth to the Moon. Hephaestation of Thebes calls him "the Divine Ptolemy."[6] His life fell approximately in the years A.D. 100-178,

---

[5]0. Neugebauer, *The Exact Sciences in Antiquity*, p. 187.

[6]*Catalogus Codium Astrologorum Graecorum*, viii 2, pp. 81-82.

covering the first three quarters of the 2nd century of our era and the reigns of Trajan, Hadrian, Antoninus Pius, and Marcus Aurelius. He was born in Egypt and did most of his work in Canopus, which was about 15 miles east of Alexandria. He is best known for his great work in astronomy: *Syntaxis mathematica*. The Arabs called this book "*al majisti*," from which it was corrupted into *Almajest*, as it is popularly known today.

In astrology Ptolemy was well aware of all previous works. Living in Egypt, he had studied Egyptian astrology (and therefore the astrology of Mesopotamia). From Plato (especially *Timeaus* and *Epinomis*) he knew of the Pythagorean theory that the science of Number itself brings us to the heavens from whose order we can divine the beauty, rhythm, and harmony of the universe. Ptolemy knew, and generally rejected, the Stoic concept of the universe. Zeno of Citium (c. 336-264 B.C.), the founder of Stoicism, brought to Greece the belief that mankind and the universe were bound together in a system of fate. Such attitudes were stimulated by astrology, and in turn stimulated astrology to further development. The Stoics were well aware of the close link of their philosophy with the astral cults: astrology. Indeed their philosophy brought out into the open the pantheism implied by the belief that the heavens controlled all that happened on Earth (the so-called "correspondence theory"). In astrology this philosophy was best expressed by Gaius (or Marcus) Manillius (fl. 1st century B.C.) in his *Poeticon asternomicon*.[7]

> "First the nature (or astrology) designed to move the minds of kings who touched the tracks of things nearest to heaven and tamed savage nations in the eastern lands. It's there the world's reborn and light comes over darkened cities. Next priests, tending with rites and temples, age on age, and chosen to offer the people's homage to gods, and win their favor, felt in pure minds the deity's mightily presence. . . ."

---

[7] *Gaius Manillius, Poeticon Asternomicon*, i:40ff (translated as in *Origins of Astrology* by J. Lindsay).

We shall see that this philosophy has a major influence on post-Renaissance and Modern astrology. But in the second century of the Christian era Ptolemy used the more reasonable writings of Aristotle to explain the workings of astrology. The viability of Aristoteliamsm is attested by the fact that it is still a force in modern thought: in the Neo-Scholasticism of Jacques Maritian (1882-1973), no believer in astrology; in recent psychology, whose behavioristic tendencies are in part a revival of Aristotelian modes of thought; in the various forms of vitalism in contemporary biology; and in the dynamism of such thinkers as Henri Bergson (1859-1941); and in the more catholic naturalism which has succeeded the mechanistic materialism of the last century, and which, whether by appeal to a doctrine of levels or by emphasis on imminent telology, seems to be striving along Aristotelian lines for a conception of nature broad enough to include the religious, moral, and artistic consciousness. Aristotle proposed a science that was both physical and mathematical—one that took account of the form and matter duality of nature. Utilizing such a philosophy Ptolemy was able to rid astrology of the superstitions of the Egyptians and the pantheism of the Stoics. But first he had to defend the science against the attacks of its critics.

Astrology had been criticized for more than 600 years. Perhaps the strongest opponent was Cicero (106-46 B.C.). Ptolemy recognized that before he could develop a truly scientific astrology he had to refute Cicero:

> ". . . If, then, a man knows accurately the movements of all the stars, the Sun, and the Moon, so that neither the place nor the time of any of their configurations escapes his notice, and if he has distinguished in general their natures as the result of previous study, even though he may discern, not their essential, but only their potentially effective qualities, such as the Sun's heating and the Moon's moistening and so on with the rest; and if he is capable of determining in view of all these data, both scientifically and by successful conjecture, the distinc-

tive mark of quality resulting from the combination of all the factors, what is to prevent him from being able to tell on each given occasion the characteristics of the air from the relations of the phenomena at the time: as for instance, that it will be warmer or wetter? Why can he not, too, with respect to an individual man, perceive the general quality of his temperament from the ambient at the time of his birth: as for instance, that he is such and such in body and such and such in soul (character), and predict occasional events, by use of the fact that such and such a temperament is favorable to prosperity, while another is not so attuned and conduces injury?"[8]

The first three chapters of Book I of the *Tetrabiblos* is the most brilliant defense of astrology ever written. It answers most of the objections, even of today. In addition, Ptolemy was particularly concerned with the admonition of Issiah, implied by the quotation used in the introduction of this book. The Babylonians, Egyptians, and later the Stoics considered astrology as a universal Truth, something akin to a religious dogma, whose prognostications were not to be questioned. With the exception of the democratic city-states of Greece, the governments of the Near East were all theocracies, and the rulers encouraged belief by the masses in the occult nature of astrology. As a scientist he knew that astrology was anything but an exact science: ". . . even though one approaches astrology in the most inquiring and legitimate spirit possible, he may frequently err because of the very nature of the art . . . for in general every science that deals with the quality of its subject-matter is conjectural and not to be absolutely affirmed. . . ."[9] Had the Babylonians the same concept of astrology as Ptolemy, Issiah's statement would have been unnecessary.

Ptolemy not only brought the scrutiny of the scientists to astrology, but in addition advanced the art by the application of mathematics, astronomy, and physics. Previously, predictions

[8]*Tetrabiblos*, i:2.

[9]Ibid.

were based on the relative positions of the planets and Earth in their revolution around the Sun. But the Earth's rotation about its axis effects apparent diurnal changes in the relative positions of the heavenly bodies. Utilizing the new trigonometry followers of Ptolemy divided the equator (the plane of rotation of the Earth) in unequal parts representing the varying length of day and night. This division of the equator is called loci or houses: and each of the different loci are correlated to distinct facets of an individual's life (see chapter II). Many changes were made in the method of computing these loci during the Renaissance, but the method of Ptolemy was first, and gave to astrology the ability to correlate celestial phenomena directly to the life of an individual.

Roman and Early Christian Influences

Ennius (239-169 B.C.) is the first Latin writer known to speak of astrologers. Among the spreaders of astrology in Rome were men brought in as slaves from the east. Pliny states that it was a slave, Antiochos, who introduced astrology to Italy. Almost from the beginning astrologers were in Rome. In 139 B.C. they were expelled from the city after being accused of having a hand in the slaves' revolt. Both Augustus and Tiberius took recourse against astrology, and they proceeded against the seers in order to inhibit speculation concerning their death dates. Thrasyllus was court astrologer to Tiberius. The interesting story of how he became so is related in the *Annals* by Tacitus. Tiberius consulted several astrologers, none of whom could convince him that they were not charlatans. These imposters were quickly killed. Thrasyllus predicted great glory for Tiberius. But the emperor, to test him further, asked if Thrasyllus had cast his own nativity: could he foresee what was going to happen in the course of the year? On that very day? Thrasyllus consulted his chart and ". . . stricken with fear, he paused, hesitated, sank into meditation ... breaking his silence at last, he said, 'I see the crisis of my fate. This very moment may be my last'. . . ." Tiberius clasped him with congratulations on his knowledge and on his escape from danger. After that he considered Thrasyllus' predictions as the oracles of truth and the astrologer was ranked high among his confidential friends.

Thrasyllus was a prolific writer on astrology. He took the views of the Egyptians, but in philosophy he was a neo-Pythagorean, and he wrote a book on numerology. Porophyry (A.D. 233-C.304) cites him as an authority on Pythagoreanism, and discusses the controversy waged by Ptolemy against the more occult aspects of Thrasyllus' doctrine.

The first three centuries of the Christian era found a systematic persecution in Rome of all astrologers who in any way touched on imperial politics. However, within the official circle the astrologer was elevated to a position of considerable power. Balbillus succeeded Thrasyllus as astrologer to Claudius and Nero. His influence is indicated by the fact that Nero's accession was planned by Agrippina with the aid of Balbillus and other astrologers; and things were held up until the auspicious moment established by Balbillus arrived. Later Balbillus was instrumental in turning Nero on the Christians for allegedly starting the great fire of A.D. 64. (By implication from Renan, *Antichrist*, analysis of Revelation xiii:15: "The second wild beast was then permitted to give life to the beast's image, so that the beast had the power of speech. . . ."). This, of course, did not serve to endear astrology to the Christians.

Despite the efforts of Porphyry in his treatise, *The Tetrabiblos of Ptolemy*, to introduce science to Roman astrology, the astrology of this period combined the fatalism of the Stoics with the superstitions of the Egyptians. The culmination was the reign of Carcalla (188-217), who ascended to the throne through the murder of his brother Geta in A.D. 212. During his reign various cults devoted to the Moon, Sun, and Hercules took hold of astrology. The art had a powerful hold on the Romans, but degenerated to necromancy, magic chants, and other superstitions.

Astrology had another set-back vis-a-vis Christianity near the end of the 3rd century with the advent of the Neo-Gnostic sect of Manichaeism. Gnosticism is the name given to a religious movement older than Christianity. Its origins lie in fusing various religious ideas and practices together. In Gnosticism only the elect who have been inflated into its mysteries can be saved. This select band usually operated through magical rites and formulae. When Christianity came along the Gnostics merely adapted their philosophy to the new religion, appealing to those who wish to consider themselves somehow superior to their fellow beings. The Persian Mani (c. 250) attempted to unite the teachings of Zoroaster with those of Christ. In terms of traditional Christian teachings his heresies were many. But for our purposes we need only note that in the secret rites of Manichaseism astrology played a prominent part. Astrology then, according to Mani, was not a science open to all, but part of a secret knowledge available only to a select few.

Constantine legalized Christianity by the Edict of Milan in A.D. 313. In 325 he convened the epoch-making Council of Nicea. This council formalized the doctrines of Christianity through the Nicean Creed; and in the process condemned the heresies of Gnosticism and Manichaeism. By implication astrology was also condemned. But not the astrology of Ptolemy. Rather it was the astrology as practiced by the superstitious or heretical cults. Sometimes a valid astrology, but with a philosophical basis anathema to science. The Church 2,000 years ago, the Church today, and the Church in the future will always condemn superstition wherever she finds it. Astrology has always had the unfortunate experience of being taken up by charlatans who associate themselves with pseudo-science and occultism for the purpose of lining their pocketbooks. As a result it has often been mistaken for that with which it has been associated. However, as will be seen, popes and cardinals have availed themselves of astrologer when these individuals were also true scientists.

The Roman Empire did not go out with a bang. Rather it slowly sunk into oblivion. Its great artists and poets were no more. Too many centuries of moral decay had left the once great city bereft of its inheritance from previous civilizations. Christianity became the state religion. But the Fathers were interested in man's relationship with God, not with his relationship with the world.

The monasteries kept knowledge alive, but did nothing to advance the level of scholarship in any field other than theology. As is so often the case when church and state is close together heresy was generally considered akin to treason. Gnosticism and Manichaeism were suppressed, and knowledge of scientific astrology was lost to Western Europe. That many in the Church remained concerned about a revival of pseudo-astrology and its attendant heresy is evident by the fact that in England Benerable Bede (673-735) attempted to substitute the names of the apostles for the signs of the zodiac: Peter (Aries), Andrew (Taurus), James the Greater (Gemini), John (Cancer), Thomas (Leo), James the Less (Virgo), Philip (Libra), Bartholomew (Scorpio), Matthew (Sagittarius), Simon (Capricorn), John the Baptist substituted for Judas (Aquarius), and Jude (Pisces).

The Islamic Contribution

Scientific astrology was dead in Western Europe. Even the superstitions of the Sun-sects and the Moon-goddess, Tanit, once so powerful, were but a vague memory. The very name of Ptolemy was unknown outside of the Arab lands. The pre-Islamic Arabs, on the other hand, were knowledgeable of Greek science in general and Ptolemy and Aristotle in particular. Consider the neo-platonic philosopher Stephanus of Alexandria. He was a contemporary of Heraclius (610-641). In the fall of A.D. 621 Stephanus calculated a horoscope for the inception of Islam! From this chart, cast six months prior to the Hijira, Stephanus predicted the course of Islam through the Abbasid Caliph in A.D. 7 55! Included in his predictions were the battles of Jalula (637), Nahavend (641), and the civil war in A.D. 660. He predicted the defeat of Suleiman at the gates of Constantinople (717-718) and the preservation of Christianity through the defeat of Abd er-Rahman at Pointiers (Tours) by Charles Martel in 732.

Astrology as a scientific discipline was well established in Islam during the Dark Ages in Europe. Al-Kindi (d. 873) was a great Arabian follower of Aristotle. Of the tribe of Kindah, he wrote on geometry, astronomy, arithmetic, music (which he developed on arithmetical principles), physics, medicine, psychology, meteorology, and politics. It is not spoken of in scientific circles these days, but al-Kindi also wrote several treatises on astrology summarizing this knowledge in light of current science. But perhaps the greatest Arabic astrologer was a follower of al-Kindi: Muhammad ibn Ahmad al-Biruni. Al-Biruni traveled to India and wrote a commentary on Indian science including astrology. For our purposes it is his great book on astrology that is most remarkable: *The Book on Instruction in the Elements of the Art of Astrology*. This book was written in A.D. 1029, but was first translated into English in 1934 by Professor R. Ramsay Wright. Only 100 copies of this English translation are extant. It contains many elements of astrology that cannot be found in any of today's books. Also some of the astrological techniques in use today are quite different in al-Biruni's book. A complete discussion of this book would take us too far afield. Al-Biruni, however, was a true student of Ptolemy, and fully recognized the place of astrology in the scheme of scientific knowledge. His book is in five parts: mathematics, astronomy, geography, chronology, and astrology. This order is not accidental. Following Ptolemy, al-Biruni considered astrology not a part of any one science per se, but rather a logical extension of other scientific disciplines.

With the rise of Islam, Israel, left the yoke of Rome to be taken into the camp of the Prophet. The Jews brought to Islam their expertise in philosophy, science, astrology. The best known of the Jewish astrologers of the Middle Ages was Masha'allah (known as Messahala in Europe). He wrote an astrological world history called *On Conjunctions, Religions, and Peoples*. This work which showed that all important religious and political changes are indicated by conjunctions of the planets Saturn and Jupiter, related the history of the world from the Deluge (c. 3350 B.C.) to the rise of the Buwayhids (A.D. 928).[10] Masha'allah also computed the ac-

[10]The companion book to this volume, *Fixed Stars and Judicial Astrology*, presents some remarkable modern discoveries relating the solar cycle to this theory.

cession horoscopes for all the caliphs through Harun al-Rashid, and wrote a book on nativities. Analysis of the works of Nostrodamus suggest that the great prophet was quite knowledgeable of Masha'allah and used his theories extensively.

It was through the Jewish astrologers that Europe learned again of the scientific astrology of Ptolemy. The most influential of these astrologers as the poet, mathematician, and philosopher Abraham ben Meir ibn Ezra (1092-1167). Abraham ibn Ezra's philosophical influence was restricted to the Jewish world; to the Christians he was known mainly as an astrologer. He made significant contributions in exegesis, philosophy, grammar, poetry, and mathematics. He was one of the most famous Jews produced at any time and in any clime. The great orientalist, Leopold Dukes, said of him:[11]

> "Every literature occasionally has a man to boast of, who, equipped with the knowledge of his time, finds himself in a position to survey it, although his age is unable to appreciate him. Such men see far beyond the intellectual horizon of their contemporaries, and hang aloft their lantern, from which later generations kindle their light. Such a man was Abraham ibn Ezra."

Ibn Ezra was inclined toward judicial astrology, but also wrote on nativities. He wrote eight astrological treatises in Hebrew: *The Beginning of Wisdom*, *The Book of Reason*, *The Book of Nativities*, *The Book of Consultations of the Stars*, *The Book of Selections*, *The Book of Lights*, and *The Book of the World and the Conjunctions*. These books were written c. 1146 but were cited throughout the following centuries by men such as Christopher Columbus. Ibn Ezra's astrology is basically that of Ptolemy. However, the pure rationalism of Ptolemy was modified significantly by large doses of Jewish mysticism and a tendency towards Stoic fatalism. These elements are present even today in most books on astrology. This mysticism does not go so far as the occultism of the Egyptians, nor is the fatalism as absolute as that of the Stoics and

[11]Leopold Dukes, *Der Orient*, 1843, p. 657.

Gnostics. Indeed the sophisticated Hebraist would not consider them superstitions at all in themselves. But Renaissance Man was not yet sophisticated, and his interpretation of ibn Ezra yielded an astrology that led to its own demise with the advent of the mechanistic materialism of the eighteenth and nineteenth centuries.

The treatises of ibn Ezra were translated into French in 1273. The first of these treatises, *The Beginning of Wisdom*, contains 120 aphorisms useful in prognostics. These were discovered by Johannes Campanus (c. 1260),who attested their viability to, Pope Urban IV. The pope made Campanus his personal physician and astrologer. Campanus was a mathematician noted for his .translation of Euclid. In astrology he invented a method of loci (house) division based on the trisection of the prime vertical. As Ptolemy's method of loci division had not yet been distributed in Europe, Campanus had to improvise based on incomplete descriptions in ibn Ezra. Campanus was successful, however. Scientific astrology had returned to Western Europe.

The Renaissance and Astrology's Glory

The rediscovery of scientific astrology took Europe by storm. Some of the best minds of the day took up serious study of astrology. For example, the greatest mathematician of his century was Johann Muller (1426-1476), more generally known by the Latinized form of his birthplace of Konigsberg, as Regiomontanus. His treatise *De triangulis omnimodis*, written about 1464, was the first systematic European exposition of plane and spherical trigonometry considered independently of astronomy. In 1475, he was invited to Rome by Pope Sixtus IV as court astrologer and to partake in the reformation of the calendar. Regiomontanus also invented a system of loci division that carries his name. In this instance it was the equator that was divided. But unlike Ptolemy who used time arcs, Regiomontanus used spatial arcs.

If it seems that there was a great deal of confusion as to the correct method of loci division, the answer is "quite so!". The earliest edition of Ptolemy in Europe is dated 1484, and the earliest commentary by near contemporaries such as Porphyry is even later: 1559! The only link to the classical methods of scientific astrology were writers such as Masha'allah and ibn Ezra. Butthese writers wrote for Arabiac readers who were well versed in the classical methods. Hence their books were sketchy on the methodology of chart construction, emphasizing instead the interpretation.

When the *Tetrabiblos* finally came to Europe along with the *Paraphrase* of Proclus and Phorphyr's commentary in the middle of the sixteenth century, the situation vis-a-vis classical astrology got worse instead of better. In the first place, some readers misinterpreted Porphyry and divided the ecliptic instead of the equator. (This error has persisted to this day in attributing to Porphyry a method he did not use). The *Almagest*, which contains Ptolemy's method[12], is difficult to read unless you are an accomplished mathematician. As a result there were at least four methods of loci division competing for recognition. Except for a very few sophisticated scientists all of these methods seemed equally valid. Therefore it wasn't too long before there were many different methods of loci division. Every astrologer, it seemed, had his own that he hawked as being the only "true" one that would allow this astrologer, and only this one, to prognosticate correctly. When the smoke cleared, the method of Regiomontanus was the one preferred by most serious astrologers. Regiomontanus was better known that Ptolemy; and in the last analysis astrologers had to retreat to a known position in order to clear up the confusion as they had no way at that time to determine the truth or falsity of the competing claims.

The method of Ptolemy was used by the more scientific astrologers of the 16th century, however. There is in the Victoria and Albert Museum in London a statuette of Mercury wrought in 1527 by Antonio Minelli and consecrated by a Venetian partician,

[12]More precisely, the *Almagest* contains the basic information on which Ptolemy's method of loci division is based. It does not specifically detail the astrological problem of loci division.

Marcantonio Michiel. The statuette carries a horoscope with a graphic demonstration of the planet Mercury's position according to the Ptolemic method of loci division, and was probably cast by the mathematician and astrologer Girolamo Cardano (1501-1576).

One of the most gifted and versatile men of his time, Cardano wrote a number of works on arithmetic, astronomy, physics, medicine, and astrology. His greatest work in his *Ara magna*, the first Latin treatise devoted solely to algebra. He learned astrology from his father through the works of the Arabians. He was imprisoned for a time for heresy because he published a horoscope of Christ's life. However, on his release he went to Rome where he became a distinguished astrologer, receiving a pension as astrologer to the papal court.

It is generally believed that the demise of astrology began with the verification of the heliocentric theory of Nicolai Copernicus by Johann Kepler in 1609. Nothing could be farther from the truth. However to appreciate how astrology got to its present state we must digress to consider the Copernican controversy in a bit of detail.

As early as the sixth century B.C. the solar system was regarded by the Greeks as a stationary Earth, around which revolved the Sun, the planets, and the stars. These bodies were assumed to revolve eastward around the Earth in a circular orbit, pausing periodically to retreat toward the west against the turning background of the constellations. The problem of planetary motion that the early Greeks undertook to solve was kinematical: by what combinations of uniform circular motions centered on the Earth could the looped movements of the planets be best represented? The best answer was the proposed by Ptolemy in his *Almagest*. In its simplest form Ptolemy's theory envisioned each planet moving in a small circular orbit centered on the planets orbit around the Earth (see chapter V). Further study of planetary movements by Arabs, however, led to epicycles piled upon epicycles until the whole construction became very cumbersome.

Nicolas Copernicus (1453-1543) attempted to simplify the ancient theory. In his book, *De revolutionubus orbium coelestium*, published shortly before his death, he showed that all the motions of the planets can be explained by assuming the Sun stationary, and the planets and the Earth revolving about the Sun. His arguments, however, were mainly heuristic and his theory remained just that: unproven conjecture.

Nor was Copernicus the first to propose such a theory. Centuries before, Hipparchus analyzed such a theory and rejected it on what would be valid scientific grounds even today: if Earth moved about the Sun, there must be an observable stellar parallax, and none could be observed. It was not until 1727 that the English astronomer James Bradley (1693-1762) demonstrated the Earth's motion through the discovery of the aberration of starlight; and the stellar parallax was not finally proven until 1838 when F.W. Bessel (1784-1846) first measured the parallax of the star 61-Cygni. Hence the Copernican hypothesis was not proven until 400 years after its conjecture, and 200 years after Galileo's troubles with the church.

Tycho Brahe (1546-1601) was an extraordinary observer of the heavens. He invented non-telescopic instruments that allowed him to determine the places of celestial bodies in the sky with an average error of less than a minute of arc. These observations led him also to discard the Ptolemaic system. But rather than repudiate completely the geocentric solar system as did Copernicus, Tycho's system had the planets while the Sun revolved around a stationary Earth. Tycho made most of his observations from the island of Hven, northeast of Copenhagen. However, he was an excellent astrologer (having accurately predicted the achievements and time of death of Gustavus Adolphus), and was invited to the court of Rudolf II of Austria. He brought with him as a protege a young astronomer that was already being talked about for his brilliant theories: Johann Kepler (1571-1630).

Tycho took on Kepler because of his ability as an astronomer. But the Emperor Rudolph agreed with the appointment because of Kepler's astrological ability. Kepler had already prophesied from the stars a hard winter, and so it had proved; and had also prepared horoscopes for the great Wallenstein and other notables in Germany. Therefore it is not surprising that Kepler's first assignment was astrological; in 1602 he published *De fundamentis astrologiae certiorbus*: a treatise whose purpose was "to distill and preserve" the truths of astrology. In 1603 Kepler wrote the *Judicum de trigonoigneo* in which he proposed what are today called the minor aspects: senii-quartile, sesquiquadrate, quincunx, and semi-sextile (see Chapter V).

Two years after Kepler arrived in Prague, the great Tycho Brahe died and left the records of his life s work to his protege. Using the detailed observations of his former master, especially those on Mars, Kepler was able to formulate his first two laws of planetary motion. Published in 1609 in *Astronomia nova* these are:

> 1. The orbit of each of the planets is an ellipse with the Sun at one of the foci.
>
> 2. Each planet revolves so that the line joining it to the Sun sweeps over equal areas in equal intervals of time.

Further study enabled Kepler to publish his third law, from which Newton was later able to develop the well known law of gravitation. This was published in the treatise *De harmonica mundi* in 1619:

> 3. The squares of the periods of any two planets are in the same proportion as the cubes of their mean distances from the Sun.

Kepler's first love was astronomy, although he continued to publish treatises on astrology (e.g., *Tertuis interueniens* in 1610). He wrote that he "played with the foolish daughter only to be near the wise mother, as the scanty rewards of an astronomer would not provide me with bread, if men did not entertain hopes of reading the future in the heavens." Both astrology and astronomy claim Kepler as one of theirs. Both are correct.

Our story is not complete without reference to the problems

confronting Galileo Galilei (1564-1642). Galileo invented the telescope and through his observations, such as the phases of Venus and the sunspots, was able to completely discredit the Ptolemaic system. In 1613 the Cardinal Mafeo Barberini, later to become Pope Urban VIII, wrote to compliment Galileo on his work. Had there been only one competing theory Galileo would have had no problems. Unfortunately, there were two, and Galileo opted (correctly) for the Copernican hypothesis. While Galileo's observations repudiated Ptolemy, they left in doubt the correctness of the theories of Copernicus and Tycho.

Centuries before, Saint Augustine and Saint Thomas Aquinas had written that the Bible was not intended to teach science, and therefore its authority could not be invoked in scientific disputes. But at the beginning of the seventeenth century both Scientists and Church were unable to obey the admonitions of the Holy Fathers. What could not be demonstrated by scientific observation could be proven by reference to scripture. Galileo was no match for his within the Church. Even his friend Pope Urban VIII was forced to give in. Galileo was censured for his views and prohibited from ever promulgating them in any form whatsoever. He was never imprisoned as some imagine, but a century later (and even today) this tragic incident is used by those who wish to discredit previous authority as relating to a current controversy: in this instance the viability of astrology.

Copernicus initiated the concept, Kepler using the observations of Tycho developed the theory, and Galileo with his new invention, the telescope, provided the experimental evidence. The science of astronomy, and with it all human knowledge, was on the verge of a revolution. Astrology, however, was not considered discredited! Jean Baptiste Morin de Villefranche (1583-1656), for example, authored *Astrologia gallica*, was astrologer to Cardinal Richelieu, and correctly predicted the deaths of Richelieu, Louis XIII, and Wallenstein. His scientific credentials included being a doctor of medicine and a professor of mathematics at the Paris University. Even later was the monk Placidus de Tito (1603-1668) who was a professor of mathematics at the/University of Padua. Both Morin and Placidus invented systems of loci division that bear their names. But by a quirk of history the system of Placidus has become that which is most well known today.

Astrology as a Pseudo-science

The death blow to scientific astrology was given by Sir Isaac Newton (1642-1727), albeit inadvertently. Utilizing the papers of Sir Isaac Barrow, Newton (and Leibniz in Germany) developed the mathematics of the infinitesimal: today called calculus. The tools were now at hand. Next Newton, using the results of Kepler and Galileo, formulated the laws of motion and gravitation in his great work *Philosophiae naturalis principia mathematica.* Scientists from that day to this have given up the serious study of astrology. Astrology is an inexact art or science at best. The new theories, using the calculus, promised a rigor in the physical sciences that had never before been possible. The intellectual challenge was the development of mathematics and the new physics based on Newtonian mechanics. Those scientists that still considered as viable the correlations of the positions of heavenly bodies with events on earth had no time to apply their talents to astrology. The practice of astrology was left to those with little or no scientific training.

The most noted of these non-scientist astrologers was William Lilly (1602-1681). Lilly practiced astrology using the same techniques as his scientist colleagues. He was consulted by King Charles I in 1647 as to his escape from Carisbrooke Castle: and in 1666 he was summoned to appear before a committee of the House of Commons, appointed to inquire into the cause of the great fire of London which he had accurately predicted. Despite the flight of scientists from the practice of astrology to the more satisfying studies of mathematical physics, astrology continued to be considered a respectable science well into the 18th century. In England astrological evidence was received in a court of justice as late as 1758; and Sir Walter Scott made Guy Mannering cast a horoscope for the young laird of Ellangowan that the latter preserved all his life. But without the scientist astrology began to deteriorate to the type practiced in the latter days of the Roman Empire.

Neo-Manichaeism and Stoicism flourished from the earliest introduction of the Jewish astrologers to Europe at the end of the 13th century. Europeans of the early Middle Ages were still quite superstitious. Most had only recently been converted to Christianity and the remnants of their ancient pagan beliefs were still to be found. Elements of Jewish mysticism (misinterpreted) tended to fortify the ancient superstitions. Jewish astrology, therefore, became the vehicle for fusing the older European Animism with the newer Near Eastern Christianity.

An example of this tendency is the famous alchemist Paraceleus (fl. 1493). He believed that "all influences that come from the Sun, the planets, and the stars, act invisibly on man, and if these are evil, they will produce evil effects." Also, he directed that a person deficient in the element whose essence radiates from Mars should be given iron. He said, "If a person gets angry, it is not because he has too much bile, but because the Mars correlative in his body is in a state of exaltation."

As long as scientists remained active in astrology this kind of thinking could be kept in perspective. Stoicism could be minimized, and the more speculative concepts relegated to a position outside the mainstream of scientific astrology. However, when the scientists left the practice of astrology, these self-same Stoics became the major spokesmen for the ancient art. In addition, the philosophy of science was undergoing a dramatic change: all the truths of the universe, it was thought, could be explained in terms of Newtonian mechanics—astrology was unnecessary. Indeed, along with religion, it was just another ancient superstition that man had now outgrown. Two hundred years later science was to reassess its position in regards to such absolutism. In the meantime astrology declined from a valid scientific discipline to a superfluous pseudo-science.

Followers of men such as Paraceleus did not make things easier for astrology. In the light of the new science of the day such concepts were ripe for ridicule. It is not unlikely for example, that the decadence of astrology in England was hastened by the publication of Samuel Butler's *Hudibras*, in which, astrology and its (then) greatest living, exponent William Lilly, under the title of Sidrophel, were so successfully and popularly satirized. Among its passages we read of astrologers:

"... in one case they tell, more lies

In figures and nativities

Than th'old Chaldean conjurors

In so many hundred thousand years ..."

But Samuel Butler was not alone. A few years later the great satirist Jonathan Swift followed in the same vein in his Predictions for the Year 1708 by Isaac Bicerstaff, Esq. By the beginning of the 19th century astrology was so discredited that some scholars were doubting Ptolemy's authorship of the *Tetrabiblos*. (No astronomer would ever practice astrology; Ptolemy was one of the world's greatest astronomers; ergo, Ptolemy could not have written a treatise on astrology).

In 1795 two men were born who were to be responsible for the resurgence of astrology: Morrison (later known as Zadkiel), and R.C. Smith (later known as Raphael). These two Englishmen were competitors in the publishing of almanacs for use in astrology. Neither were well educated, and both were actually mediocre astrologers more interested in their publishing business than in truly advancing astrology. For example, Smith (Raphael) was unable to compute loci cusps mathematically. The only available "Tables of Houses" was one based on the system of Placidus de Tito. These were incorporated in his almanac; and the Placidian system of loci division became the standard in England and the United States. The reason for this, of course, is that the users of *Raphael's Almanac* were even more unsophisticated in astrology than was the author. As to Raphael's competence, it need only be pointed out that early editions of his tables of houses had errors of as much as a degree of arc for the Horoscope (Ascendent). While they are to be commended for at least attempting to keep astrology alive, men such as Morrison and Smith have served mainly to prove astrology nothing but a pseudo-science.

The Resurgence of Scientific Astrology

The best astrologers of the 17th century were French, (Morin for example). Hence it is only just that it was the French that finally "rediscovered" the traditional scientific astrology. In 1897, the Abbe' Charles Nicoullaud (Fomalhaut) published *the Manuel d'astrologie spherique et judicaire* in which 33 years before the event he predicted the existence and named the planet Pluto. Next, Morin was introduced with Henri Selva's *La theorie des determinations astrologiques de Morin de Villefrance.* Finally, Paul Choisnard was the first to apply the modern scientific methods of statistics to astrology in 1908 in his *Preuves et bases de I'astrologie scientifique.*

At the beginning of the 20th century another revolution was brewing in science. Einstein's theories were questioning many of the implications of Newtonian physics. And Heisenberg proved that in many instances it was impossible to know with certainty what was going to happen. The only thing that could be known was the probability that an event would occur. The ancient philosophical basis of astrology, first formulated by Ptolemy, was finally being demonstrated.

The great scientific discoveries of the first half of the 20th century were German; and it was the Germans that first used the interdisciplinary approach in the study of astrology. The science of applied mathematics is basically interdisciplinary in approach; and astrology is a branch of applied mathematics. During World War II teams of scientists composed of everything from anthropologists to zoologists, and headed by mathematicians, were put together for the purpose of the analytical study of warfare. The resulting discipline is called operations research, and was responsible (for example) for the Allied victory over the German submarine fleet.

But all this was anticipated vis-a-vis astrology in 1927 when the Germans formed the *Deutche Kulturgemeeinschaft zur Pflege der Astrologie*. This society was composed of professors of mathematics, palaenthology, philosophy, and other *herren doktoren*. Significantly absent were representatives of the physical sciences, but the scientist had returned to astrology after a hiatus of almost three hundred years!

These scientist-astrologers were violently opposed by the hermetical and theosophical astrologers. These latter sects are the direct descendants of the Gnostics and Manichaeists of the previous centuries. In post-World War I Germany, there were by far the most numerous and influential of those who practiced astrology. Magic and occultism has never been able to remain supreme in any field once the scientists enter it. Therefore the theosophists worked to ingratiate themselves to those most likely to be in power. Hitler was a follower of astrology, and it was the hermetical and theosophical brand that he preferred. The scientists were arrested and their society was disbanded. The remarriage of science and astrology ended in a violent divorce almost as soon as it had begun.

The decades following World War II have been typified by a rejection of previous modes of thought, and a willingness to explore even areas that have been rejected. Astrology, both the theosophical and the scientific brands, have benefitted in the process. That which was begun again in Germany in 1927 has been given another lease on life, especially in the United States.

There is today a significant movement of scientists (including those from physics and astronomy) towards again considering objectively the claims of astrology. Michael Gauquelin, in France, has collected very large amounts of data relating occupations with planetary positions at birth. In the United States the National Council for Geocosmic Research encourages the application of sophisticated statistical and mathematical techniques to the problems of scientific astrology. The desire to once again make astrology a recognized scientific discipline is there. Unfortunately very few of the practitioners have the requisite education. The misuse of statistical methods is the rule rather than the exception. For example, Gauquelin's data is too subjective to be amenable to real scientific analysis. However numerous investigators have published "analyses" claiming to have found "valid statistical correlations." But most of those who practice what today has become to be called "humanistic" astrology. As its best, humanistic astrology attempts to correlate celestial positions with psychological archetypes, (for example those defined by C.G. Jung and his followers). At its worst it becomes little more than pseudo-psychology. In either event the use of solid analytical techniques is sadly lacking.

The real advances in legitimizing astrology have been made by those outside the field entirely. The Russians have long been interested in finding methods for predicting future events having a major impact on their society: famine, epidemics, depressions, etc. Professor A.L. Chizhevskiy (1892-1964) long ago recognized the possibility of relating sunspot activity to human affairs. As a result he founded the (in Russia) respected science of heliobiology: the science dealing with the influences of solar activity and other cosmic factors on the terrestrial biosphere. This definition is his, not mine! If it sounds vaguely familiar remember that the practice of astrology is harshly, very harshly, dealt with in the Soviet Union. And Professor Chizhevskiy's work continues. A Soviet scientist, V. Desyatov, has related suicides and automobile accidents to solar flares.[13] And other investigators have shown a statistically significant relationship between such diverse elements as air temperature, precipitation, river run-offs, water levels of lakes and ground water, crop yields, and diseases in man.[14] Furthermore, as is shown in my next book, *Fixed Stars and Judicial Astrology*, the solar cycle is directly relatable to many of the observations of classical astrology.

Where all this will lead only the future knows. And astrology

[13]D.P. Konstaninov and V.D. Pekelis, eds., *Inhabited Space*, NASA TT F-819, NASA Technical Translation, Washington, D.C., 1975.

[14]I..P. Druzhinin and N.V. Khamaova, *Solar Activity and Sudden Changes in the Natural Processes on Earth, a Statistical Analysis*, NASA TT F-652, NASA Technical Translation, Washington, D.C., 1976.

(at least of the classical scientific kind) does not pretend to see into the future in any such depth.

It will be noted by the astute student that much has been left out of this all too short account of the history of astrology. We could have written a great deal on the interrelationship of astrology with the religion of the Babylonians and Egyptians, for example. Or, the connection between astrology and alchemy in the Middle Ages could have been expanded on in depth. The list of the history of astrology could fill several volumes. The interested student is directed to the bibliography for further material in this interesting area.

Review Questions

1. What is the difference between judicial and genethliacal astrology?

2. Explain the relationship between the calendar and the zodiac.

3. The vernal equinox will soon be rising with the constellation Aquarius, initiating the Age of Aquarius. However, the first day of spring will still mark the beginning of Aries. Explain.

4. Recently a Sunday supplement magazine challenged astrologers to give the name and date of the next public figure to be relieved from his job is disgrace. According to Ptolemy is this a valid question to put to astrology? Explain.

5. Is the practice of astrology against the tenets of traditional Christianity? Explain.

6. Name five mathematicians who were also astrologers.

7. What is the relationship between the astrology of ibn Ezra and that of Paraceleus?

8. What method of loci division was most used in the Middle Ages?

9. What is the difference between the theories of Planetary movement according to Ptolemy and Tyco Brahe?

10. Why is astrology considered a pseudo-science?

Chapter II

Genethliacal Astrology

The Branches of Astrology

Astrology has been defined as the correlation of events on Earth with the relative positions of the heavenly bodies. Traditionally there are five divisions of astrology. The first of these has to do with widespread phenomena such as earthquakes, floods, very large storms, and tides. The second division concerns more limited events that effect whole populations: famines, epidemics, revolutions, emergence of new religions or sects, etc. The third division is especially concerned with the environment of the individual human, the events which affect him in the course of his life, and the influences which remain behind him in his progeny. The fourth division has to do with human activities and occupations. The fifth division of astrology seeks solutions of immediate problems.

The third and fourth of these divisions are what is called genethliacal astrology, or the science of nativities. Most of the first division has been incorporated into such sciences as geophysics or meteorology. Astrology is still valuable in determining some of the long range trends within the first division, but the astrologer who is not also a meteorologist or geologist is likely to make a fool of himself in this field. The second division comprises what is today known as mundane astrology. The fifth division is known as horary astrology. Al-Biruni has this to say of horary astrology:[1]

> "... Here astrology reaches a point which threatens to transgress its proper limits, where problems are submitted which it is impossible to solve for the most part, and where the matter leaves the solid basis of universals for one of particulars. When this boundary is passed, where the astrologer is on one side and the sorcerer on the other, you enter a field of omens and divinations which has nothing to do with astrology.. ."[1]

The tools of astrology are observational astronomy in combination with other sciences. We have already mentioned the necessity of mastering meteorology and geology for the practice of astrology of the first division. Mundane astrology requires a knowledge of political science, history, and (in some instances) econometrics. Genethliacal astrology requires an in-depth knowledge of psychology, sociology, and biology (especially genetics). Most of the errors of modern astrologers can be traced to a lack of preparation in these basic disciplines. The reading of one or two books on psychology at the college sophomore level just does not suffice. And astrology proper requires an understanding of observational astronomy and the necessary accompanying mathematics.

The Astronomical Basis for Astrology

Before proceeding to describe in detail the nature of genethliacal astrology it is best to digress and review a bit of the astronomical background. Our Earth is a planet revolving about a small star we call the Sun. The Sun is situated in a spiral arm of a galactic system that encompasses the luminous girdle of the Milky Way. The Sun is near the principal plane of the system, 26,000

[1]Al Biruni, *The Book of Instruction in the Elements of the Art of Astrology*, p. 615. Most branches of astrology that writers speak of today fall into one of these five divisions. Esoteric astrology, or the study of hidden meanings and aspects, is part of the occultism of the neo-gnostics. Some of those who practice medical astrology are making noises akin to those emanating from a certain aquatic feathered vertebrate.

light years from the center, which is situated in the direction of the constellation Sagittarius. About the Sun revolve nine planets, including the Earth, and an asteroid belt that may be the remains of a tenth. Some of these planets have satellites revolving about them. The satellite of the Earth we call the Moon.

Astrology, however, does not use astronomy as it is, but as it appears to be. The Earth and the planets revolve about the Sun. But for an observer on Earth, the Sun and the other planets appear to revolve about the Earth. The Earth rotates on its axis from west to east, and makes the Sun appear to move from east to west. It is this latter apparent motion that astrology uses. Indeed, it makes not one bit of difference to astrology whether or not a heliocentric or a geocentric solar system is true, whether the stars are near or far, or whether they are fixed or move. What astrology uses is the relative positions of the stars and planets as referenced from the Earth. It is these relative positions that Ptolemic astronomy attempts to explain. Therefore for the purposes of astrology a geocentric explanation is the more viable.

The Classicists believed that the celestial sphere is a body like a ball revolving in its own place; it contains within its interior objects whose movements are different from those of the sphere itself, and the Earth is in the center of it. There are eight such spheres enclosed one within the other, like the skins of an onion. The smallest sphere is that which is nearest to the Earth, within which the Moon is always traveling alone, rising and setting, within its limits. The second sphere above that of the Moon belongs to the planet Mercury, the third to Venus, the fourth to the Sun, the fifth to Mars, the sixth to Jupiter and the seventh to Saturn. These seven spheres[2] belong to the planets; but above them all is the sphere that was known as that of the fixed star. Figure 1 depicts this Ptolemaic concept of the celestial sphere.

---

[2]The extra-Saturnian planets, Uranus, Neptune, and Pluto, had not yet been discovered. On their discovery, modern astrology immediately attempted to incorporate them into the science. These planets are discussed in Chapter IV; however, as they are not visible to the naked eye, it is doubtful that the classical astrologer would have considered them as proper to the body of astrology.

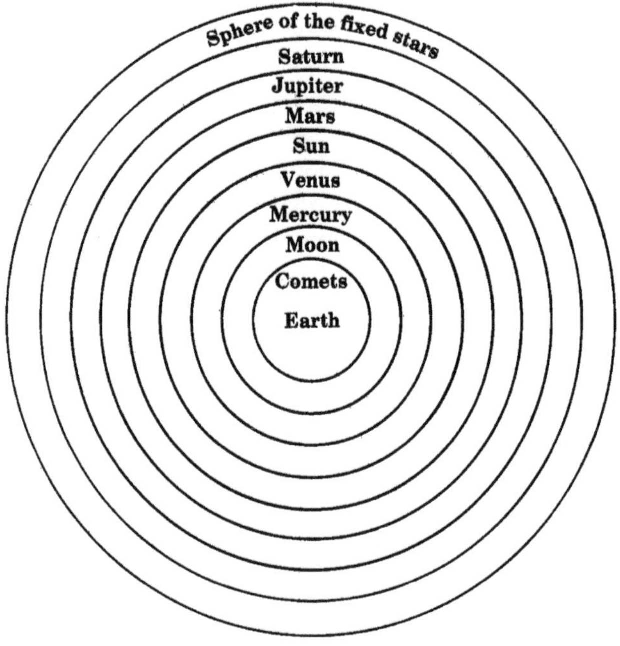

Figure 1. Ptolemaic Concept of the Universe.

As observed from the Earth constellations appear in the evening sky at the different seasons. From night tonight at the same time each star is found a little farther west. This steady westward march of the constellations during the year is caused by the Sun's apparent eastward movement among the star. The apparent annual path of the Sun's center on the celestial sphere is called the ecliptic. The ecliptic is a great circle inclined 23½ degrees to the celestial equator.

The celestial sphere is the conventional representation of the sky as a spherical shell on which the celestial bodies appear to be projected. Its center is usually taken as the observer's position. The point on the celestial sphere vertically overhead of the observer is called the zenith; and the nadir is the opposite point, vertically un-

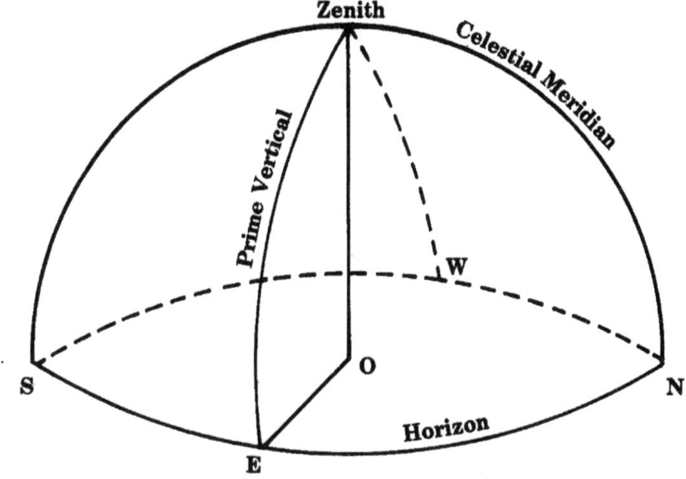

Figure 2. Zenith and Horizon.

derfoot. The celestial horizon is the great circle on the celestial sphere halfway (90°) between the zenith and the nadir. Vertical circles are great circles which pass through the zenith and the nadir, and are therefore perpendicular to the horizon. The vertical circle that crosses the horizon at its north and south points is the observer's celestial meridian; and the vertical circle at right angles to the meridian is called the prime vertical, and it crosses the horizon at its east and west points. Figure 2 shows these relationships.

The westward movement of the Sun across the sky, which causes it to rise and set, is an example Of a motion that all the celestial bodies have. In geocentric terms it is as though the celestial rotation, or diurnal motion, of the heavens is an effect of the Earth's rotation about its axis from west to east. Every star describes its diurnal circle around the sky daily. However there are two points on the celestial sphere having no diurnal motion. They are the points towards which the Earth's axis is directed, and are called the north and south celestial poles. The celestial equator is the great circle of the celestial sphere halfway between the north and south celestial poles. It is in the same plane as the Earth's

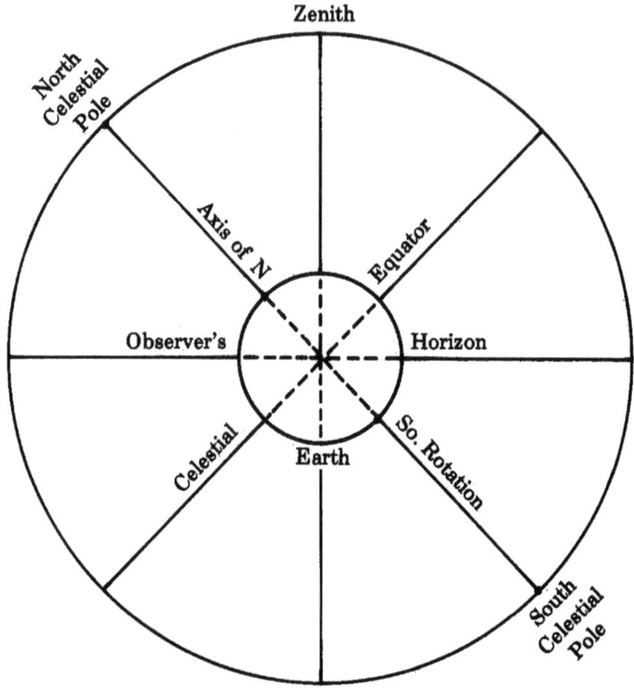

Figure 3. The Celestial Equator.

equator, and is the largest of the diurnal circles. Figure 3 depicts the relationship of the celestial equator with the horizon.

All the diurnal circles of the stars are parallel to one another. At the Earth's poles they are parallel to the horizon, and at the Earth's equator they are perpendicular to the horizon. Elsewhere on the Earth the star's diurnal circles are oblique to the horizon. The diurnal circles are always parallel to the celestial equator. The Sun, Moon, and planets however appear to move along a different path: the ecliptic. These celestial bodies move among the stars in a non-parallel manner. Where the ecliptic intersects the equator are the two equinoxes; and where it is farthest are the two solstices. With these definitions in mind we can now begin our discussions of genethliacal astrology.

The Tools of Astrology

The science of nativities begins with the birth of the individual. At this instant of time, where the prime vertical intersects the eastern horizon, some particular star is beginning to rise. This point (where the prime vertical intersects the horizon at the time of birth) is called the horoscope (ASC); and the rising star is called the ascendant[3]. The ascendant has been correlated with the native's temperament, and the type of individual he will be[4]. From the horoscope also can be determined the length of the native's life, his physical characteristics, inherent abilities, mentality, and personality[4]. At the instant of birth where the meridian intersects the ecliptic is called the medium coeli (MC), or middle of the sky. Relationships of the stars with the MC have been correlated with the native's actions throughout his life, his success or lack thereof, and, as with the horoscope (ASC), the length of life itself[5].

The horoscope (ASC) and MC and their two complementary points, the descendant and imum coeli (IC), are called angles. These four points are the primary references for relations between the planets and stars for delineating various facets of an individual's life. In addition to the angles, the signs of the zodiac in which are posted the various planets, stars, and reference points (such as the angles significantly modify the interpretations that may be given.

A given planet has varying correlative efficacy in different parts of the sky. In one sign of the zodiac it will correlate positively with various events, and in other signs there will be a negative correlation, or even no correlation at all. Even within a given sign certain degrees seem to imply a greater or lesser validity in terms of

---

[3]Modern terminology has confused the identification of the horoscope with the ascendant.

[4]Strictly speaking, from the relationships of various stars, including the ascendant, to the horoscopic point.

[5]Not all of these relationships were considered equally strong even by the Classicists. The limits of delineation in these areas will be developed in subsequent chapters.

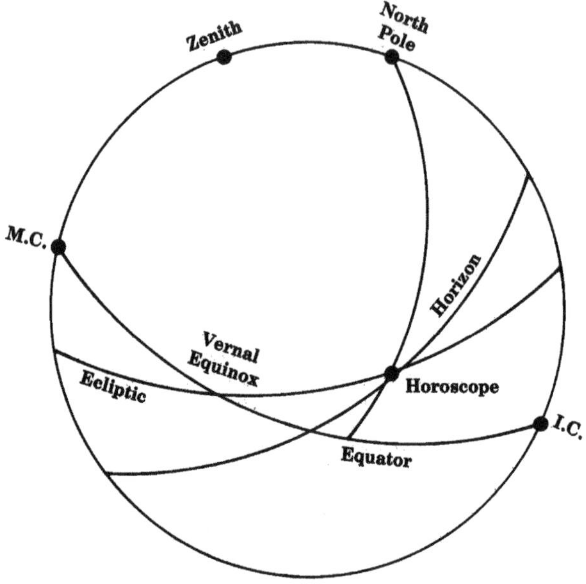

Figure 4. Relationship Between the Ecliptic and the Equator.

correlations with events on Earth. In the same manner some parts of the sky tend to submerge the correlations of one planet with those of another. Hence astrology requires not only the relationships of the planets (and stars) with the angles, but also the positions of the celestial bodies themselves in the sky. These peculiar sections of the heavens will be indicated in their proper places in this and subsequent chapters.

The relationships of the planets between themselves, to the angles and other reference points, and to the various signs of the zodiac are called aspects. For example two planets may come to the same point in the sky. Such a relationship is called a conjunction. Or one planet may be 90 degrees from an angle or from another planet. This aspect is called a quartile. The correlative effects of the different aspects are themselves different. The theory of aspects will be left to Chapter V. Suffice to say here that the aspects are a complex set of observational relationships that include various types of risings, culminations, and settings and angular and other references between the stars, planets, and various other reference points in the sky and on Earth.

The Loci

The tools of genethliacal astrology include the planets, signs of the zodiac, and various reference points and aspects that can be observed in the sky and on Earth. In addition there are a set of reference points and areas that can be obtained only mathematically. As the ecliptic is divided into twelve equal areas measuring the apparent annual movement of the Sun, so the equator and observer's horizon is divided into 12 unequal areas measuring the apparent diurnal movement of the Sun. These areas, projected onto the ecliptic, are called loci[6]. As explained in Appendix B, the loci are unequal due to the fact that the hours of the day that the Sun is above the horizon are not, in general, the same as the number of hours that the Sun is below the horizon. Appendix B presents the theory of the development of the loci. In this chapter we shall discuss their significance to the science of nativities.

The horoscope determines the beginning of the loci as determined by the Sun. That is the size of each of the loci is based on the length of time between sunrise and sunset on the day that the Sun rises at the horoscopic point. The planets and stars posited in these loci constitute what is known as the Solar Horoscope. This is the most well known and popular horoscope, and in genethliacal astrology indicates the quality of action of the native[7]: the series of probable events that constitute the life of the native together with his conduct and behavior.

In addition to the solar horoscope based on the Sun there is another division of the loci based on the Moon. That point on the horizon that has the same relationship to the Moon as the horoscope

[6]Today these divisions are incorrectly called houses. The term house will be defined in its proper context in Chapter IV.

[7]The native is the individual whose horoscope is being delineated.

has to the Sun is called the Part of Fortune. The Part of Fortune determines the beginning of the division of the loci of the lunar horoscope. The Lunar Horoscope indicated the quality of the native's soul: his moral and emotional nature, his temperament and psychological characteristics, and his intellect and mental acuteness. The lunar horoscope is unknown to most modern astrologers. The solar horoscope is used in its stead to delineate the quality of the soul. While leading to some errors this is not altogether inappropriate as much of what is in the lunar chart is also in the solar one.

The chart, or horoscope, as it is popularly called, is a map of the positions of the stars and planets as seen from the Earth. The loci of the chart are areas on the horizon projected onto the ecliptic. Each locus, or area, is physically one-twelfth the time required for the Sun to rise and then set; and is indicative of some particular facet of an individual's life or personality. The first three loci are indicative of those facets that combine both the body and the soul; the next three loci (4, 5, and 6) of those facets that concern the body alone without the soul; the 7th, 8th, and 9th loci concern events that are essentially independent of both body and soul; and the last three loci (10th, 11th, and 12th) concerns the soul alone without the body.

Those readers familiar with the philosophy of Aristotle will have no problems in interpreting the meanings of "body" and "soul" as used above. For others a bit of explanation is in order.

The hylemorphic theory of Aristotelianism states that every object in the sense world is a union of two ultimate principles: the material constituents, or matter; and the soul which is the form, or essence, which makes the matter (or body) the determinate kind of being that it is. This union of matter and form is not an arbitrary one. Matter is in every case to be regarded as possessing the capacity for form—as being potentially formed matter. Likewise the soul has being only in the succession of its material embodiments. Matter, then, must be conceived as a locus of determinate potentialities that become actualized only through the activities of form. The soul is the substantial form of the body and the only origin of all vital and mental performances. The soul without the body is an incomplete substance whose characteristics can only be manifested through the body.

The Meanings of the Loci

The first three loci are therefore the most deterministic. They denote that peculiar combination of matter and form that constitute the individual as he was born. The next three loci indicate those facets of the native's life that have potential actuality, given the cooperation of his temperament and personality. Loci 10,11, and 12 indicate events that emanate from the soul but that must be given actuality by the body. Loci 7, 8, and 9 are facets of life brought about through the accidents of the native's environment. These divisions are quite general however. It is now necessary to consider the meanings of each locus independently.

The first locus indicates the native's temperament and personality. The psychology of the native, his education and mental abilities have been correlated with the first locus. In addition those events in very early childhood can be delineated. The horoscopic point and cusp of the first locus are also important in determining the length of the native's life. Note that the native's temperament and personality are determined from the first locus of the lunar horoscope, while early childhood events and the length of life are correlated to the first locus of the solar chart.

In modern astrology the second locus concerns pecuniary matters: the native's income and possessions. This is only partially correct. In the lunar chart the second locus indicates the individual's feelings about money and possessions, and to some extent his-ability to acquire these things. As an acquisitive nature is likely to lead to wealth, the second locus does indeed have a tendency to indicate its acquisition. But in the solar horoscope it is events that lead to the native's manner of earning a livelihood that are correlative. Again, as some professions are more richly rewarded than others, the acquisition of wealth may be delineated. The native's propensity to command or follow (lunar), and those whom he commands or follows (solar) are also indicated by this locus.

The first locus deals with the native's innate mental abilities and education in general. The third locus indicates acquired mental activity: the ability to apply his mentality to such areas as literature, law, theology, and the like (lunar). Also included here is the direction his education is likely to take (i.e. the native's mental interest). In the solar chart the third locus indicates events concerned with the native's brothers, sisters, and other close relations including in-laws. Also correlative are short journeys, changes of domicile, and the like. In the Middle Ages this locus was considered indicative of knowledge of Holy Scripture and Canon Law.

Remember that the first three loci require a combination of matter and form. Therefore any events. Propensities, or abilities indicated by these loci not complementary to both of these factors in the native cannot transpire.

The fourth locus concerns the native's home and parents, especially the father. It is also correlative of real estate, farms and mines. It is indicative of the grandparents, and of immediate descendants. The solar horoscope's fourth locus presages events concerning these elements. Aristotelianism recognizes that the soul has accidental qualities as well as its inherent qualities. These accidental qualities are a product of the environment and receive their form from the soul. Hence the accidental qualities of the soul are as the body.

The fifth locus indicates children (especially sons, love affairs, and personal pleasures and enjoyments. In the Middle Ages this locus was also considered correlative of small acquisitions of wealth through such ventures as agriculture (i.e. success, or lack of same, of crops, etc.). Friendships in general, and business contacts in particular are also of concern here. In the lunar horoscope the fifth locus is indicative of the native's creativity. In this regard it is the first and third loci that determines the creative ability, the fifth locus determines the outward manifestation of this ability.

The sixth locus is correlative of sickness and health, and of accidents and loss of property (especially through confiscation). In classical astrology this locus was considered indicative of fraud and calumny and unjust imprisonment (or sometimes imprisonment whether just or unjust). In those times and places for which servants and maids are common, this locus also indicates the quality and loyalty of this kind of help. As a matter of conjecture, in a society such as the United States the locus might prognosticate concerning any type of employee or tradesman (plumber, milkman, etc.) that the native comes in contact with. In the lunar horoscope this locus concerns mental illness, especially as such an illness will affect the body.

Marriage, love affairs, and mistresses are presaged by the seventh locus. Business affairs, such as partners and lawsuits, are also indicative of this locus. Very close friendships are indicated by the seventh too. As is often the case in astrology, and in Aristotleanism in general, opposites are closely connected. The seventh locus is therefore correlative of open enemies, and losses through theft. As the seventh, eighth, and ninth loci concerns events independent of the native's body and soul the lunar chart must be used with care when considering facets of life in connection to them. However the soul is affected by the environment every bit as much as by inherent factor. An unhappy love affair will make at least a temporary change in an individual's personality, for example. The lunar horoscope must therefore be examined in light of the events predicted by the solar chart in these three loci.

The eighth locus is called "The House of Death"! Popular opinion to the contrary, this locus does not indicate the time of death. Rather it is indicative of the quality of death: the manner of death, whether immediate or lingering, whether by sickness or accident, and the like. As a corollary this locus predicts inheritance (especially through the death of the wife or husband). In the Middle Ages this locus also presaged murder, especially through poisoning, and the evil effects of drugs (very pertinent in today's society). This locus is also correlative of separation from one's loved ones, of fear, of grief, and of ruin (e.g., extreme poverty). Some modern astrologers attribute psychic ability to the eighth locus.

There is no historical evidence for this, but if true it would be found in the lunar horoscope.

"The House of Dreams" got its name from the ninth locus' indication of the native's ability in the interpretation of visions and dreams. This is the locus of psychic ability and experiences, of attainment of knowledge from the stars and divination, of religion and service dedicated to God. It is correlative with long journeys, distant roads, and messengers. Modern astrology also attributes in-laws to this locus, but classical astrology puts in-laws in the third locus which is more logical. The ninth locus concerns philosophical accomplishments and knowledge which comes through a revelation of one form or another (the long journeys and messengers contributing to this knowledge).

The tenth locus is perhaps the most important in the chart. Traditionally the first locus is the more powerful; but for some applications, such as the chart for a reigning ruler or of a nation, the tenth locus is even more powerful than the first. This is the locus of authority and success, or lack of same. It is correlative with the native's reputation and honor—both personal and professional. The tenth locus contains the MC, which is the primary prerogative place of the length of life (the others are the 1st, 11th, 9th, and 7th loci). This locus also refers to the mother (not the father as modern astrology has it). While this locus is indicative of fame and success (or lack of it) in the solar horoscope particular attention must be given to the Lunar tenth. The tenth, eleventh, and twelfth loci are all concerned with the soul alone without the body. There can be no success, nor honor, without a correlative indication in the lunar tenth. What an individual thinks of himself is all important in this regard; and the lunar horoscope will indicate this basic factor.

The solar eleventh is correlative of the native's friends and companions. It is also indicative of happiness and of concern for life and death. Traditionally this locus is called "The House of Hopes and Wishes." The lunar horoscope's eleventh locus concerns all that the native hopes to obtain in this life and in the next. The praise of colleagues, the friendship of women, wealth, heaven, all that man dreams and hopes for in the innermost depths of his psyche is revealed here.

"The House of Sorrows" indicates grief, indigence, envy, animosity, fear, tricks, prisons, captivity, disgrace, exile, disease, and enemies. However the twelfth locus is different from the sixth and eighth loci in that these troubles emanate from the native himself, and not from accidents of the environment. The lunar twelfth is called "The House of One's Undoing"! In the lunar horoscope all those defects of the soul that lead an individual to get himself into trouble are revealed. The lunar twelfth should be considered in conjunction with the solar and lunar first when delineating an individual's character and personality.

The correlative facets of life indicated above for the various loci go back almost 2,000 years, although there were some additions during the Middle Ages. The names of the loci were different in classical times however. At the beginning of the Christian era the names of the loci were: 1st, Horoscope; 2nd, Gate of Hades; 3rd, Goddess; 4th, Lower Midheaven; 5th, Good Fortune;6th, Bad Fortune; 7th, Occident; 8th, Beginning of Death; 9th, God; 10th, Midheaven; 11th, Good Daemon; and 12th, Bad Daemon.

Astrological Terminology

Loci 1, 4, 7, and 10 contain the angles and are called the poles (leading houses according to modern terminology). Loci 2, 5, 6, and 11 are supports for the poles (succedent houses); and the 3rd, 6th, 9th, and 12th loci are called the wanes (cadent houses). The poles are more important, or powerful, than the supports; and the supports are more powerful than the wanes. But this is only a generally true statement. Each of the loci have been determined to have a given relative efficacy to one another in terms of their importance in delineating a chart. Table 1 presents the relative importance of the loci. In Table 1 the lower the number, the greater the importance of the locus.

In addition to the relative powers of the loci as shown in Table 1, the table also presents other data handed down to us from classi-

Table 1: Characteristics of the Loci

Locus	*Years of Life*	*Rank or Power*	*Joy of the Planets*	*Powers of the Planets*
1	Infancy	1	☿	
2	Rest of Childhood	10		♃
3		8	☽	♂
4	Old Age and Death	6		☽
5		5	♀	
6		12	♂	
7	Prime of Life	4		♀
8		9		♄
9	Beginning of Youth	7	☉	☿
10	Middle Life	2		☉
11	End of Youth	3	♃	
12		12	♄	

cal times concerning elements peculiar to the various divisions of the equator. For example it was mentioned above that the first locus was indicative of events of very early childhood. Events throughout the rest of the native's life are correlative of other loci as shown in Table 1. Ages of these "years of life" are not given as they will vary among individuals.

The terminology of astrology is rife with words and phrases that today seem to smack of either stupidity or of naive superstition. However a study of the manner in which these terms came to be indicates a remarkable sophistication of thought. In studying correlations between the positions of the planets and events on Earth (particularly events concerning individuals) it was observed that certain planets when posited in a given locus very often indicated a future favorable circumstance of a nature connected with that locus. As it could then be expected that the native would be excited in expectation of this favorable circumstance, the Classicists called these combinations of planet and locus joys. When a planet is posited in such a locus, as when Mars is in the sixth locus, the planet is said to be in its joy.

Different individuals vary in those events that have the most marked influence on their life. When certain planets are posited in a given locus the events indicated by that locus will very often have a most powerful influence on the native. This combination of planet and locus is called powers. When a planet is posited in such a locus, as Venus in the seventh locus, the planet is said to be in its power; and that locus can be expected to exert a potent influence on the native. Table 1 gives the joys and powers of the planet/locus combinations.

Chart Construction

To set up a chart for the time of birth of an individual, or for any other time, the clock time of birth must first be converted to star time, or sidereal time[8]. The sidereal time together with the location of birth, as measured by geographical latitude and longitude, can be entered into the equations in Appendix B to determine the celestial longitude of the angles and cusps of the loci[9]. These positions are then plotted in a circular form with the horoscope at "9 o'clock" and the MC at "12 o'clock."

This can be readily accomplished on a piece of polar-coordinate graph paper, or specially designed astrological chart paper, in which the circle is divided into 360 degrees. Zero degrees of the sign of the zodiac containing the horoscope can be conveniently chosen so that the horoscope is at "9 o'clock."

---

[8]The conversion of clock to sidereal time is taken up in Appendix A.

[9]The construction of an astrological chart requires a certain sophistication in mathematics. In order that the non-mathematical reader not be confused in learning the elements of astrology, most of the mathematics has been deferred to the appendices. It is recommended that readers with the ability proceed to the appendices prior to reading Chapter III.

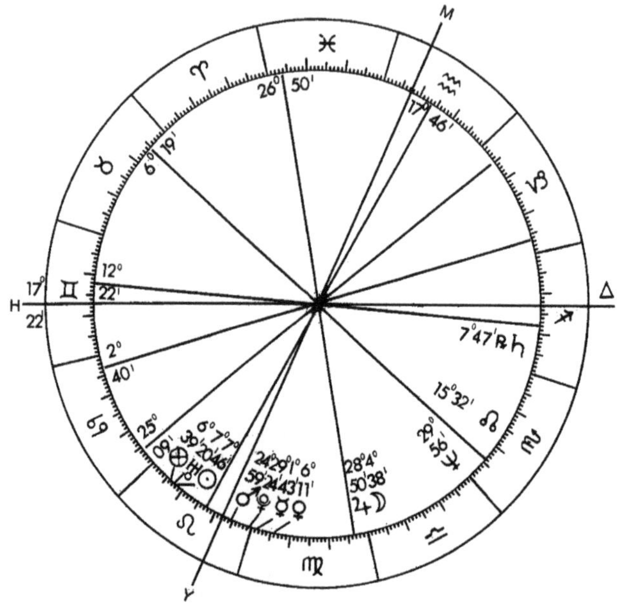

Figure 5.

Starting at zero degrees of the sign containing the horoscope the circle is then laid off into equal 30-degree segments, each segment denoting a sign of the zodiac. The signs are entered, beginning with the ascending sign, in the order of the succession of the signs (the order indicated in Table 2). The loci are then laid off, and the angles entered as indicated according to their celestial longitude. Figure 5 shows the result of these divisions for an individual born at 0200 hours Eastern Daylight Time on July 31, 1957 at New York City.

For the individual born at this time and place it is found (Appendix B) that the horoscope (ASC) is at 17 Gemini 21, and the MC is at 22 Aquarius 37. The descendant and IC are, of course, 180 degrees from these points. The loci are: 1st, 12 Gemini 21; 2nd, 3 Cancer 39; 3rd, 25 Cancer 09; 10th, 17 Aquarius 45; 11th, 26 Pisces 50; and 12th, 6 Taurus 19. The complementary loci, 4th,

Table 2. Astrological Symbols.					
Sign	Symbol	Planet/Angle	Symbol	Aspect	Symbol
Aries	♈	Moon	☽	Conjunction	☌
Taurus	♉	Mercury	☿	Quartile	□
Gemini	♊	Venus	♀	Trine	△
Cancer	♋	Sun	☉	Opposition	☍
Leo	♌	Mars	♂	Sextile	⚹
Virgo	♍	Jupiter	♃	Semi-quartile	∠
Libra	♎	Saturn	♄	Sesquiquadrate	⚼
Scorpio	♏	Uranus	♅	Quincunx	⊼
Sagittarius	♐	Neptune	♆	Semisextile	⊻
Capricorn	♑	Pluto	♇	Quintile	Q
Aquarius	♒	Horoscope	H	Biquintile	BQ
Pisces	♓	Medium coeli	M	Parallel	∥
		Descendant	Δ	Equipollent	∦
		Imum coeli	Y	Part of Fortune	⊗

5th, 6th, 7th, 8th, and 9th can be found by projection of the others. Table 2 presents the symbols used above for the signs and planets and other elements of the chart. Some of these symbols, such as the aspects, will be defined in later chapters. They are collected here as a matter of convenience.

Note that in Figure 5 the MC is in the ninth sign from the horoscope (ASC). In such a position the angles are called cadent. Had the MC been in the tenth sign the angles would be erect, and if in the eleventh sign, succedent. Erect angles are more powerful than succedent ones, which are more powerful than the cadent angles.

The planets are entered in the chart from an ephemeris. Most ephemerides contain the positions of the Sun, Moon, and planets computed for either noon or midnight Greenwich Mean Time (GMT). Clock time of birth is converted to GMT according to the method set forth in Appendix A. The planets' position for the time of birth are then interpolated from the entries in the ephemeris using standard mathematical methods.

For the birth data given for the chart in Figure 5 the planets' positions are: Moon, 4 Libra 37; Mercury, 1 Virgo 43; Venus, 6 Virgo 11; Sun, 7 Leo 45; Mars, 24 Leo 59; Jupiter, 28 Virgo 50; Saturn, 7 Sagittarius 47; Uranus, 7 Leo 20; Neptune, 29 Libra 56; and Pluto, 29 Leo 23. These data, entered into the chart in figure 5, constitute the solar horoscope.

Another important point in the solar chart, and required for the lunar chart, is the Part of Fortune. This point is computed on the equator, in right ascension[10], and translated to celestial longitude according to the formulae in Appendix B. The Part of Fortune is computed as follows:

Part of Fortune = ASC + ☽ - ☉

Translated to the ecliptic, the Part of Fortune has the position 6 Leo 39. This point now becomes the cusp of the first locus of the lunar horoscope. The other loci are found using the formulae in Appendix B. The angles of the solar chart are also the angles for the lunar chart. Only the cusps of the loci are changed; and, of course, the loci within which are posited the planets. Figure 6 is the lunar chart for the individual whose birth data has been given.

As explained above, the solar horoscope is a map of the positions of the stars and planets at the time of birth. The horoscope (ASC) represents the eastern horizon, or orient; and the descendant represents the western horizon, or occident. Therefore the stars and planets in the upper part of the chart, from the horoscope to the descendant, are above the horizon; and the stars in the lower part of the chart are below the horizon. For example, the Sun will be in the upper part of the chart if the birth was during daylight; and in the lower part of the chart if the birth was at night. The Moon in the up-

[10]Traditionally the Part of Fortune is computed in longitude rather than in right ascension. However, for this point to have the relationships mentioned as the "Lunar Horoscope" it must be computed as shown. For other applications, as for example in horary astrology, the traditional computation for the Part of Fortune is used.

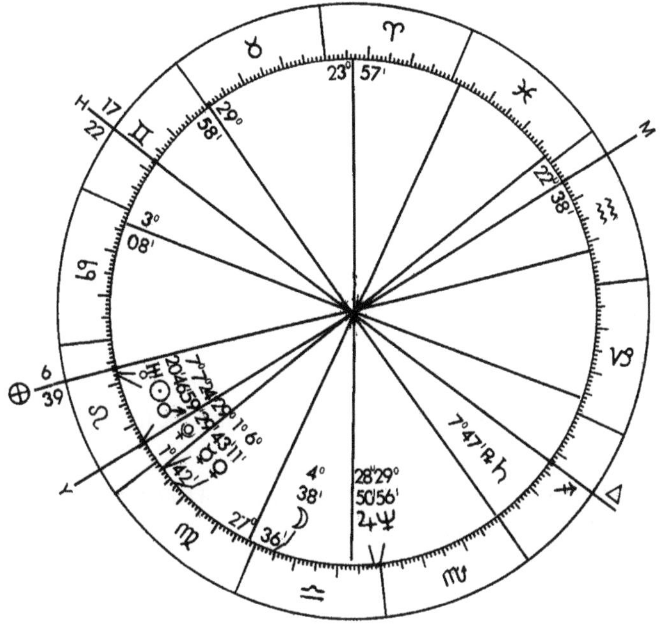

Figure 6.

per part of the chart, and the Sun in the lower portion, indicates a nighttime birth with the Moon visible in the sky.

This chapter has indicated the nature, and some of the tools of genethliacal astrology. The correlative nature of each of the loci has been discussed, and the method of chart construction has been outlined (albeit in a very cursory manner). It now remains to examine the charts depicted in figures 5 and 6 in detail and to investigate the elements contained therein. This will be done in the following chapters.

Review Questions

1. An individual comes to an astrologer in an attempt to locate a lost piece of jewelry. What branch of astrology would the astrolo-

ger be if he were to agree to help? What was the opinion of the Classicists of the use of astrology in such cases? Explain.

2. What is the difference between the celestial meridian and the prime vertical?

3. If the Medium coeli is at 22 Capricorn and the horoscope is at 17 Aries, where are the descendant and Imum coeli?

4. What is the significance of the Moon in the 4th lunar locus?

5. In a chart the second lunar locus and the third solar locus have very favorable indications. However, the lunar tenth and lunar twelfth have unfavorable indications. Comment.

6. The right ascension of the Moon is 185°,of the Sun 167°, and of the horoscope 65°. What is the right ascension of the Part of Fortune?

7. What planets can be seen in the sky at 2:00 a.m. July 31,1957, in New York City? Explain.

8. Both the 5th and the 7th loci are indicative of love affairs and friendships. Explain the difference.

9. Using the following information construct a solar chart.

Locus/Angle	*Longitude*	*Planet*	*Longitude*
Horoscope (ASC)	28 ♑ 22	Moon	20 ♑ 45
Medium coeli	21 ♏ 00	Mercury	25 ♑ 54
10	16 ♏ 54	Venus	15 ♒ 08
11	9 ♐ 41	Sun	12 ♒ 30
12	1 ♑ 29	Mars	22 ♐ 32
1	23 ♑ 22	Jupiter	25 ♑ 09
2	29 ♒ 30	Saturn	13 ♊ 46
3	8 ♈ 30	Uranus	23 ♎ 03
		Neptune	7 ♐ 05

Chapter III

The Signs

The Aristotelian Basis for Astrology

It is a generalization, of course, and many exceptions may be found, but in the Northern Hemisphere the quality of the winds as they blow from the various points of the compass is a constant that can be associated with the seasons of the year. Aristotle called the wind a "breath." However the same word, breath, also meant (in Greek science) a substance found in plants and animals, and pervading everything that brought life and generation. The signs of the zodiac are also associated with the seasons, and the scientific Greeks looked to the quality of the various winds to explain observations of the correlative indications of the signs.

"The knowledge of these facts (the quality of the winds) is useful to enable one to form a complete judgment of the temperatures (personality, character, etc.) in individual instances. For it is easily recognizable that, together with such conditions as these, of seasons . . . there is a corresponding variation in potency of the stars' faculties, and that in the conditions akin to them their quality is purer and their effectiveness stronger. Those that are heating by nature, for instance, have a greater potency in heat; and those that are moistening, in the moist. Under opposite conditions the stars' power is adulterated and weaker: the heating stars in cold periods and the moistening stars in dry periods are weaker. . . ."[1]

Ptolemy theorized that the stars, like the seasons and the winds, have a quality of being hot, cold, moist, and dry. Greek scientists had noted that winds from the east had a quality of dryness, for at the time of year the east wind was prevalent (autumn) the season was dry[2]. The Greeks called the east wind Apeliotes or "the wind from the sun" (it will be seen in the next chapter that the sun is correlated to the qualities of heat and dryness). During the summer the wind comes from the south. The south wind is called Notus and it is hot and rarefying. The west winds of spring are called Zephyrus and are fresh and moist. The Boreas is the cold north wind of winter.

The qualities of hot, cold, moist, and dry had a much wider meaning to the Greeks than they do today. They are the "elements" of Aristotelian physics. This is what it was composed of: the

substance pervading everything. The breaths of the various winds are associated with particular seasons, and the signs of the zodiac are likewise associated with the seasons. The quality of the winds have a certain affinity (by name) with the primary elements, hence it is reasonable to explain the correlative indications of the signs in terms of their having various admixtures of these elements (or so thought the Greeks of 2,000 years ago).

Now Aristotelian physics *qua* physics has been proven false. However many of the various observed correlative facts concerning the signs, stars, and planets are only indicated in the astrological literature by their explanations in terms of the ancient science. For example, the ancients believed that moisture was a feminine quality. If an individual exhibited a trait considered peculiar to the female (sympathy for instance) it was because of an increase of the element "moisture" in the body. No one seriously considers "moisture" to be an element anymore. Indeed, today there is even controversy as to whether any traits at all can be said to be peculiarly

[1] C. Ptolemy, *Tetrabiblos*, i:10.

[2] This is true of the lands along the Eastern Mediterranean. Most of Europe also has a relatively dry autumn.

male or female. But sympathy, for instance, is still a trait that one exhibits or does not exhibit. Insofar as the positions of heavenly bodies indicate such facts it is immaterial as to whether or not they are described in terms in Aristotelian physics; and such a description does not, in and of itself, prove the falsity of such observations.

So well known was the physics of Aristotle that descriptions of the correlative indications of the signs, stars, and planets was generally limited to a cursory statement of the "active" and "passive" elements thought to be contained in the nature of these bodies. Ptolemy, for example, devotes only one very short chapter to the nature of the signs[3]. And al-Biruni[4] merely presents the following table:

Table 3. The Triplicities.

	Dry	*Moist*	*Dry*	*Moist*	*Dry*	*Moist*
Hot	Aries	Gemini	Leo	Libra	Sagittarius	Aquarius
Cold	Taurus	Cancer	Virgo	Scorpius	Capricornus	Pisces

and then states:

> ". . . When therefore you know the active virtues of a sign whether hot or cold, and the passive virtues, whether dryness or moisture, it will not be concealed from you what particular element of the world and what particular humour of the body each sign resembles. . . ."

During the Middle Ages when astrology was being reintroduced into Europe writers of astrology, such as ibn Ezra, went into much more detail in describing what they called the "nature" of the signs and planets. The Europeans of this period had very little knowledge of Aristotle. The prevalent philosophy was the neo-Platonism of Augustine, and Aristotelianism was learned by the educated few only at the end of the 13th century. Because of the lack of knowledge of Aristotelianism the description of the

[3]*Tetrabiblos*, i:18

[4]Al-Biruni, *The Book of Instruction in the Elements of the Art of Astrology*, p. 347.

signs and planets was necessarily simplistic. Such naive descriptions of the signs are unfortunately still in use today. For example, Taurus, Virgo, and Capricorn are said to be of the "element" earth; and individuals with the sun in one of these signs are supposed to have a tendency to be practical and cautious (these traits being correlated to the "element" earth). This is all true, of course, but really only a small part of what is meant.

To begin with "earth" is not an element. Nor is "fire", "air", or "water." In the Aristotelian sense fire, earth, air, and water are primary bodies out of which all other bodies were assumed to be made. An element is that into which other bodies are analyzed, but which itself cannot itself be analyzed further. The compounds contain other elements—even potentially. The elements are the opposite, or contrary, qualitites hot and cold, dry and moist. The reason these contraries, and not some others, are elements is explained by Aristotle[5]. We shall take it on faith and proceed.

Hot and cold are active elements. In Aristoteliansism hot is that which associates things of the same kind or class, (and hence destroys that which is foreign). But cold is that which brings together both things which are of the same kind, and things which are not of the same class.

The moist and the dry are passive elements. The moist being that which, though easily adaptable to form (e.g. capable, as it were, of "filling something up"), cannot be confined within limits of its own. That is—the moist requires a "container" or a form (in the Aristotelian sense) other than itself in order to exist. The dry, on the other hand, is that which is easily confined within its own limits, (e.g. requires no "container," and hence is its own form). But the dry is not easily adaptable to form. That is it cannot completely fill a "container," or take another's form. That is it cannot completely fill a "container," or take another's form as can moist.

Elements are either active in that they act on something else, or they are passive in that they are acted upon by something else.

---

[5]Aristotle, *De Generatione Et Corruptione*, ii.

The hot and cold are active elements because they act on other things to bring them together. The moist and the dry are passive because they are acted upon by form, (which, as was discussed in the previous chapter, is analogous to "soul").

The Triplicities

There are six mathematically possible ways to combine the four elements, but two of these combinations (e.g., hot-cold and moist-dry) are not physically or logically possible. The other four combinations are the primary bodies (or "elements" in the medieval literature) of Aristotelianism.

Fire is that primary body which has the combination of the elements hot and dry. Aries, Leo, and Sagittarius are of the "nature" of fire (see Table 3). By this is meant that events in which these signs are part of the correlative indicators are explainable in part by the elements hot and dry. Anger, for example, disassociates strife from love (things of a different kind) and associates together the passions of hate and fear (things of the same kind). Anger manifests itself through a "form" of its own: e.g., it is easily definable both in terms of the act and of the object of the act; it does not, as it were, completely "fill the container," but leaves room for other emotions (you may be angry at one you love, etc.). Therefore, anger is both hot and dry: it is of the nature of fire. Events, then, in which the fiery signs are a part of the correlative indicators may be the result of anger or a similar intemperance. Some of this is found in modern astrological texts which claim that those born with the fiery signs predominant exhibit a rash, feverish, easily excited or impulsive nature. Such an individual may incline to a high level of activity (equals friction and heat), and be very enthusiastic in every undertaking. But this description is an over simplification of the nature of fire. For example, the love of one individual for another would also be of the nature of hot and dry; although self-love sometimes tends to be hot and moist. Why? Again, the acquisition of a headlight or tire manufacturing company by an automobile manufacturer is also of the nature of fire, as is the formation of a political or religious organization, (as opposed to the joining of a religious organization which can be hot and moist). The list could go on indefinitely. The point here is that modern astrology tends to oversimplify what it calls the "nature of fire" together with the natures of the other "elements."

Earth is that primary body which has the combination of the elements cold and dry. Taurus, Virgo, and Capricorn are of the nature of earth. Sex, as opposed to procreation, is correlative with earth as it brings together dissimilar things (male and female); and it has a form of its own (e.g. has a well defined object). But sex is not an end in itself and, hence, does not generally completely "fill the container." Other things of the nature of earth include conglomerate corporations, nations such as the United States and Australia with their heterogenous populations, and universities (as opposed to, say, divinity schools, law schools, or teachers colleges), and the like. Such concepts are not discussed in modern astrology however. Indeed, many modern astrologers would have difficulty in identifying Aristotle, let alone describing his philosophy. The best that one can get today are lists of traits of those born with earthy signs predominant in their charts: i.e., nervous temperament (noticed especially in Virgo and Capricorn) and individuals who are dependably practical and hard working in "sensible" or conservative" ways. Needless to say this hardly does justice to what the classical scientist-astrologer meant.

The signs of Gemini, Libra, and Aquarius combine the elements of heat and moisture. They are of the nature of air. As indicated previously self-love has this quality. It associates things of the same kind (self); and, while not having a form of its own, can completely fill the form of he who has it. Now in Aristotelian philosophy, fire and air have a natural movement toward infinity, while earth and water have a natural movement toward the center (of the Earth or universe). The propensity of those with the fire and air signs predominant in their charts is therefore toward the extrovert, while the earth and water signs indicate the introvert. Modern astrology stresses the intellectuality and communication of the airy signs. It is said that such individuals are inclined to reasoning, intelligent pursuits, and working in the realm of ideas. However modern astrology also tends to neglect the fact that these same traits are also fiery, the particular primary body prevalent depends on how all-consuming the trait is. Does it or does it not, "completely fill the container." Other things that have the nature of air include religious experiences, the emotion of hate (as opposed to anger), and revolutionary activities.

Finally, the elements of cold and moist make up the elemental body water. Procreation is a primary example of something of the nature of water. It brings together dissimilar classes (male and female), but it does not have a form of its own. Procreation is wholly and solely the nature of that which it attempts to bring about (as a child is the object of the act of procreation between human beings). The signs of Cancer, Scorpio, and Pisces are watery signs. Classical astrologers, such as Ptolemy and al-Biruni, classified these signs as fecund. Modern astrologers find that individuals with these signs predominant are emotional, unstable, and sensitive. The individual is apt to be a creature of his environment—shaped, as it were, by his contact with other people. But this is also the nature of airy signs. The difference lies in the contrast between the elements heat and cold (e.g., in the manner is which the individual becomes the same as, or different from, his environment and those he associates with).

It should be evident from what has been said that the elemental bodies can change, one into another. The theory of how this happens is described in Aristotle's *De generatione et corruptione*. This book, and Aristotle's companion works, *Physicia*, *De caelo*, and *Meteorologica*, should be studies in depth by those wishing to really know and understand the natures of the signs and planets as postulated by the Classicists. Suffice to say here that the addition of the element cold to the elemental body fire will result in the elemental body earth. In like manner if moisture is added to fire the result is air, and so forth (see Table 3).

Each of the planets have a quality as one of the elements

(Chapter IV). Hence the planets moving through the signs affect changes in them. The Sun, which is hot when in Cancer, will tend to change the correlative indications of Cancer from that of water to that of air. If but one element only need be changed, as when going from water to air, the change is easy and fast. If both elements need be changed, as when going from water to fire or from earth to air, the change is difficult and slow.

In modern astrology the hypothesis is that each sign is of a fixed nature, and that the planets manifest themselves in different modes according to the sign of the zodiac in which they are posited. Hence the Leonian person is described as dignified, commanding, powerful, strong-willed, generous, etc. In classical astrology, on the other hand, it is the planet's nature that is fixed. This nature can be modified by the aspects (Chapter V) and other relationships, but in comparison to the signs it is the planetary natures that are constant[6]. The signs, on the other hand, change from the nature of one elemental body to another. This changing of coming-to-be and passing-away of elemental bodies, and hence of the natures of the signs, is affected by the movements of heavenly bodies (planets) in orbits and at speeds which do not coincide with those of the fixed stars. Hence in classical astrology the Leonian person exists if, and only if, the "nature" of Leo has not been changed by the movement of one or more of the planets.

The Sects

In addition to likening of the correlative effects of the signs to the combinations of the elements and the elemental bodies, the signs are divided into two sects: masculine and feminine, diurnal and nocturnal, positive and negative. Aries is masculine, diurnal, and positive: Cancer is feminine, nocturnal, and negative. These sects alternate around the zodiac.

Modern texts of astrology mention the sects (through the word "sect" is seldom used) without attempting to describe how they

[6]A planet's potency, or ability to act decisively according to its nature, varies among the signs. The basic nature of the planets, however, is invariant.

come about, or they may make an attempt at some occult explanation. However, both Aristotle[7,8] and Ptolemy[9] make it quite clear that the division of signs according to sect is not arbitrary. The elemental qualities are contraries; and each contrary has either a positive or negative element, with hot being positive and cold being negative. Therefore, Aries, Gemini, Leo, etc., being hot are positive while Taurus, Cancer, Virgo, etc., are cold and negative. Also that which is male must hold the first place (or so thought the Greeks of 2000 years ago), and as Aries is the starting point for the zodiac it must be male. In like manner Aries must be diurnal as it marks the beginning of spring and "a new day." The sects then change in succession in alternating order around the signs of the zodiac.

The Quadruplicities

The final major classification of the signs is according to the seasons: the so-called quadruplicities of modern astrology. This distinction divides the zodiac into the solstitial, equinoctial, solid, and bicorporeal signs. The sostitial signs are Cancer and Capricorn; the equinoctial, Aries and Libra; the solid, Taurus, Leo, Scorpio, and Aquarius; and the bicorporeal are Gemini, Virgo, Sagittarius, and Pisces. Modern astrology names the sostitial and equinoctial signs cardinal, the solid signs fixed and the bicorporeal signs common or mutable. Today the opinions as to the "natures" of the signs as related to the quadruplicities is confused and contradictory. For example Llewellyn George states[10] that individuals in which the cardinal signs dominate will be versatile and adaptable, while the nature of the bicorporeal signs will indicate an unstable individual. Margaret Hone, on the other hand, insists[11] that the na-

[7]Aristotle, *De Caelo*, ii:3.

[8]Aristotle, *De Generatione Et Corruptione*, ii:10.

[9]*Tetrabiblos*, i:12

[10]L. George, *A to Z Horoscope Maker and Delineator*, Llewellyn Publications, St. Paul, Minnesota, 1972.

[11]M. Hone, *The Modern Textbook of Astrology*, Fowler, London, 1969.

ture of the common signs is an indication of adaptability, and that the cardinal signs presage an individual to be outgoing—an extrovert. Amazingly, they both agree that the nature of the solid signs is "a resistance to change." Here is yet another example of confusion and inaccuracy in modern astrology caused by a lack of knowledge of the scientific astrology of the Classicists.

Traditionally[12], the natures of the signs are determined by the seasons that take place in them. Al-Biruni gives the following descriptions[13] that are confirmed in all the ancient texts. Aries, Taurus, and Gemini are vernal, changeable, govern childhood, the east and the east wind, and first watch of night (the first three civil hours after sunset). Cancer, Leo, and Virgo are vestal, restful, govern youth, the south and the south wind, and the second watch. Libra, Scorpio, and Sagittarius are autumnal, changeable, govern adult life, the west and the west wind, and the third watch. Finally, Capricorn, Aquarius, and Pisces are hibernal, peaceful, govern old age, the north and the north wind, and the last three civil hours before sunrise (the fourth watch).

The first sign of each season are the tropical signs. When the Sun is in the solstitial signs the Sun "begins to reverse its latitude (in the terminology of the ancient Greeks) causing summer in Cancer and winter in Capricorn. The nature of these signs is therefore change. When the Sun is in Aries or Libra, on the other hand, the days (sunrise to sunset) and the nights (sunset to sunrise) are of equal time. Hence it is the nature of the equinoctial signs to be unchanging or constant in temperament. The tropical tetragons, taken as a whole, have correlative indications of gentleness, purity, and sociability, with a tendency towards science and detail.

The solid signs of Taurus, Leo, Scorpio, and Aquarius are those which follow the tropical signs. The seasons which began in the preceding signs are now firmly established. It is not the nature of these signs to be "resistant to change"; rather, it is their nature to be "inured to change," to find what has changed acceptable, or at

[12]*Tetrabiblos*, i:11.

[13]Al-Biruni, p. 380.

least bearable. (In a sense, of course, this implies a resistance to further change). The correlative indicators of this tetragon are also mildness, thoughtfulness and justice. Al-Biruni says that in many cases these signs indicate litigiousness and pugnacity, and sometimes endurance in adversity and patience in trouble and justice (an effect of being inured to change).

Gemini, Virgo, Sagittarius, and Pisces (the bicorporeal signs) follow the solid signs and precede .the tropical ones. The seasons in these signs are those of the solid signs in the beginning, and those of the, tropical signs at the end. Hence they share, as it were, two kinds of weather. The terms "adaptable" and "unstable" are both correct description of the nature of the bicorporeal signs. They also indicate amiability, levity, playfulness, thoughtlessness, discord in business, capriciousness, and duplicity.

The correlative indications of the solid signs is generally quite strong, that of the bicorporeal signs more obscure, and those of the tropical in between.

The Decanates

Ptolemy determined by experience and observation that the general descriptions of the natures of the signs are modified somewhat in different parts of the signs. He found that individual thirds (in longitude) of each sign, and their northern and southern parts by latitude, have different "atmospheres." That is, when these different parts of the signs become indicators of an event the interpretations differ. The thirds of the signs are variously called "faces," "figures," and "decanates" according to Arab, Greek or Hindu custom. Modern astrology uses the Hindu decanate for the 10n degrees of a third of a sign. We shall use the same terminology. Finer divisions of the signs were also sometimes used by astrologers: the novena (Hindu "navamsas") or one-ninth of a sign, and the dodecagon (Hindu "dwadashamsa") or one-twelfth of a sign. These finer divisions of the signs were looked down upon by the best of the ancient astrologers. They will be discussed in part in later chapters however.

Ptolemy determined the "atmospheres" of the decanates and the northern and southern parts of the signs to be as indicated in Table 4. Remember that the "natures" of the signs are analogous to the weather indicated in the sign. The first decan of Aries, for example, would presage the more intemperate aspects of the elemental quality air.

The Nature of the Signs

It now remains to consider each sign of the zodiac in turn to describe thousands of years of observational results concerning their correlative indications.

Aries is the dreaded sign, indicating passionate temper and bodily hurt. In his *De revolutione annorum mundi* (Noribergae, 1549), Masha'allah wrote of the Creation having taken place when the seven planets (Sun, Moon, Mercury, Venus, Mars, Jupiter, and Saturn) were in conjunction here, and foretold of the destruction of the world when they should be in the same position in Pisces. Pliny wrote that the appearance of a comet within its borders portended great wars and wide-spread mortality, abasement of the great and elevation of the small, with fearful drought in the regions over which the sign predominated. However ibn-Ezra calls Aries one of the good and agreeable signs. Closer to the truth would be:

> "First Golden Aries shines, and as he oft does lose
> His fleece, and then as frequently renews,
> 'Twixt sudden ruin, and a fair estate
> He fixes the variety of fate;
> He gets, then loses, then returns to gain
> The loss steals in, and empties all his pain . . ."[14]

According to the Classicists this sign is indicative of houses of worship and the seats of justice. The people corresponding to this sign are kings who practice justice and generosity, the leaders in battles, fire, slaughter and bloodshed. In ancient times it was also

[14]M. Manilius, *Astronomicon*, iv:10.

Table 4. The Decanates

Sign	Whole Part	North Part	South Part	1st Decan	2nd Decan	3rd Decan
Aries	thunder & rain	bringing heat & destruction	bringing cold & ice	wind, rain & thunder	temperate	bringing hot plague epidemics
Taurus	heat inclin-ning to moisture	temperate	unsettled conditions	earthquake & hot wind	temperate	heat, light-ing, thunder
Gemini	temperate	winds dry-ing up ground	scorching heat	destructive moisture	temperate	unsettled
Cancer	improvement warm	scorching heat	scorching heat	hot winds earthquake	temperate	winds
Leo	heat	wind	moisture	hot depress-ing atmosp.	temperate	winds
Virgo	moisture & thunder	wind	temperate	very hot & destructive	temperate	destructive moisture
Libra	changeable	great heat	moisture bringing epidemics	fine weather	temperate	very wet
Scorpio	thunder & lightning	wind	moisture	snow & wind	temperate	earthquake
Sagittarius	windy	wind	very wet & unsettled	moisture	temperate	very hot
Capricorn	very wet	very wet & bringing destruction	very wet & changeable	great heat destruction	temperate	rains
Aquarius	cold & wet	great heat	wind & snow	very wet	temperate	winds
Pisces	cold & wet	wind	wet	moderate	very wet	very hot

indicative of "those who walk on roads." Today the meaning would include all those who travel a great deal over land. Traditionally this sign is also indicative of those who are eager for marriage. Their families will be small, however this sign can also favor the production of twins. As a result of what has been said the sign is considered to be of two natures.

In physical characteristics those born with Aries rising will be of medium height, thin, short-sighted, glance upcast, eyes dark or grey, and reddish curly hair. Modern astrologers add a ruddy complexion, an active walk, and a longish stringy neck. However in this regard, care must be taken of Ptolemy's admonition[15] that heredity and environmental factors take precedence over the astrological. Two blue eyed parents can only have blue eyed children regardless of the time of birth or of the rising sign! The physical descriptions of natives born under a given sign must be considered only a tendency. In like manner an individual's personality can be largely a product of his environment. It is to the discredit of modern astrology that today the non-astrological factors are not given their proper place in astrological delineations.

In personality those born with Aries as the indicative sign will have a weak but pleasant voice, always laughing and talkative but with a tendency to be sharp-tongued. He will be kingly and haughty, fond of poetry, lustful and brave. Ibn-Ezra remarks that "he will want to eat copiously, be irascible, and be fond of justice." Those born in the first decanate of Aries (or with the Sun in this decanate) will have numerous friends and will abhor evil, in the second decanate will be easily aroused to anger and not be able to control this emotion, he will have numerous enemies, and he will have high principles and an understanding of their correct applications. Those born in the third decanate of Aries will combine traits of the other two.

Modern astrologers attribute the following characteristics to Aries: courageous, restless, hot-tempered, strong-willed and independent, ambitious, energetic, selfish, crude, aggressive and reckless.

As to the professions, the Classicists mentioned kings, bankers, coiners, blacksmiths, coppersmiths, butchers, shepherds, spies, and thieves. The Modernists add soldiers and surgeons.

Taurus marked the vernal equinox from about 4000 B.C. to 1700 B.C. In all ancient zodiacs preserved to us it began the year.

[15]*Tetrabiblos*, i:2.

The Druids considered Taurus an important object to worship, their great religious festival, the Tauric, being held when the sun entered its boundaries. In Hebrew lore the sign is assigned to the tribes of Manasseh and Ephriam, from Moses' allusion to their father Joseph in the 33rd chapter of Deuteronomy: "his horns are the horns of the wild ox."

Its part of mankind includes procurers, those who like to eat, drink, and make merry, and "all those longing for coition." The sign in indicative of those who are eager for marriage, and like Aries is also correlative of small families. The first part (decanate) of Taurus is even considered to indicate sterility. On the whole the Classicists considered Taurus an unfortunate sign, although a manuscript almanac of 1386 had: "Whoso is born under yat syne schal have a grace in bestis"; and thunder, when the sun was in Taurus, "brought a plentiful supply of victuals."

In physical characteristics the Taurean native will be tall with a broad forehead and black downcast eyes with small whites. Their nose will be broad with the point upturned. They will have a large mouth, thick lips, black hair, and a strong neck. The modern astrologers add that he is usually heavy, and that his movements are apt to be deliberate.

In personality this sign is indicative of those who are very lustful and gluttonous, and have a habit of contraries. They will exercise good judgment, but will have a tendency toward negligence. Those born in the first decanate will be noble at heart, will enjoy all kinds of delight, and will have numerous friends; in the second decanate the native will have a generous soul and will be intelligent; in the third decanate the native will have a tendency to suffer from overwork, and they will have no luck in their dealings with the opposite sex.

Modern astrologers attribute the following characteristics to Taurus: patience, jealous, obstinate, affectionate, indifferent, and sometimes hot-tempered.

As to the professions the Classicists mention sellers, tailors, weighers of grain, fishermen, cobblers, agents, and farmers. The

Modernists add art dealers, financiers, and singers.

Gemini, the Twins were placed in the sky by Jove in reward for their brotherly love so strongly manifested while on Earth. In classical days the sign was often symbolized by two stars over a ship. For their efficient aid in protecting their fellow Argonauts in the storm that nearly overwhelmed the Argo, the Gemini were considered by the Greeks as propitious to mariners. In Acts xxviii:11 we read:

> "And after three months, we sailed in a ship of Alexandria that had wintered in the island, and whose figurehead was the 'Heavenly Twins'."

Jove appointed the Twins as the guardians of Rome, and they generally appeared on all silver coinage of the Republic from about 269 B.C. That the Gemini were invoked by the Greeks and Romans in war as well as in storm as is attested in Macaulay's *Lays of Ancient Rome* that so stirred the schoolboys' heart in the days of classical education.

Those born within the sign of Gemini will be crafty in the good sense of the word, in all their work and in all their tasks. Among them will be writers, mathematicians, astronomers, and famous sages. They will be truthful individuals and moderate in their fear of God. In terms of children, the Gemini are specially charged with the production of twins. This sign was given the name of "many faced" in ancient times because it denotes riot only twins, but three or more children at a single birth.

In physical appearance the Geminian will be of medium height, good appearance with a fine face, sharp-sighted with broad shoulders and a strong voice. The hair will be curly and the eyes beautiful. Al-Biruni adds that the shanks will be long in comparison with the forearm. Modern astrologers say that the native of the Gemini will have a youthful appearance all through life, a slender build, a springy walk, and an alert expression.

The Gemini produces a generous and chaste personality. Individuals excelling in games and fond of philosophy and astronomy are also indicative of the Gemini, as are also those who are magnanimous, munificent, and (sometimes) violent. The first decanate indicates those who are not irascible, those who will suffer from overwork, and those who are unlucky in their dealings with the opposite sex; the second decanate is correlative of those with pleasing speech, well bred, noble, and those who associate with people in high places; the third indicates those who are sexually promiscuous, those who use vulgar and filthy language, and those who prevaricate.

Modern astrologers attribute the following to the Gemini: clever, intuitive, restless, heartlessness, undependability, inquisitive, lack of perseverance, and sometimes too clever.

Classicists say that the Geminian follow the professions of kings, calculators, teachers, hunters, dancers, musicians, painters, and tailors. The Modernists add: journalists, novelists, lecturers, linguists, commercial travelers, and pupils.

Cancer is the most inconspicuous asterism in the zodiac. The is explained in mythology by the story that when the crab was crushed by Hercules for pinching his toes during his contest with the Hydra in the marsh of Lema, Juno exalted it to the sky. Yet few heavenly signs have been subject to more attention in the early days, for, according to Chaldean and Platonist philosophy, it was supposed to be the "Gate of Men" through which souls descended from heaven into human bodies. Egyptian records of about 2000 B.C. describe Cancer as a Scarabeaus, sacred, and a symbol of immortality. Cancer is the house of the Moon (see Chapter IV), and there is an early belief that this luminary was located here at the Creation.

It is one of the more unfortunate signs; and when the Sun is within Cancer thunderstorms are indicative (in ancient times) of commotions, famines, and locusts. Berossos (fl. 3rd century B.C.) asserted that the Earth was to be submerged when all the planets met in Cancer, and consumed by fire when they meet in Capricorn. Individuals born under Cancer are lovers of mankind and highly respected, but women for which this sign is the horoscope (ASC) may be beset by difficult undertakings. Ibn Ezra[16] remarks that those who are born under this sign may be deaf and dumb. Cancer is one of the fecund signs and is indicative of large families.

In physical appearance the Cancerian is of moderate height, with thick limbs and fine frown rather long hair. He will have a crooked nose and uneven teeth, his look will be downcast and he will have a tendency toward corpulence. Al-Biruni states that his shanks will be longer than his forearms. Modern astrologers add that he is apt to be soft and not very muscular, and have a round face.

Those born under the sign of Cancer will be indolent, dumb, fickle, and changeable. Those born in the first decanate will have a good soul, many friends, and he will be an expert in fraud. The second decanate indicates an individual beloved by all creatures, and the third those who will suffer a great deal by themselves.

Modern astrologers assert that the sign is correlative of selfishness. The native will be devoted to his country and his family. His feelings will be easily hurt and he may become moody and sullen. He is kind and self-reliant, but can be restless. They have strong feelings, especially strong feelings of compassion.

The Classicists assert that the Cancerian natives are good sailors, swimmers, and canal diggers. Al-Biruni also includes water diviners. The Modernists add innkeepers, caterers, nurses, housewives, mothers, social workers, and the like.

In Greek and Roman mythology, Leo the lion represented the Nemean Lion, originally from the Moon, and, after his Earthly stay was carried back to the heavens with his slayer, Hercules, where he became the poet's "Nemeasus." The Egyptian king Necepsos, and his philosopher Petosiris, taught that at the Creation the sun rose near Denebola; and hence Leo was "Domicilium Solis": the emblem of fire and heat. Throughout antiquity the lion and Leo have always been identified with the Sun and great dynasties, even ap-

[16]Abraham ibn Ezra, *The Beginning of Wisdom*, 1148. This and other references on the natures of the signs continues throughout the text and will not be repeated.

pearing on the royal arms of England. But the lion is also the tribal sign of Judah as recorded in *Genesis* lclix:9:

> "Judah is the lion's whelp . . . resting thou has couched as a lion, and as a lioness, who shall rouse him."

And this is confirmed in the Apocalypse of St. John, v:5:

> ". . . Weep not; behold the lion of the tribe of Judah, the root of David. . . ."

The lion is a most fortunate sign. Those born under it will be valiant and irascible. They will be educated and clever individuals, relying on themselves in cases of danger or of major problems. In the horoscopes of women Leo prognosticates modesty. Ibn-Ezra states that natives of Leo have a nature of that of wolves, very gluttonous and fond of all food. Ancient physicians thought that when the Sun was in this sign medicine was a poison, and even a bath could be harmful. In the Middle Ages it was said that thunder, when the Sun was in Leo, foretold of sedition and the deaths of great men. As to children, Leo indicates sterility.

The Leonian person will be of fine appearance. He will be of full height, with a broad face and grey eyes, a large nose and a wide mouth. He will have slender thighs, and his hips will be on the large side. His hair will be of chestnut color, his fingers thick, and he will have a prominent belly. Modernist add that he will have a strong, well formed back, and that his lips will be of good color. The Leonian will have a dignified poise, and his manner and walk can be described as quick.

In personality those born under the sign of Leo are kingly, formidable, sharp-tongued, hard-hearted, litigious, knavish, forgetful, and bold. They tend to be powerful by nature, and al-Biruni asserts that they are sinners and have many troubles. Those born in the first decanate will be well known among men, and Ibn Ezra adds that they will be modest while associating with kings; in the second decanate they will be magnanimous .and honored by their people; and those born in the third decanate of Leo will have many friends and enemies, and ibn Ezra says that they will also be powerful, fond of women, and have abundant ailments.

Modern astrologers add that the Leonian person is creative, courageous, joyful, impulsive, egotistical, just, altruistic, conceited, and forgiving.

The Classicists say that the professions of those born under the sign of Leo include horsemen, joiners, and falconers. Modern astrologers add actors, goldsmiths, jewelers, managers, monarchs, professional athletes, and film stars.

Virgo is the older, purely allegorical representation of innocence and virtue. Eratosthenes (276?-196 B.C.) identifies her with the Egyptian goddess of nature, Isis. According to early Greek tradition the Sphinx was constructed with Virgo's head on Leo's body because the Sun passes through these two signs during the inundation of the Nile. Others, however, have identified Virgo with Ishtar, the Babylonian and Assyrian goddess of fertility. This latter deity is the Astarthe of *3 Kings*, xi: 5-33, whom Solomon worshiped to his regret.

Virgo is an unfortunate and sterile sign, signifying barrenness or few children, especially of male issue. Those born under her will be learned and intelligent, and will be good looking. They will have a tendency to be impotent, but will have a kind soul and be an advocate of justice. According to Pliny the appearance of a comet within its borders implied many grievous ills to the female portion of the population.

In physical characteristics those born under Virgo will be medium stout inclining to being tall. They will have long hair and flat noses. Al-Biruni says that they will have moles on their chest and abdomen. Ibn Ezra asserts that they will be attractive in posture, and have broad shoulders and non-curly hair. Modern astrologers add that like Gemini, the Virgo person will keep a youthful appearance well into old age.

The personality of those born under Virgo will be thoughtful, lively, playful, and truthful. They will have good manners, be well-informed, and fond of dance and music. They are liberal in the modern sense of the word, pious, and have a tendency to judge others harshly. Those born in the first decanate will have a pleasing face, will be a writer, and will be an expert in mathematics. Those born in the second decanate will be well bred, candid, endowed with magnanimity and fond of receiving compliments. The third decanate indicates those who will be educated, truly intelligent, humble, and wise.

Modernists claim that the Virgo person is critical and exacting. They are said to tend to neatness in everything, and can have an exaggerated attention to detail. They are altruistic, just persnickety, clever, and intuitive.

Professionally the Virgos will be secretaries, supervisors, ordinary people, dancers, and singers. Al-Biruni asserts they will also be viziers and eunuchs. Modern astrologers add accountants, agents, craftsmen, critics, doctors, teachers, farmers, dietitians, inspectors, and health officers.

Despite the fact that Libra is an equinoctial sign ushering in the beginning of autumn, it is one of the last of the 12 signs of the zodiac identified. In very ancient times the stars of Libra were called the "Claws of the Scorpion" and were part of Scorpio. The Egyptian historian Manetho said that Libra originated when on the equinox and so represented the equality of day and night. Libra is identified with the balance, and is considered to have influence over the legal profession:

> "What he determines, that for right shall stand,
> As justice weigh'd her balance in his hand,
> This ruled at Servius's birth, who first did give
> Our laws a being . . ."[17]

The general horoscope for those born under this sign is that they will be sensible and well bred persons with pleasant speech. They will be capable of plying any trade, will be musicians and be capable of composing music. Ibn Ezra says that they will be fond

[17]M. Manilius, Astronomicon, iv:16.

of women and will enjoy the hunt. Astrologers of the 14th century insisted that "Whoso es born in yat syne sal be an ille doar and a traytor." Those born in the first decanate will have beautiful countenance, will suffer from overwork, and will be humble and refined; in the second decanate will be liberal and affable; and those born in the third decanate will be known and respected by his people. As regards to marriage and family Libra favors large families and an eagerness for wedlock.

As to appearance, the Libran will be of moderate size, good looking with grey eyes, good nose, and good feet. Al-Biruni says that they will be inclined to brown and yellow and have distinctive marks on the neck and waist. Modern astrologers assert that the native of this sign will be well proportioned with regular features, good color, and gentle eyes. They will have a spontaneous smile and a tendency to dimples.

The personality of the Libra native will tend toward the thoughtful, polite, and generous. He will be a just judge, excited in speech, and may be a musician and singer, he will be of, or identify with, the plebeian class; and can become indolent and cowardly. Modernists add that those born under this sign will be intuitive, harmonious, refined, affectionate, intelligent, indecisive, too demonstrative, modest, and tactful in his dealings with others.

The professions include (in addition to musicians, composers, and singers mentioned above) philosophers, geometricians, merchants, and grammarians. Al-Biruni adds privy-counselors, merry makers, and devotees. Modern astrologers include artists, diplomats, generals, and staff officers.

Scorpio slayed the giant. The giant was then relegated to the sky where, as Orion, he sinks below the Scorpion still in fear of it. Early dwellers of the Euphrates consider Scorpio a symbol of darkness, showing the decline of the Sun's power after the autumnal equinox, then located in this sign. Legend has it that the sign as the scorpion or serpent whereby Pharaoh, King of Egypt, was enforced to let the children of Israel depart out of his country.

Scorpio is one of the fruitful signs, "active and eminent"; but ancient astrologers also knew it as the accursed sign—the baleful source of war and discord. Those born in this sign will have an unpleasant voice and enunciation (or so said the classical astrologers). Ibn Ezra asserts that they will be homely; have many children; and will be destructive, deceitful, irascible, a prevaricator, a calumniator, melancholy, generous, refined, unreliable, and astute. Pliny states that a comet in Scorpio portended a plague of reptiles and insects, especially locusts. In ancient times the setting of the constellation exerted a malignant influence and was accompanied by storms. In the Middle Ages the alchemists held the sign in high regard, for only when the Sun was in Scorpio could the transmutation of iron into gold be performed.

The Scorpionic person will be good looking have small eyes with yellowish whites, and hold his head erect. He will have a round face, a narrow forehead, broad nose, and coarse hair. He will have slender thighs and ankles, and a broad chest and shoulders. Al-Biruni says that there will be a mark on the back. Modern astrologers add that the eyes will tend to be deep-set with the bone above the eyes prominent.

Those born under the sign of the scorpion will be generous by nature. They will be anxious, deceitful, bold, rough, morose, and sharped-tongued. Al-Biruni asserts that in addition they will be a slayer, a fool, indolent, bold, and overly pleased with themselves. Those born in the first decanate will be well educated, sensible, and glib in speech; in the second decanate they will be well bred and loquacious; and those born in the third decanate will be fond of gluttony and sex, and, according to ibn Ezra, will be very dejected.

Modernists assert that the Scorpionic person will be secretive, passionate, strong-willed, restless, jealous, hot-tempered, exacting, unbegrudging, and have a magnetic personality.

The professions of those born under this sign are physicians and sailors. Al-Biruni also includes enchanters and magicians. The Modernists add butchers, coroners, detectives, pharmacists, and psychologists.

Cuneiform inscriptions designate Sagittarius as the "Strong

One," the "Giant King of War," and as the "Illuminator of the Great City," personifying the archer god of war, Nergel of *4 Kings*, xvii: 30. Early tradition had the constellation put into the sky so that the Archer could guide the Argonauts in their expedition to Colchis. Like Aries, Sagittarius promises a variety of indications. Manilius put it: "The double centaur different tempers breed." The sign is the principle house of Jupiter (chapter IV); however it was also the domicile of the goddess Diana, one of whose temples was at Stymphalus, the home of the Stymphalian birds. When these birds were slain by Hercules they were transferred to the sky as the paranatellons of Sagittarius: the stars Aquila, Cygnus, and Vultur Cadens.

Sagittarius is a fortunate sign. Those born under it will be jovial, strong, and generous. Ibn Ezra says that they will be agile in jumping, fond of horses, a geometer, will have a weak voice and few children. On the debit side the native will be sly and inconsistent. A 12th century astrologer wrote that a man born under this sign would be thrice wedded, very fond of vegetable, would become a matchless tailor, and have three special illnesses (the last at eighty years of age). Our medieval sage may have been a bit far out, but ibn Ezra was correct as to the number of children. From antiquity Sagittarius presages a great desire for marriage, but small families.

In appearance the Sagittarian will be tall and good looking especially from the back view. He will be of light, even red, complexion. He will have good eyes, a large belly, and his shanks will be longer than his thighs. In classical times a long beard, coarse nose, and marks on the arms and legs were usually added. Modern astrologers assert dignity of carriage and a high, dome-shaped forehead.

Those born under the sign of Sagittarius will be a capable mathematician, thoughtful about the next world, fond of horses, and particular as to food, drink, and clothing. He will be kingly, virile, reticent, liberal, and on the bad side tricky and prejudiced. Those born in the first decanate will uphold all that is good, and according to ibn Ezra, will associate kings and magnates; those born in the second decanate will be restless; and in the third decanate modest, helpful, and well bred.

Modern astrologers assert that those born under this sign will be sympathetic, just, intelligent and a deep thinker. He will also be impulsive, and may have a hot temper. There is also a tendency for the native to be brusque and boisterous, and as a result is likely to be misunderstood.

The professions of the Sagittarians are surveyors, horse dealers and, according to al-Biruni, middle class people and busy-bodies or meddlers in other people's business who excite strife (albeit with honest intentions). Modern astrologers add lawyers, horse trainers, jockeys, ministers, philosophers, publishers, and sportsmen.

In ancient Babylon, Capricorn was an amphibious character—the Sea-Goat. In later times Ptolemy and his contemporaries had the sign as a complete goat-like animal. But in astrology Capricorn has always been regarded as the "Mansion of Kings." The Goat was the natal sign of the emperor Augustus, and Capricorn was shown on the silver coins of that emperor. The sign was also frequently on uranographic amulets of the 14th and 15th centuries, and was worn as a kind of an "astral defensive armor." The Platonists held that the souls of men ascended to heaven through the stars of Capricorn, whence the sign was called the "Gate of the Gods"; and the old books of Sargon asserted that the world would be destroyed by a great conflagration when all the planets were in conjunction in this sign.

Those born under the sign of Capricorn will be irascible and destructive. At times their actions will seem futile, and they will lack energy. They are endowed with education, deceit, and great sorrow. The almanac of 1386 has: "Whoso is borne in Capricorn shal be ryche and we lufyed." Capricorn is the very pet of all signs with classical astrologers through the ages. It is extremely fortunate, and both the emperors Augustus and Vespasian were born in the sign of Capricorn. Ibn Ezra maintains that Capricorn natives will acquire great wealth through kings; but that they are also "addicted to sexual intercourse and fornication, will have a large family including twins, and that they will be subject to a serious mishap because of a woman." A 16th century astrologer claimed that a man born under this sign "would be a great gallant, would have eight special illnesses, and would die at sixty." Traditionally, the first part of Capricorn indicates sterility, while the last part presages the birth of twins. Al-Biruni says that the forepart of Capricorn and Scorpio indicates hermaphroditism. It is said that those born under this sign will also be eager for marriage.

The Capricornian person will have a slender and erect body, a fine figure, and a goat-like face with wide grey eyes and crooked ears. They will have little hair, thin legs, and an active gait. Men will have a longish beard and will be handsome. Modern astrologers add that the native will have a bony look, especially about the knees and knuckles; and the Modernists say that there is apt to be long deep creases at the sides of the mouth.

Those born under this sign will be arrogant, impetuous, changeable, anxious, quarrelsome, opinionative, fond of games and life, crafty, forgetful, and bold. Al-Biruni adds false, choleric, and evil-thinking. Those born in the first decanate will be intelligent, modest, refined, and magnanimous; in the second decanate the native will have the intention of doing evil, and will be irascible but ingratiating; in the third decanate he will be easily aroused to anger, will abhor evil and long for the companionship of the opposite sex. He will also be refined and sociable if born in the third decanate of Capricorn.

In modern astrology the Capricornian is said to be self-reliant, refined, oratorical, prudent, cautious, proud, selfish, deep-thinking, independent, and can sometimes become mean and miserly. Overall, however, their personality can generally be described as magnetic.

In classical times the professions of those born under the sign of Capricorn included hunters and slaves. Modern astrologers add civil servants, mathematicians, osteopaths, and politicians.

Aquarius was represented as a man or a boy pouring water from a bucket even on very early Babylonian stones. To the Magi and the Druids this sign represented the whole science of astronomy. In China it was the symbol of the emperor Tchoun Hin, in whose reign was a great deluge; and the Epic of Creation has an account of the Deluge in its 11th book, corresponding to this eleventh sign. Aquarius is the "Place of Good Fortune" and the ancient Egyptians imagined that the setting of Aquarius caused the rising of the Nile as he sank his huge um in the river to fill it.

Those born under this sign will be magnanimous, attractive, and self-laudatory. Their sole ambition will be to increase their wealth and they will either be impotent or will have very few children. In the Middle Ages it was considered a sign "of no small note, since there was no disputing that its stars possessed influence, virtue and efficacy, whereby they altered the air and seasons in a wonderful, strange, and secret manner." When Saturn is in this sign the Classicists asserted that he had man completely in his (Saturn's) clutches. Early almanacs state that when Aquarius was on the horizon with the Sun the weather was always rainy.

In physical appearance the Aquarian will be of medium height tending to tall. They will have a narrow forehead and dark grey to black eyes, with the black part being wider than the white. They will have coarse lips, a broad chest, a downcast look, and the overall appearance will be of a good looking individual with a well filled out body. Modern astrologers add that the complexion is usually fresh and well colored.

In personality the native will be well-disposed, chaste, eager to accumulate riches, eager for magnificence, a gourmet, bad-hearted, inert, indolent, restful, and too anxious about world affairs. Men will want to assert their manliness. Those born in the first decanate will be refined, gregarious people; in the second face ibn Ezra asserts that "he will be grieved all his life"; and those born in the third decanate will be fond of the opposite sex.

Modern astrologers assert that the personality of the Aquarian native includes helpful, altruistic, detached, scientific, too bold, apt to go to extremes, outspoken, rude and tactless, clever, intuitive, refined, modest, cranky, and original.

The professions include servants, traders, and makers of glass and jewelry. Al-Biruni also included ass-drivers, uneducated people and grave robbers. Modern astrologers add airmen, broadcasters, inventors, photographers, radiologists, and scientists.

When Venus was frightened by the attack of the monster Typhon, she threw herself, and her son Cupid, into the Euphrates in order to escape. Two fishes came along and carried Venus and Cupid to safety. As a reward these fishes were placed in the sky as the twelfth sign of the zodiac: Pisces. Within Pisces, in the year 747 auc, three conjunctions of the planets Saturn and Jupiter took place. This is the year, 7 B.C., that many assign to the birth of Christ. This conjunction is in striking agreement with Saint Matthew's account of the Star of Bethlehem. Masha'allah in the 9th century asserted that this conjunction ushered in the Birth of Jesus; and the opinion that these appearances guided the Magi in their visit to Judea was advanced by Kepler, and worked out in 1826 by Ideler, and in 1831 by Encke. It is remarkable that the Rabbis held tradition, recorded in the 15th century by the Jewish scholar Abrabanel (1487-1508), that a similar conjunction took place in Pisces three years previous to the birth of Moses; and that they anticipated another such conjunction in Pisces at their Messiah's advent.

Jewish astrologers considered Pisces a malignant influence in human affairs, "a dull, treacherous, and phlegmatic sign." But this opinion was probably given them by their Egyptian teachers of astrology who are said to have abstained from eating sea-fish out of dread and abhorrence; and when they would express anything odious, represented a fish in their hieroglyphics. It is ibn Ezra's opinion that those born under the sign of Pisces will "indulge freely in sleeping, gluttony, and inebriety. He will not be peremptory, but he will be irascible, polite, and deceitful." Pliny asserted that the appearance of a comet here indicated great troubles from religious differences. These troubles were said to be other than was and pestilence. The sign has traditionally been predominant in influence with mariners. Pisces is one of the fecund signs, and presages large families.

In physical appearance those born in this sign will have a good figure, but with delicate joints. They will have a smooth skin and a fine handsome face. They will be of medium stature with a fairly broad chest, narrow shoulders, small head, narrow forehead and black eyes. Their look will be downcast. Modern astrologers add that the chin is somewhat weak and indeterminate, the nose is large, and the eyes slightly protuberant.

The personality of the Piscean person is generous and elegant. They are of good disposition, unstable in their opinions, of good faith, and mediocre in business. They can be lustful, tricky and deceitful. Al-Biruni adds that they are forgetful, liable to err, foolish, and bold. Those born in the first decanate will be seekers after truth; in the second decanate they will be hostile to all men; and in the third decanate the natives so born will be often ill and have a tendency to suicide (or so said the classical astrologers).

Modern astrologers assert that the personality traits of those born under the sign of Pisces include the attributes of being helpful, just, misunderstood, stubborn, vague, sentimental, impressionable, kind, intuitive, worrying, modest, and too affectionate.

The professions of those born under Pisces are those of the most revered and religious of people (e.g. priests, ministers, and rabbis). Al-Biruni says that the last part of the sign indicates blind men (and those that operate on them for cataracts), and sailors. The Modernists add artists, mediums, poets, psychics, spies, wine merchants, and all those professions having to do with the sea.

Some Peripheral Descriptions of the Signs

It cannot be emphasized too strongly that the descriptions of the "natures" of the signs as just presented must not be taken too seriously. These are merely a compendium of the observations and opinions of astrologers from antiquity to the present. Modern astrologers have a tendency to lean on such descriptions in the delineation of charts, as in the "keywork" method as proposed by Margaret Hone[18]. This is in error! The true "nature" of the signs is to be found in the elements and seasons as modified by the planets. In this regard attention is requested to the first part of this chapter, and to the applicable parts of the next chapter. The personality physical characteristics, professions, and fortunes of the native are found only through a complex analysis of the planetary positions among the signs. These general descriptions of the signs should be used only as a guide, not as a crutch.

To complete the descriptions of the signs various other indicators must be given. These are necessary if the student is to read with understanding the classical astrologers, and it may also help later in the delineation of charts. Care must be taken, however, as most of the more fanciful of these descriptions were discarded by the more scientific of even the most ancient of the astrologers.

Aries, Taurus, Leo, and Pisces are described as maimed. The first three because the ancients imagined that their feet were cut off at the hoofs and claws, and Taurus in addition because it is "only half an ox cut in two at the navel." Pisces was included because of the absence of limbs. Aries, Libra, and Sagittarius are described as erect. Gemini, Virgo, Libra, and half of Sagittarius and Aquarius are represented as human. The other signs are non-human. The four-footed figures are Aries, Taurus, and Leo; while the hinder half of Sagittarius, and sometimes the front half of Capricorn, are also considered to be the same. Of these Aries and Taurus have cloven feet, Leo claws, and Sagittarius hoofs.

---

[18]M.D. Hone, *The Modern Textbook of Astrology*, Fowler, London, 1969. In the "keyword" method the signs and the planets are given a designated keyword, e.g., Venus: "harmony", "unison"; Aries: "assertive", "energetic". The method, then, is that the planet designates the principle, and the sign the mode of action. Therefore, Venus in Aries would be given the interpretation; "The 'harmony' and 'unison' of Venus in Aries will be expressed 'assertively' and 'energetically.'"

Gemini, Virgo, and Libra are said to be loud-voiced, and of these Gemini is said to be capable of speech. Aries, Taurus, and Leo are said to be half-voiced; Capricorn and Aquarius are weak voiced; while Cancer, Scorpio, and Pisces are voiceless. A knowledge of voice and speech is essential when assessing indications of difficulties in these signs. The louder the voice, the greater the extremes in this regard.

Al-Biruni asserts that as regards the conduct of women, "Taurus, Leo, Scorpio, and Aquarius denote reserve and abstinence; Aries, Cancer, Libra, and Capricorn corruption and bad conduct; while Gemini, Virgo, Sagittarius, and Pisces denote a mean in this regard: of the four Virgo is the most virtuous."

In medieval astrology a great deal of importance was attached to the colors indicated by each sign. Modern opinion differs widely on this matter: each astrologer indicating a different set of colors. While there are some differences in classical astrology, the following is taken from the most ancient manuscripts:

Aries: white and reddish.

Taurus: white and brownish, not shining.

Gemini: greenish yellow.

Cancer: smoke colored, not quite black.

Leo: whitish red.

Virgo: whitish yellow.

Libra: white tinged with black.

Scorpio: golden.

Sagittarius: reddish.

Capricorn: colors mixed like a peacock.

Pisces: white.

Places Indicated by the Signs

In classical astrology each of the signs were indicative of various types of places or habitation. Traditionally these are:

Aries: deserts, pasturing places for beasts of burden, wood sheds, places where fire is used, thieves' dens, and places where jewelry is manufactured.

Taurus: mountainous places, orchards, pasture land, storehouses for food, cow and elephant sheds.

Gemini: mountains, hills, mounds, hunting-grounds, riversides, resorts of acrobats and gamblers and musicians (i.e., Las Vegas, Atlantic City, etc.), and kings' palaces.

Cancer: reservoirs, reed-beds, river-margins, cultivated places, trees, wells, rivers, and places of worship.

Leo: mountains, fortresses, high sanctuaries, kings' palaces, desert places, quarries, and barren saltish ground.

Virgo: divans, women's quarters, musicians' houses, threshing floors, and cultivated fields.

Libra: small mosques and places of worship, castles, cultivated areas, palm groves, observatories, plains, orchards, and the tops of mountains which are cultivated.

Scorpio: high places, pools of bad water, prisons, places of grief and mourning, scorpions' holes, deserted places, vineyards, and mulberry groves.

Sagittarius: level plains, Magian temples, Christian churches, arsenals, cattle-stalls, lime pits, and irrigated orchards.

Capricorn: castles, ancient reservoirs, harbors, fireplaces, slaves' sleeping places, holes of dogs and foxes, lodging for strangers; and the first part of the sign indicates stone and gravel quarries, and buildings containing water wheels.

Aquarius: running and standing water, heated bath water, taverns, brothels, canals and ditches, birds nests, and the resorts of aquatic birds.

Pisces: abodes of angels, places frequented by holy men and Magian priests. Also mourning places, cane-breaks, lake shores, salt marshes, and granaries.

Parts of the Body and Diseases Indicated by the Signs

In relation to the parts of the body the Classicists and modern astrologers are not at all in agreement. This is not surprising, as Modernists cannot agree among themselves as to the correct relationship. Some, for example, placing the sides under Cancer and the lungs under Gemini; while others place the sides under Leo and the lungs under Cancer. This lack of consistency prohibits a complete discussion of all the modern positions. The interested student is commended to the bibliography for a fuller treatment of the signs and the parts of the body in modern astrology. The Classicists listed these relationships as follows:

Aries: the head and face.

Taurus: the neck and windpipe.

Gemini: the arms and hands.

Cancer: the chest, breast, sides, stomach, and lungs.

Leo: the heart.

Virgo: the womb, and its contents.

Libra: the back and buttocks.

Scorpio: the genitals.

Sagittarius: the thighs.

Capricorn: the knees.

Aquarius: the shanks.

Pisces: the feet and heels.

These parts of the body have an obvious relationship to the use of astrology in medicine. As we have seen the signs are intimately connected to the various "winds." And Greek medicine looked to these same "winds" to explain the nature of disease. As a result astrology was considered a natural tool of medicine by reputable scientists almost to modern times.

Medical astrology is today in less than good repute in the best of modern astrological circles. However many non-scientific astrologers are still interested in this subject. Much of what passes today for "scientific" astrology is attempts to correlate tendencies toward such diseases as cancer with various astrological phenomena. In addition Russian scientists (not astrologers) have correlated various diseases with the solar cycle[19].

It is instructive, therefore, to consider the opinion of classical astrologers in these matters. The following is a summary of the ancient opinions as to the general health and sickness as it is related to the sign.

Aries: at first very strong; but afterwards weak and liable to disorders. These disorders are especially in the head such as baldness, blood to the face, rashes, lepra (psoriasis) and scabs. The individual will be sweet smelling, but will have tired and worn out limbs, and will be phlegmatic.

Taurus: at first the native will be very strong. But toward the end he will be lean and sparse, and will be only moderately subject to disorders. These illnesses will most likely include diseased to the neck such as scrofula (swelling of the glands) and quinsy (inflamation of the throat). He will also be subject to ozaema and marks on the back and breast.

Gemini: the native will have a healthy and sweet smelling body. Such illnesses as he may get will not be serious. He is subject to catarrh and gout, but these conditions will not cause much distress.

Cancer: the native will be sick and weakly, and will be subject to such diseases as gout, catarrh, cancer, baldness, eczema, deafness, ringworm, dandruff, leprosy, pimples, piles, and heaviness in the left foot and fingers.

Leo: at first the native will be strong; but afterwards he will be weak and liable to diseases, especially of the stomach, he will also be subject to pain in the eyes, loss of hair, and offensive breath.

Virgo: the native will be strong and only moderately subject to

[19]I.P. Druzhinin and N.V.Khasaow, *Solar Activity and Sudden Changes in the Natural Processes on Earth, a Statistical Analysis*, NASA TTF-662, NASA Technical Translation, Washington D.C., 1976.

sickness. The most likely is loss of hair.

Libra: strong and sound.

Scorpio: at first the native will be strong and thickset, but at the end of life he will be weak and sickly. The most likely illnesses are chiefly deafness and dumbness, cataracts, cancer, eczema, ringworm, leprosy, retention of the urine, and eunuchism.

Sagittarius: the native will be strong with a moderately healthy body. At the end he will be weak and sickly. The most likely diseases are gout, catarrh, blindness, blind in one eye, baldness, epilepsy, superfluous fingers, headaches, and marks on the legs.

Capricorn: the native is basically weak and sick, but with sound limbs. Illnesses include deaf and dumb, ophthalmia, bleeding, itching, scrofula, cancer, baldness, and tumors. The ancients considered a tendency toward baldness much stronger in this sign than in any other.

Aquarius: at first strong, although weak at the end. Sound limbs. Diseases are those of the tongue, jaundice, catarrh, gout, bilious headaches, pain in the eyes, vertigo, rupture, epilepsy, and ozaema.

Pisces: the native is weak, thin, and sickly, especially in the limbs. Illnesses include gout, sleeping of the limbs, eczema, ringworm, leprosy and catarrh.

Classical astrology must be read very, very carefully, the more especially so when specific elements of fate are mentioned. The scientific classical astrologer did not believe that all those born under Sagittarius, for example, would be blind. Nor did they believe that those born under other signs would not be blind. The specific diseases itemized under each of the signs were merely early attempts to assess the tendency of the natives of a given sign to contract a given disease or condition. What is actually being given are the results of observations of the correlative indications of disease with the signs of the zodiac. An early attempt to "play the odds," so to speak.

It goes without saying that modern science would not consider such observations as valid. Baldness, we now know, is the result of hereditary influences having nothing at all to do with any astronomical phenomena. But our ancient scientist was nonetheless an astute observer, and it would be an interesting study to determine the limits of validity of ancient medical astrology.

Flora and Fauna Indicated by the Signs

Classical astrologers also considered the trees, crops, and animals that are correlative with the various signs. These are:

Aries: all hoofed animals, wild and domestic, such as goats, sheep, rams, and deer.

Taurus: crops from the setting out of cuttings, fruit, artichokes, bastard saffron, cows, calves, elephants and other such animals that become attached to man.

Gemini: tall trees, domestic fowls and such birds as become tame, gazelles, and homed vipers.

Cancer: medium trees, rice, cane sugar, reptiles, aquatic and terrestrial animals that are numerous in the desert such as beetles and poisonous lizards.

Leo: wild horses, tame lions, and all animals with claws, and black snakes.

Virgo: berries, herbs, ordinary seeds, magpies, black crows, bulbuls, sparrows, parrots, and large serpents.

Libra: date palms, birds, leopards, and according to the Arabs the jinn (or jinni) is correlative with Libra.

Scorpio: reptiles, aquatic animals, destructive wild beasts of prey, many footed animals like scorpions and wasps, and poisonous insects.

Sagittarius: solid-hoofed animals especially pack-horses, mules, and asses. This sign is also correlative of birds and reptiles.

Capricorn: crops, herbage, and the like, such as do not require to be sown. Also fruit, kids, lambs, animals that are herded, creeping thins, and locust.

Aquarius: bipeds, vultures, eagles, beavers, sables, ermines, and aquatic birds (especially black ones).

Pisces: cotton, sugarfruit, large and small fish, aquatic carnivores, and serpents.

This completes the correlative indications of the signs of the zodiac as handed down to us by the ancients. Where possible, comparisons with modern astrology have been made. Unfortunately in most instances Modernists have either contradictory opinions or none at all concerning these matters. Other indications and comparisons of the signs in different contexts will be made in subsequent chapters as applicable.

The Years of the Signs

To complete this discussion of the signs of the zodiac, it remains to investigate areas and degrees within each sign that have a special significance in terms of the efficacy or type of predictions that can be made there. Table 5 gives the years of the signs. It would take us too far afield to discuss in any depth the derivation and use of this table at this time. The data are collected here as a matter of convenience. Its derivation will be discussed in the next chapter. The table is not used at all in modern astrology, but it is required for the methods of prognostication practiced by the Classicists, where it is useful in the timing of events.

The Meanings of the Degrees of the Signs

It was mentioned that each sign is of a given sect: male or female, diurnal or nocturnal, positive or negative. Within each sign the Classicists found that individual degrees could themselves be classified as male or female, positive or negative, etc. This does not mean that the sect of a male sign, for example, is changed in its female degrees. Rather these degrees have the effect of accentuating or deemphasizing the sign's sect. A male planet (see Chapter IV) in a male degree of a male sign would be considered to affirm

Table 5: The Years of the Signs

	Primary Years			*Secondary Years*	
Sign	*Years*	*Months*	*Days*	*Days*	*Hours*
Aries	15	15	37	3	3
Taurus	8	8	20	1	16
Gemini	20	20	50	4	4
Cancer	25	25	62½	5	5
Leo	19	19	47½	3	23
Virgo	20	20	50	4	4
Libra	8	8	20	1	16
Scorpio	15	15	27½	3	3
Sagittarius	12	12	30	2	12
Capricorn	27	27	67½	5	15
Aquarius	30	30	75	6	6
Pisces	12	12	30	2	12

most strongly the male nature of the sign; but that the same planet in a female degree of a female planet would be said to "be out of sect," and its efficacy would be markedly reduced. The male (M) and female (F) degrees of each of the signs are presented in Table 6.

In classical astrology the brighter the planet or star the more indicative it is concerning whatever is bing correlated. A dim star, even in a strong position, is not given a great deal of significance in the delineation of a chart. These degrees of significance were given names corresponding to descriptions of the apparent brightness of stars.

The Classicists distinguished five classes of degree of brightness: bright (B), liminous (L), void or neutral (V), dusky (D), and dark or shadowed (S). Table 7 presents these bright and dark degrees of the signs of the zodiac. A beneficial planet (chapter IV) when posited in a bright degree has a greater efficacy than if in a luminous degree, and this same planet in a dark or shadowed de-

Sign	1	2	3	4	5	6	7	8	9	10	11	12	13	14	15	16	17	18	19	20	21	22	23	24	25	26	27	28	29	30
♈	M	M	M	M	M	M	M	F	F	M	M	M	M	M	M	F	F	F	F	F	F	F	M	M	M	M	M	M	M	M
♉	M	M	M	M	M	M	M	F	F	F	F	F	F	F	F	M	M	M	M	M	M	M	M	M	M	M	M	M	M	M
♊	F	F	F	F	F	F	M	M	M	M	M	M	M	M	M	M	M	F	F	F	F	F	F	M	M	M	M	F	F	F
♋	M	M	F	F	F	F	F	M	M	M	F	F	M	M	M	M	M	M	M	M	M	M	M	F	F	F	F	M	M	M
♌	M	M	M	M	M	F	F	M	M	M	M	M	M	F	F	F	F	F	F	F	F	F	F	M	M	M	M	M	M	M
♍	F	F	F	F	F	F	F	M	M	M	M	M	F	F	F	F	F	F	F	F	M	M	M	M	M	M	M	M	M	M
♎	M	M	M	M	M	F	F	F	F	F	M	M	M	M	M	M	M	M	M	M	M	F	F	F	F	F	F	F	F	F
♏	M	M	M	M	M	M	F	F	F	F	F	F	F	M	M	M	M	F	F	F	F	F	M	M	M	M	M	M	M	M
♐	M	M	F	F	F	M	M	M	M	M	M	M	F	F	F	F	F	F	F	F	F	F	F	F	M	M	M	M	M	M
♑	M	M	M	M	M	M	M	M	M	M	M	F	F	F	F	F	F	F	F	M	M	M	M	M	M	M	M	M	M	M
♒	M	M	M	M	M	F	F	F	F	F	F	F	M	M	M	M	M	M	F	F	F	F	F	F	F	M	M	M	M	M
♓	M	M	M	M	M	M	M	M	M	M	F	F	M	M	M	F	F	F	F	F	M	M	M	M	M	M	M	M	M	M

Table 6. Male and Female Degrees.

Sign	1	2	3	4	5	6	7	8	9	10	11	12	13	14	15	16	17	18	19	20	21	22	23	24	25	26	27	28	29	30
♈	D	D	D	S	S	S	S	S	D	D	D	D	D	D	D	D	B	B	B	B	S	S	S	S	B	B	B	B	B	S
♉	D	D	D	L	L	L	L	L	L	L	D	D	B	B	B	B	B	B	B	B	V	V	V	V	V	B	B	B	B	B
♊	V	V	V	V	V	B	B	D	D	D	B	B	B	B	B	V	V	B	B	B	B	B	B	D	D	D	D	D	D	D
♋	D	D	D	D	D	D	D	B	B	B	B	B	D	D	L	L	L	L	S	S	B	B	B	B	B	B	B	B	S	S
♌	B	B	B	B	B	B	B	D	D	D	S	S	S	S	S	S	V	V	V	V	V	B	B	B	B	B	B	B	B	B
♍	D	D	D	D	D	L	L	L	L	V	V	B	B	B	B	B	B	V	V	V	V	S	S	S	S	S	S	S	V	V
♎	B	B	B	B	B	D	D	D	D	D	B	B	B	B	B	B	B	B	D	D	D	B	B	B	B	B	B	B	L	L
♏	D	D	D	L	L	L	L	L	V	V	V	V	V	V	L	L	L	L	L	L	S	S	L	L	L	L	L	D	D	D
♐	B	B	B	B	B	B	B	B	B	D	D	D	B	B	B	B	B	B	S	S	S	S	D	D	D	D	D	D	D	D
♑	D	D	D	D	D	D	D	B	B	B	S	S	S	S	S	B	B	B	B	D	D	L	L	L	L	B	B	B	B	B
♒	S	S	S	S	B	B	B	B	B	D	D	D	D	D	B	B	B	B	B	B	B	B	V	V	V	L	L	L	L	L
♓	D	D	D	D	D	D	D	B	B	B	B	V	V	V	V	V	V	L	L	L	D	D	D	D	D	D	D	D	D	D

Table 7. Bright and Dark Degrees.

gree will have its power markedly reduced. The opposite is true of a malefic planet (Chapter IV), of course—in a dark or shadowed degree the efficacy of these planets is maximized, while in a bright degree it is minimized.

There are also degrees which increase and diminish fortune. If the Sun in a diurnal chart, the Moon in a nocturnal chart, the degree of the horoscope (ASC) or the Part of Fortune are found in a fortunate degree, the good luck and power of these entities are doubled. The degrees of diminished fortune are called pits. If a planet is in a pit it is enfeebled in its action, being neither able to effect good if lucky, nor evil if unlucky—the tendency therefore is toward peace.

The fortunate degrees and pits are:

Aries: fortunate 19th;

pits 6th, 11th, 17th, 23rd, and 29th.

Taurus: fortunate 8th;

pits 5th, 13th, 18th, 24th, 25th, and 26th.

Gemini: fortunate 11th;

pits 2nd, 13th, 17th, 26th, and 30th.

Cancer: fortunate 1st, 2nd, 3rd, 14th, and 15th.

pits 12th, 17th, 23rd, 26th and 30th.

Leo: fortunate 5th, 7th, and 17th;

pits 6th, 13th, 15th, 22nd, 23rd, and 28th.

Virgo: fortunate 5th, 7th, and 17th;

pits 8th, 15th, 16th, 21st, and 25th.

Libra: fortunate 2nd, 5th, and 12th;

pits 7th, 20th, and 30th.

Scorpio: fortunate 12th, and 20th;

pits 9th, 10th, 17th, 22nd, 23rd, and 27th.

Sagittarius: fortunate 13th, 20th, and 23rd;

pits 7th, 12th, 15th, 24th, 27th, 30th.

Capricorn: fortunate 12th, 13th 17th, and 20th;

pits 2nd, 7th, 17th, 22nd, 24th, and 28th.

Aquarius: fortunate 7th, 16th, 17th, and 20th;

pits 1st, 12th, 14th, 23rd, and 29th.

Pisces: fortunate 12th and 20th;

pits 2nd, 9th, 24th, 27th, and 28th.

Review Questions

1. Aries, Leo, and Sagittarius are all of the nature of fire. However, Aries is tropical, Leo is solid, and Sagittarius is bicorporeal. Explain how the love of one individual for another would differ if influenced by each of these signs.

2. How do the natures of Taurus and Capricorn differ?

3. How do the natures of Gemini and Libra differ?

4. How do the natures of Scorpio and Pisces differ?

5. It is the nature of the Moon to be moist and of the Sun to be hot. Describe the effect of the Moon in Leo.

6. Describe the effect of the Sun in Taurus.

7. Describe the effect of the Sun and the Moon together in Scorpio.

8. How might the places indicated by the signs be of use in astrology?

9. How might the correlative indications of flora and fauna with the signs of the zodiac be of use in astrology?

10. The Sun is a male planet and Moon is a female one. Let the Moon be in the 17th degree of Gemini and the Sun be in the 11th degree of this same sign. Comment on all the effects.

Chapter IV

The Planets

The Nature of the Planets

The active power of each of the planets is as one or more of the elements. It is through the planets that the natures of the signs of the zodiac are changed. The imagined process of this change is as explained by Aristotle in the manner cited in the last chapter. The interest in this process of change is not because of any scientific or other truth, but because it is the easiest manner of explaining the astrological attributes of the planets and signs working together. The "natures" and correlatives of planets recognized by the Classicists are given below. The modern theory of the trans-Saturnian planets is explained in a special section at the end of this chapter.

Traditionally the planet farthest from the Earth is considered first. Saturn, until the discovery of Uranus by Herschel in 1781, was considered the most elevated and farthest from both the Earth and the Sun. As a result its basic quality is to be cold. But because of its distance from the Earth and its moisture[1], this planet is also considered to be somewhat dry. Now for the reasons enumerated by Aristotle[2] the ancients believed that the elements of hot and

[1]C. Ptolemy, *Tetrabiblos*, i:4.

[2]Aristotle, *Meteorologica*, lv:l.

moist were fertile and brought forth life, while those of the contraries—dry and cold—were destructive and brought forth death and decay. It is not surprising, therefore, that Saturn is considered a maleficent planet in both classical and modern astrology. The Classicists realized that despite its destructive nature, the correlative indications of this planet could sometimes be quite beneficial. This was explained by Ptolemy[3] in his theory of diurnal and nocturnal planets. The daytime is considered masculine because of the active force of its heat and the nighttime is feminine and moist. Saturn is then a diurnal planet, and the heat of the day alleviates its extreme cold to produce that which is beneficial. In like manner Saturn is a masculine planet. In modern astrology the planets have lost their identification with the sects of the Classicists. However, they have kept their general natures throughout the ages. Modern textbooks on astrology attribute the keywords "limitation" and "cold" to this planet, and assert that "difficulties" will follow those with whom this planet is prominent in their charts.

Saturn is called the greater malefic and al-Biruni states[4] that it is ". . . disagreeable and astringent, offensively acid, and the coldest, most stinking, and most powerful of things." The planet is also associated with shortness, dryness, hardness, heaviness, and barren mountains. In medieval times its day was Saturday and Wednesday night; and its color was jet-black mixed with yellow.

Individuals dominated by Saturn will, according to the Classicists, be fearful, timid, anxious, suspicious, miserly, a malevolent plotter, sullen and proud, melancholy, truthful, grave, and unwilling to believe good of anyone. This planet is also indicative of an individual so engrossed in his own affairs that the indications are for discord and either ignorance or intelligence, but with any ignorance well concealed by the native. As a result of his own trickery (or that of others) the native will either acquire great wealth, or will end his days in exile and poverty. Note here the great extremes of Saturn. Nothing in moderation!

---

[3] *Tetrabiblos*, i:6,7.

[4] Al-Biruni, The Book of Instruction in the *Elements of the Art of Astrology*, pp.

Those dominated by Saturn may attempt to dominate and enslave other human beings through treachery and fraud; or through such actions as weeping, wailing, and lamanations (al-Biruni). According to ibn Ezra[5] the native will "deceive consistently with little benefit and great harm."

Modernists indicate such character traits as aspiring, careful in speech, cautious, controlled, just, patient, practical, responsible, and serious as being the positive correlatives of this planet. On the negative side, Saturn is said to presage such traits as depressive, dogmatic, dull, fearful, grasping, limited, mean, severe, unappreciative of beauty, and uninspired.

In modern astrology occupations are generally correlated with the signs. Planets merely reinforce that which the signs have already indicated. Classical astrology, on the other hand, put the emphasis on the planets, with the signs playing the more subservient role. The occupations correlative with Saturn in classical astrology are building, paymaster, farming, reclaiming land and distribution of water, apportioning money and heritages, and grave digging. Al-Biruni adds[6] the selling of things made of iron, lead, bone, hair, copper, the selling of black slaves; and the application of knowledge used for bad purposes such as acts of government as lead to evil oppression, wrath, captivity, and torture. It is ibn Ezra's opinion[7], however, that the occupations correlated with Saturn is "any one which requires much work and which yields little reward: menial tasks such as chopping stones, cleaning cisterns, and any sordid job."

Jupiter, according to the Ptolemic scheme of the solar system, is below Saturn and above Mars. Because Jupiter's movement takes place between the cooling influence of Saturn and the burning power of Mars the planet was said[8] to both heat and humidify.

---

[5]Abraham ibn Ezra, *The Beginning of Wisdom*, p. 194ff.

[6]Al-Biruni, p. 435.

[7]Ibn Ezra, cited above.

[8]The same references as applied to Saturn apply to the other planets as well, and so will not be repeated.

Because of the heating power of Mars and the Sun (the next closest celestial body to the Earth after Mars according to the ancients), Ptolemy reasoned that Jupiter's heating power was greater than its moistening power, and that the two combined so that the planet produced fertilizing winds. Because of this heat and moisture Jupiter is called the greater benefic. It is a masculine planet and it also is diurnal. Unlike Saturn, therefore, both of its sects are compatible, and aid in the beneficial nature of Jupiter. Al-Biruni calls Jupiter the best and easiest of things. He associates the planet with moderation, solidity, and smoothness. In medieval times its day was Thursday and Monday night, and its color was dust and white mixed with yellow and brown. Today Jupiter is considered "the planet of opportunity" and its keywords are "expansion" and "preservation."

Jupiter is correlative of individuals with a good disposition and of those who are high-minded, devout, learned, noble and a friend of good government. They make honorable, trusty and responsible custodians of other persons and property. It was also stated by the Classicists that this planet endowed natives to be devoted to religion and good works, and eager to obtain both education and wealth. Al-Biruni added that these natives were "inspiring, intelligent, patient, chaste, cautious in friendships, egotistic, responsible, uxorious, laughing, and eloquent . . . and in addition to affability and some levity the native tended to recklessness. . . ."

Ibn Ezra states that the planet's nature "denotes affection, justice, peace, faith, humility, good reputation, nobility of heart, freedom of mind in telling the truth, and reliability in keeping covenants." Ibn Ezra also affirmed that Jupiter "prognosticates life, any increase in well being, productivity, development, and talk of justice and righteousness."

Today the positive characteristics of Jupiter include expansive, fond of sport, fortunate, generous, good conversationalist, jovial, and optimistic. Negatively the planet indicates a correlative with individuals who may be extremist, improvident, jocose, have no sense of detail, or are over-trusting to luck. In this vein Jupiter is also indicative of those who are provocative or wasteful.

Traditionally the occupations correlative of Jupiter are judges, scholars, those who serve God, goldsmiths, bankers, and those who sell old gold and silver. It was also added that those who do good works, the meek, the noble, and the just of whatever occupation were indicative of this planet.

The next most distant planet from the Earth in classical times was Mars. This planet's sphere of movement was envisioned to be just above that of the Sun. Because of its nearness to the Sun and because of its color, Mars' nature is considered to be very dry and hot. The excessive dryness of Mars makes this planet the lesser malefic, but because of its heat there are beneficial correlatives associated with it too. So its sects are nocturnal (giving the moisture of night) and masculine. The Classicists used such descriptors as hot, hard, sharp, dryness, and coarseness as indicative of the planet. Its color is dark red, and its day is Tuesday and Saturday night. The modern keywords of Mars are energy, heat, and activation. Note here that modern astrology has the tendency to assert the more positive correlators of both the planets and the signs. Hence while Ptolemy emphasizes Mars' dryness, the Modernists emphasize the planet's heat.

The Martian native may have confused opinions and be ignorant, rash, licentious, bold, quarrelsome, unsteady untrustworthy, violent, shameless, and unchaste (al-Biruni); and medieval authors add a bad companion, solitary, spiteful, and tricky, and generally engaging in evil conduct; but also being quickly repentant for his evil deeds. Ibn Ezra asserts that the Martian character includes strength, a desire for victory and power, a willingness to engage in disputes and combat, and to assault all that which is prohibited by law. Character traits given by modern astrologers include combative, constructive, courageous, energetic, forceful, good leader, impulsive, justly indignant, passionate, and quick. On the negative side it is aggressive, angry, cruel, destructive, foolhardy, impatient, pugnacious, rampageous, rude, sensual, and thoughtless.

The Martian is apt to wander from one spot to another, running risks and afflicting those he comes in contact with. He may be the cause of marriages and businesses going to ruin, or to the leading of others into captivity.

Traditional occupations of the Martian are soldiers and their commanders, thieves, blacksmiths, sellers and makers of armaments, grooms, shepherds, butchers, surgeons, housebreakers, highwaymen, and grave-diggers (al-Biruni). In medieval times they were also thought of as circumcisers and the sellers of hounds, cheetahs, bears, wolves, coopers, sickles, beer, glass, boxes, and wooden cups.

The nature of the Sun is to be hot and dry, but to be mostly hot. It is a diurnal body, but is neuter as concerns sex. Indeed, as shall be seen in the next chapter, the sex of a planet changes with its relationship to the Sun. So the Sun can be considered as a determiner of sex, and it has none itself. The Sun neither is beneficent or maleficent, but rather, with Mercury, has both powers: taking that power of whichever planet it has a relationship with. The Sun is indicative of the most expert, the most noble, and of the most well-known and generous of individuals. Al-Biruni adds that the planet also indicates "revolution, mines, worn-outness, and empty and vacant places"; and ibn Ezra states that the Sun presages kings, princes, and counselors. Modern keywords correlative of the Sun are power, vitality, and self-expression. Its day is Sunday and Thursday night.

Personal qualities correlative with the Sun are intelligence and knowledge. Individuals longing for power and a strong central government, and those hankering after wealth and the management of worldly affairs are also indicated: The solar person may attempt to impose his will on the ignorant, and to be harsh with his opponents. But with good relationships to other planets (especially with the benefic ones) the individual will seek a good name for helping others or for reproving evil-doers. He will also be friendly. Other characteristics include patience, chasteness, sensual, eager for knowledge, majesty, vigorous, garrulous, has the power of repartee, and excessive desires (ibn Ezra). The modern correlatives of character are dignified, dominant, faithful, gay, magnanimous, powerful, proud, regal, truly affectionate, and vital. These characteristics are on the good side of the solar person. On the bad side, or given a poor relationship of the sun with other planets (especially the malefic ones), you will find such character traits as: arrogant, autocratic, despotic, domineering, extravagant, overbearing, and pompous.

Occupations associated with the Sun are those correlative of the sign in which it is posited. However, in the Middle Ages craftsmen of all types and especially those who dealt in gold and silver were thought correlative of the Sun.

Ptolemy states that the "nature" of Venus is warm and moist, and that the planet is more moist than warm. On the other hand the Arab and Jewish astrologers asserted that Venus is cold and moist, again with the emphasis on the moisture. From the fact that the planet is the lesser benefic and that its solar house is Libra (see below) the opinion of Ptolemy seems to be the more logical. The planet is of the female and nocturnal sects, and al-Biruni asserts that it is "the-most agreeable and delicious, the most beautiful, and the softest and ripest of all things." Among the qualities of Venus are the lustful mind, fructification, growth, dispersion, and smoothness. Modern keywords are harmony, unity, and relatedness. Its day is Friday and Tuesday night, and its color is white.

Among the most important human qualities indicative of this planet are individuals who are good natured and inclining to love and sensuality, friendliness, generosity, laughter, joy, dancing, and pleasant conversation. Al-Biruni states that the Venusian native may also be "lazy, fond of wine, chess, droughts, cheating, ornaments, perfume, song, and fine clothes." Ibn Ezra adds "cleanliness, mockery, lust, carnal intercourse, and an inclination towards inebriety and an incessant longing for coition, both legitimate, and illegitimate." All authorities agree that the planet is correlative of those who are fond of children and friends, and ordinarily have a devotion to justice and to the temples of divine service. Those character traits emphasized in modern textbooks on the subject include adaptable, artistic, indecisive, indefinite, companionable, gentle, graceful, languid, lazy, harmonious, loving, placid, unreliable, weak, and tactful.

Of the occupations, Venus is indicative of works of beauty and magnificence. Natives with this planet prominent in their charts may be goldsmiths, tailors, dealers in pearls, gold and silver, singers, composers of song, and musicians or artists. During the Middle Ages work in bazaars and measuring by weight, length, and bulk were also considered Venusian occupations.

The second closest planet to Earth according to the Classicists is Mercury. By nature this planet is alternately hot and moist, and cold and dry. As a result it is neither a malefic or a benefic, but takes its power from those planets in a relationship to it. Mercury is diurnal when it is a morning star, and nocturnal as an evening star. It takes its sex from whatever planet it is connected with by any of the relationships that are discussed in Chapter V. Al-Biruni says that Mercury is a "mixture of moderate things." Its day is Wednesday and Sunday night, and its color is sky blue. In modern astrology the keyword "communication" is used to describe the nature of Mercury.

The characteristics of those born with Mercury strong in their charts include a sharp intelligence manifested in speech, thought, and wisdom. He is apt to be eloquent and have a good memory for stories. Other qualities include affability, gentleness, elegance, farsightedness, changeable, and eager for pleasure-seeking friendships of people. It was said in medieval times that the Mercurian person was deeply interested in business and longed for power, reputation, and approval; and that he attempted to keep away from trickery, strife, malevolence, bad-heartedness, and discord. Al-Biruni adds that he "keeps secrets and preserves true friends and withdraws from bad ones . . . (that he) may ruin prospects by too great an anxiety and misfortunes . . . and (that he) is eager to buy slaves and girls, and may be a busybody, calumnious and engage in thieving, lying, and falsifying." According to ibn Ezra, the Mercurian person will "be adept at astrology, sorcery, and any kind of magic. He will have an accuracy in expression, an ability in homiletics, and a talent for composing poetry. His characteristics will also include pity, affection, avoidance of evil, the ability to play musical instruments, a fondness of any small thing, and ability to argue verbally without resorting to blows; and any kind of astuteness, trickery, and the forging of false documents." The Mercurian characteristics in modern astrology include on the positive side adroit, apt, clever, expressive, intelligent, logical, talkative, and versatile; and negatively artfully critical, diffuse, loquacious, nervous, and sly.

Occupations correlative with mercury are merchants, calculators and surveyors, geometricians, philosophers, and poets. In classical times it was said that the Mercurian's hand could be trained to perform any trade, and that "he will be very eager to do any work, to acquire wealth and to squander it." In the Middle Ages the professions of astrologer, necromancer, and fortune-teller were also considered indicative of Mercury. Al-Biruni mentions the selling of slaves, hides, books, and coins; and the profession of barber and the manufacture of combs.

The closest celestial body to the Earth is the Moon. Because of its nearness to the Earth, which Greek science assumed to exhale moisture from its atmosphere, the Classicists asserted that the Moon's nature was primarily humid. Ptolemy stated that the Moon also "shares moderately in heating power because of the light which it receives from the Sun"; but the Arab and Jewish astrologers claimed that the Moon is somewhat cold and primarily moist. Al-Biruni called the Moon the "thickest, densest, moistest, and lightest of all objects." Because it is seen at night, it is nocturnal. Its day is Monday and Friday night; and its colors are blue and white and other deep colors mixed with reddish yellow. Response and fluctuation are used today to describe the nature of the Moon.

By nature the lunar person is simple, adaptable, and good hearted. He may love pleasure, be over-anxious for health and comfort, and too uxorious (i.e., little conjugal happiness or too much marriage). Traditionally he will also have a tendency to be forgetful, loquacious, timid, generous, respected by people, cheerful, a lover of women, and not too intellectually strong (much talk with little thought). Al-Biruni states the lunar person is "a king among kings, a servant among servants . . . but he may be a liar . . . Ibn Ezra adds "excessive introspection, skill in magic, knowledge of stories, prevarication, calumny, a desire for victory, amnesia, and phobia" to these human traits. The positive human characteristics of the Moon in modern astrology include changeable, good memory, imaginative, indrawn, maternal, protective, receptive, sensitive, and tenacious; and on the negative side fussy, faulty, reasoning, touchy, and unreliable.

The lunar person is apt to engage in business matters and in missions and agencies. He may have skill in all branches of religion and divine law; and practice such professions as accounting, medicine, geometry, or (what the Classicists called) the higher sciences (e.g., philosophy). In the Middle Ages such occupations as "growing and cutting hair and selling such items as food, silver cups, and virgins" were also considered indicative of the Moon. Al-Biruni adds that the Moon "indicates captivity and prison through the deceptions of wizards."

The Domiciles of the Planets

The indications of a planet do not always remain constant; but they are dependent on the planet's relationship to the various signs, to other planets and the fixed stars, to its position as regards the Sun, and to the distance from, or proximity to, the Earth. As will be seen in the next chapter, the brightness, speed, and acceleration of a planet as observed from the Earth also impact on its efficacy.

The relationship of one planet to another, or to a fixed star, are called aspects. Whenever two planets are in signs which are in "aspect" to one another, the planets are also said to be in "aspect." Signs 60 degrees from each other are said to be in sextile aspect; those 90 degrees in quartile; those 120 degrees in trine; and those 180 degrees in opposition aspect. Mars in Aries is, therefore, said to be in sextile aspect to Venus in Aquarius, in quartile aspect to

Jupiter in Cancer, in trine aspect to Saturn in Leo, and in opposition to Mercury in Libra. In addition, planets in the same sign are said to be in conjunction. The effectiveness of these aspects is a complex subject that depends, among other things, on the closeness of the aspects to being exact (i.e. when two planets are exactly 60 degrees apart they are said to be in exact sextile). The theory of the aspect will be described in Chapter V. Here we note them only for completeness.

The most important relationship of the planets to the signs are the domiciles or houses. Today this relationship is called "planetary rulership of the signs." But this is a misnomer. Planets may be said to "rule" a point in the sky; but classical astrologers never thought of a planet ruling a whole sign (e.g., a whole constellation of Suns). Planetary rulership in the classical sense will be taken up in the appropriate sections of this, and later, chapters.

As discussed previously (Chapter II), the Classicists used common terms to describe the effectiveness of the planets in various parts of the shy. These colorful terms, while scientifically loose, adequately describe the varying efficacy of the planets as they move through the background of the stars. When a man is in his own house he is most influential. His servants do his bidding; his decisions are respected and, within his house, at least, have an immediate authority; and he is relatively safe from the machinations of others when he is in his own house. When a planet is posited in its domicile, the allegory expresses most elegantly what classical astrologers asserted as the influence of the planet. Figure 7 presents the houses of the planets as handed down by the Classicists.

The reason for a particular sign being designated the house of a planet is given by Ptolemy[9]. Two thousand years ago the rising of Leo signaled the beginning of the hottest time of the year in the region of the eastern Mediterranean. The Sun is at its highest in the zenith at this period too. Therefore, Leo was given to the Sun as its domicile. The Classicists believed that the relative brightness of a celestial body (apparent magnitude in present astronomy) to be di-

[9]*Tetrabiblos*, i:7.

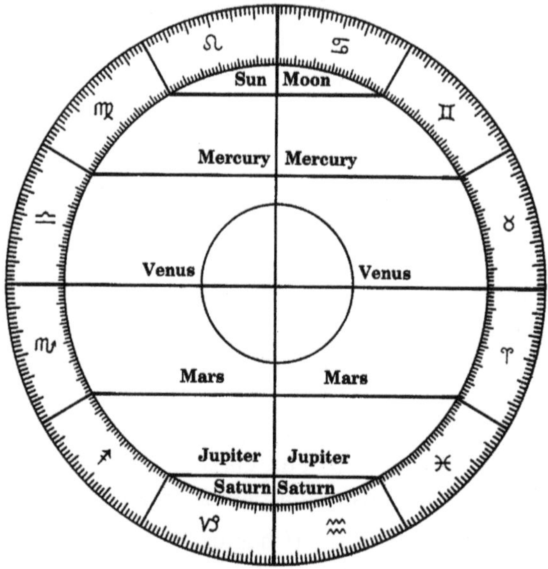

Figure 7. The Houses of the Planets.

rectly proportional to its warmth, hence Cancer was given to the Moon as its house because the next warmest month was heralded by the rising of that sign. Saturn, being the farthest from the Sun, and hence the coldest planet, was given the signs marking the coldest months: Capricorn and Aquarius. According to Ptolemy the houses of the other planets were assigned according to their relationship to Saturn in the Ptolemic concept of the solar system[10];

[10]Computation of the planetary elements (ascending nodes and perihelion) at the time when the rising of the star Mesarthim (-Ari) marked the vernal equinox indicates that the sign in which the planets were posited when brightest may have been the original houses, the Greek penchant for symmetry, and the requirement that astrology be explained by the science of the day, led to the reasons for assigning the houses as given by Ptolemy. Some investigators within the modern astrological community speculate that this assignment may have been much earlier when man mistook morning and evening risings as two separate planets, and believed that the Sun and the Moon were the same celestial body. Whatever the truth, it is highly unlikely that such relationships as the houses were arbitrary and unconnected to astronomy.

Sagittarius and Pisces to Jupiter (the next planet below Saturn); Scorpio and Aries to Mars; Libra and Taurus to Venus; and finally to the planet farthest from Saturn, Mercury, was given the signs of Virgo and Gemini as houses.

In modern astrology, Venus, for example, "rules" both Taurus and Libra. Therefore, for any chart, computed for any time, a planet posited in either of these signs comes under a relationship of dominance by Venus. Similarly, a cusp of a locus within either of these signs implies that the activities under the cognizance of that locus (see Chapter II) will be strongly influenced by Venus. Normally, therefore, each planet influences the activity of two loci in modern astrology. In classical astrology, on the other hand, the situation is quite different.

Those signs, Leo through Capricorn, on the left-hand side of Figure 7 are solar houses; while the signs on the right-hand side, Aquarius through Cancer, are designated as lunar houses. In a daytime chart, a planet posited in its solar house (i.e., Venus in Virgo or Jupiter in Sagittarius) is said to be in its proper house and its influence is markedly increased. A planet in its lunar house in a daytime chart, as Mars in Aries, has its power diminished somewhat by not being in the correct house for the time of day. Of course even being in a lunar house in a daytime chart is a better placement for a planet than in being posited in some other sign. A nighttime chart, of course, just reverses the situation as described above. As in modern astrology, one planet in another's house will come under the influence of the latter planet: as Saturn will gain some heat from Jupiter when posited in Sagittarius or Pisces. But in classical astrology, attention must be given to the difference between a diurnal and a nocturnal chart when making this assessment.

The ruler of a locus, or of the cusp of a locus, influences the activities designated by that locus[11]. But unlike modern astrology,

---

[11]"Ruler" in this context is valid. It means the planet that is most influential over the activities designated by the locus. Note that the rulership applies to human activities not to the signs of the zodiac. The Classicists used the word "familiarity" when describing the relationship of a sign to a planet: "Aries 'familiarity' to Mars is that of being the domicile of Mars."

the ruler of the locus is not determined by the sign in which the cusp is posited. Rather, rulership of the locus in classical astrology is given to that planet whose domicile has the most degrees within the boundaries of the locus. The planet whose house is the sign of the cusp becomes the ruler of the locus only in event of a tie. The ruler of the cusp of the locus is even more important in some applications than is the ruler of the locus itself. Rulership of a point (such as the cusp of a locus or of the horoscope [ASC]) is a rather complex problem that will be deferred to a later section. It suffices here to state merely that the rulers of the cusp of a locus and the rulers of the locus are not necessarily the same planet.

Face and Sect

A planet is said to be in its proper face when the sign in which it is posited has the same aspect to the sign containing the Sun or the Moon as the houses of the planet has to the houses of the luminaries[12]. Care must be exercised here to ensure that the aspect in question preserves the correct directional relationship. That is, in the original scheme, the solar houses are occidental to the Sun, and the lunar houses are oriental to the Moon. For a planet to be in its proper face, it must be in a sign of the correct aspect and either west of the Sun or east of the Moon. For example, let the Sun be in Aries. Then Venus in Gemini is in its proper face to the Sun, for Gemini is both sextile to Aries and occidental to Aries in accordance with the relationship of Venus' solar house, Libra, to the domicile of the Sun, Leo. If the Moon in the above example is in Pisces in addition, then Venus is in proper face to both luminaries—a most powerful configuration as concerns Venus. Aquarius is sextile Aries; but if the Sun is in Aries, then Venus in Aquarius is not in its proper face as regards the Sun. Why?

Both the planets and the signs are designated as male or female, and as diurnal or nocturnal. When a male planet is posited in a male sign (or a diurnal planet is posited in a diurnal sign) or vice

[12] *Tetrabiblos*, i:25.

versa, the planet is said to be in its proper sect. A planet in its proper sect is said to rejoice. A planet in a sign of the opposite sect has a part of its power paralyzed because (according to the Classicists) the dissimilarity of the signs produce "a different and adulterated nature" of the planet. A male planet in a female sign will lose its maleness (unless perhaps in a male degree, etc.).

In assessing the efficacy of a planet other factors than house, face, and sect must be taken into account. Each planet (except the luminaries) has two houses. But one house is preferred to the other. Mercury prefers Virgo, Venus prefers Libra, Mars prefers Aries, Jupiter prefers Sagittarius, and Saturn prefers Aquarius. Hindu, and many Arabic, astrologers asserted that a planet in its preferred domicile is in its proper house regardless of the time of day the chart was cast.

Debilities and Exaltations

As a planet posited in one of his houses increases in power, a planet in a sign opposite (180-degrees away) to that of his domicile loses power[13]. Signs opposite to the domicile of the planets are called the detriments or debilities of the planet. Figure 8 presents the detriments of the planets.

At the time of year when the Sun is in Aries, it begins to rise higher and higher in the sky as the days begin to get longer. Six months later, when the Sun is in Libra, the days get shorter and the Sun, at its zenith, sinks lower in the sky. The Classicists called Aries the exaltation of the Sun and Libra the Sun's depression or fall. When the Sun is in Aries, it is said to be exalted; and when the Sun is in Libra, it is said to be depressed.

The exaltation and depression of Saturn is just the opposite to that of the Sun: Libra and Aries. The reason is quite clear. Libra marks the beginning of autumn, and the weather is getting colder.

[13]The contrary and the opposite played a large role in classical science. Aristotle attempted to define all his terms in such a manner that the logical "principle of excluded middle" was applicable at all stages of the reasoning process.

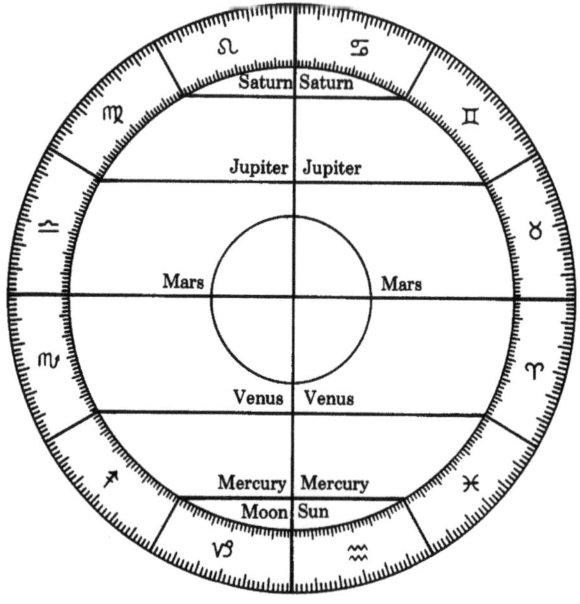

Figure 8. The Detriments of the Planets.

Therefore, cold Saturn is exalted in Libra. The reverse is true at the beginning of spring, so Saturn is depressed in Aries.

For reasons analogous to those mentioned for the Sun and Saturn, the Classicists asserted[14] that Jupiter was exalted in Cancer and depressed in Capricorn, Mars was exalted in Capricorn and depressed in Cancer, Venus exalted in Pisces and depressed in Virgo, Mercury exalted in Virgo and depressed in Pisces, and the Moon is exalted in Taurus and depressed in Scorpio. The Moon's ascending node (see below), or Dragon's Head, was considered to be exalted in Gemini and depressed in Sagittarius. The reverse is true of the Moon's descending node, or Dragon's Tail.

Ptolemy mentions only the signs in which the planets are said to be exalted or depressed. Many classical astrologers, however,

---

[14] *Tetrabiblos*, i:14.

related such a familiarity to a certain degree within the sign. There were many differences of opinion regarding this matter. Some astrologers stated that the familiarity extended in front of, and in back of, this degree a distance corresponding to the planet's orb of influence (see Chapter V); while others asserted the familiarity extended from the beginning of the sign to the degree in question. The better astrologers used the whole sign, but a special significance to the familiarity was given if the planet was posited in the neighborhood of the degree bounded by the orb of influence of the planet, and limited by the boundaries of the sign. The degrees of exaltation of the planets are: Saturn, 21 Libra; Jupiter, 15 Cancer; Mars, 28 Capricorn; Sun, 19 Aries; Venus, 27 Pisces; Mercury, 15 Virgo; Moon, 3 Taurus; Dragon's Head, 3 Gemini; and Dragon's Tail, 3 Sagittarius. The degrees of depression are, of course, 180 degrees plus or minus those given for exaltation.

Rulers of the Triplicities

In the last chapter, it was noted that signs can be grouped in triplicities having as a basic nature the same elemental quality in the Aristotelian sense. In the zodiac these signs are 120 degrees from each other and form an equilateral triangle. Greek science of 2,000 years ago maintained that a triangle is the most elementary and harmonious of geometrical forms[15]. These groupings of the signs, or trines, then have a special significance; and it is only natural that the Classicists would expect a familiarity of the trine with the planets akin to that of the individual signs to the planets (i.e. the domicile).

The fiery signs (Aries, Leo, and Sagittarius) are all of the masculine sect. As two of these signs are also domiciles of the masculine planets—the Sun and Jupiter—these planets were given rulership[16] over this trine. The earthy signs of Taurus, Virgo, and Capricorn are all of the feminine sect. Therefore, the ruler of this

[15]Nicomachus, *Introduction to Arithmetic*, ii:7.4; Plato, *Timeaus*, para 53ff; and Macrobius, *Somnium Scipionus*, i:6.22.

[16]Again, "ruler" is apt as the familiarity is not with the signs per se, but rather with the common natures of the sign triplicity.

Table 8. The Lords of the Triplicities						
	Ptolemy			Arabic		
Triplicity	Day	Night	Common	Day	Night	Common
Fiery	☉	♃		☉	♃	♄
Earthy	♀	☽		♀	☽	♂
Airy	♄	☿		♄	☿	♃
Watery	♀	☽	♂	♀	♂	☽

trine in Venus by day and the Moon by night. Saturn in a diurnal chart and Mercury in a nocturnal chart are the rulers of the masculine airy trine of Gemini, Libra, and Aquarius. This leaves only Mars. He was given the rulership over the watery trine: Cancer, Scorpio, and Pisces. But this latter trine is feminine, so Ptolemy placed as co-rulers Venus by day and the Moon by night. This is the reasoning as given by Ptolemy[17]. But the Arabs had a different scheme whereby each triplicity had one ruler by day, another by night, and a third which shared rulership by day and night. These two schemes are presented in Table 8. As will be seen later in this chapter, a planet in its own triplicity has a greatly improved efficacy and influences rulership over other areas of the chart.

Friendship and Enmity of the Planets

Using once again that colorful language of their time, the Classicists regarded the planets as being either friendly to one another, having enmity between them, or being indifferent to one another. These terms should be interpreted in the same manner in which two individuals may regard each other. Friendship, enmity, and indifference between the planets came about through an assessment of the "temperaments" and "natures" of the planets as perceived by the Classicists. For example, Saturn and Jupiter are regarded an inimical because the one is dark, malefic, and extremely distant (according to the astronomy of the period). Other considerations in the determination of friendship and enmity are

[17] *Tetrabiblos*, i:18.

the elementary qualities:[18] those planets that are fiery being inimical to those that are watery; and those that are airy being inimical to those that are earth. The great Islamic surgeon and philosopher Abu-al-Qasim[19] summarized the friendship and enmity of the planets as shown in Table 9. Friendship and enmity are not constant however, but vary according to the loci in which the planets are posited. For example, any planet whose domicile is contained in the twelfth locus from the locus occupied by another planet must be considered inimical to the latter. Also is one planet is in conjunction with another within the orb of influence of the planets (see Chapter V), and if the conjunction occurs in the 10th, 11th, 12th, 2nd, 3rd, or 4th loci, and the planets are normally friendly, the friendship becomes complete. But if under the above conditions, the two planets are indifferent to one another, they become friendly; and if the pair are inimical to one another, they then become indifferent. If the conjunction occurs in one of the other loci, the effects are precisely the reverse of those mentioned.

Rulership of the Decans

A third of a sign (10 degrees) is called a decan. This term comes from a period An antiquity when the hours of the night were marked by the culmination of certain stars[20]. Clocks had not yet

---

[18]Modern astrology assigns an analogous relationship among the signs, also based on a consideration of the elemental qualities. Classical astrology doesn't consider such relationships between the signs as valid because the natures of the signs change due to planetary movements (see Chapter III).

[19]Abu-al-Qasim (Khalaf ibn Abbas Az-Zahrawi), also known as Albucasis or Alcibitius, b. A.D. 936 near Dordoba, d. A.D. 1013. Islam's greatest medieval surgeon, he wrote "at Tasrif liman afan at-taalif" (The Method), which was translated into Latin in the 12th century and became the leading text on surgery in Europe for the next 500 years. Modern astrologers erroneously attribute to him a house division system analogous to that called the Classical system in this book. However, the system attributed to al-Qasim was ancient in A.D. 450: almost 600 years before he lived.

[20]O. Neugebauer and R.A. Parker, Egyptian Astronomical Texts, Brown University Press, Providence, Rhode Island, 1960. As mentioned in Chapter II, the hours are unequal: an hour of the day being one-twelfth the time from sunset to sunrise.

Table 9. Friendship and Enmity of the Planets				
Planet	Mutually Hurtful with	Injurious to	Offering Friendship to	Asking Friendship from
♄	☉ & ☽	♃	♂	♀
♃	♂ & ☿	☿	♀	☽
♂	♀ & ☿	☽	☉	♄
☉	♄	♀		♂
♀	♂ & ☿		♄	♃
☿	♀ & ♃	♀	☿ neither offers nor asks for friendships	
☽	♄	♂	♃	♀

been invented, and the daytime hours were determined by the position of the Sun. The time at night was told by the stars; and 36 stars were designated as the timekeepers. As each of these stars culminated, a new hour of the night began. Thirty-six stars were used (rather than 12) because of the seasonal movement of the stars. This movement required that a star indicating a given hour be changed every ten days. In the ancient terminology, each of the 36 decanal stars ruled a particular hour for a period of ten days. Additional stars were added to account for the epagomenal days at the end of the year. It is obvious that this technique for telling time was not very accurate. Why?

In Hellenic times, each of the decanal stars was identified with the third of the sign in which it was posited. Based on the nature of these stars, astrologers then gave rulership of each of the decans to one of the planets. Rulership here should not be interpreted as applying to the portions of the sign so much as to the star or (varying) hour that the decan represents. The decanary stars themselves will be discussed in a later chapter. Table 10 gives the planetary rulership of the decans.

The rulership of the particular hour of the day or night (as opposed to the varying hours of the decans) is as given in Table 11. In this table the first hour of daytime begins with sunrise, and the first

Table 10. Lords of the Decans			
Sign	*Decan*		
	0-10	*10-20*	*20-30*
♈	♂	☉	♀
♉	☿	☽	♄
♊	♃	♂	☉
♋	♀	☿	☽
♌	♄	♃	♂
♍	☉	♀	☿
♎	☽	♄	♃
♏	♂	☉	♀
♐	☿	☽	♄
♑	♃	♂	☉
♒	♀	☿	☽
♓	♄	♃	♂

hour of nighttime begins with sunset. The lord of the first hour of daytime is also the ruler of that particular day: as Mercury rules Wednesday and Saturn rules Saturday.

The signs have also been divided into nine parts (3°20'), and 12 parts (2°30'). These divisions are also given a rulership by the various planets. However, the best of the classical astrologers neglected these divisions as being absurd and of having no basis in physical fact: e.g., of not having any connection with observational astronomy. We shall not consider the ninth and twelfth of a sign in this book.

The Terms

There is another, unequal, division of the signs that the Classicists thought extremely important. These divisions are the terms, or termini, literally boundaries. The lordship of the terms are given only to the five true planets: the Sun and the Moon do not participate. Several schemes of lordship of the terms have been proposed through the ages. The Chaldeans and the Egyptians each had one, and Astaratus[21] presents a third. The astronomical significance of the terms must be said to be unknown. It is known, however, that they are related to the years of the planets (see below). And the dispute over the validity of the competing systems was entered into by all the noted scientist-astrologers of the classical period. As will be seen in subsequent chapters, the terms play a prominent role in the efficacy of their five planetary rulers, and are important in determining rulership of points in the native's chart. The terms and their rulers used by the best of the astrologers are those given by Ptolemy. Ptolemy attributed his terms to a (then) ancient manuscript he found[22]. Table 12 presents these Ptolemic terms and their rulers. The interested reader is commended to the bibliography for a fuller discussion of the other systems. But note that many modern astrologers (of the very few that even know of the terms) opt for the Chaldean system because they believe it to be the oldest. Modern astrology, of course, gives little more than lip service to the observational astronomical basis for astrology.

Rulership of a Point in a Chart

It has been noted previously that the rulership of a point, such as the cusp of a locus or of the horoscope, is a relatively complex operation. Indeed, such a rulership implies that the lord of a point have either a large number of familiarities, or some very important familiarity, with the point in question. That is, those factors we have already been considering (e.g., house, exaltation, trine, decan, sect, and term) are used to establish the lordship of any point in a chart. Ptolemy wrote[23] that planet with the largest number of these familiarities to the point in question was the ruler of that point. The Arabs improved on this scheme by the extension of assigning weights to each of these factors:

[21] An early astrologer mentioned by Abue Mashar, Masha'allah, and al-Biruni.

[22] *Tetrabiblos*, i:22.

[23] Ibid, iii:2.

Day	Daytime Hours												Nighttime Hours											
	1	2	3	4	5	6	7	8	9	10	11	12	1	2	3	4	5	6	7	8	9	10	11	12
Sunday	☉	♀	☿	☽	♄	♃	♂	☉	♀	☿	☽	♄	♃	♂	☉	♀	☿	☽	♄	♃	♂	☉	♀	☿
Monday	☽	♄	♃	♂	☉	♀	☿	☽	♄	♃	♂	☉	♀	☿	☽	♄	♃	♂	☉	♀	☿	☽	♄	♃
Tuesday	♂	☉	♀	☿	☽	♄	♃	♂	☉	♀	☿	☽	♄	♃	♂	☉	♀	☿	☽	♄	♃	♂	☉	♀
Wednesday	☿	☽	♄	♃	♂	☉	♀	☿	☽	♄	♃	♂	☉	♀	☿	☽	♄	♃	♂	☉	♀	☿	☽	♄
Thursday	♃	♂	☉	♀	☿	☽	♄	♃	♂	☉	♀	☿	☽	♄	♃	♂	☉	♀	☿	☽	♄	♃	♂	☉
Friday	♀	☿	☽	♄	♃	♂	☉	♀	☿	☽	♄	♃	♂	☉	♀	☿	☽	♄	♃	♂	☉	♀	☿	☽
Saturday	♄	♃	♂	☉	♀	☿	☽	♄	♃	♂	☉	♀	☿	☽	♄	♃	♂	☉	♀	☿	☽	♄	♃	♂

Table 11. Lords of the Hours and Days of the Week

ARIES	♃ 6 / 6	♀ 8 / 14	☿ 7 / 21	♂ 5 / 26	♄ 4 / 30
TAURUS	♀ 8 / 8	☿ 7 / 15	♃ 7 / 22	♄ 2 / 24	♂ 6 / 30
GEMINI	☿ 7 / 7	♃ 6 / 13	♀ 7 / 20	♂ 6 / 26	♄ 4 / 30
CANCER	♂ 6 / 6	♃ 7 / 13	☿ 7 / 20	♀ 7 / 27	♄ 3 / 30
LEO	♃ 6 / 6	☿ 7 / 13	♄ 6 / 19	♀ 6 / 25	♂ 5 / 30
VIRGO	☿ 7 / 7	♀ 6 / 13	♃ 5 / 18	♄ 6 / 24	♂ 6 / 30
LIBRA	♄ 6 / 6	♀ 5 / 11	☿ 5 / 16	♃ 8 / 24	♂ 6 / 30
SCORPIO	♂ 6 / 6	♀ 7 / 13	♃ 8 / 21	☿ 6 / 27	♄ 3 / 30
SAGITTARIUS	♃ 8 / 8	♀ 6 / 14	☿ 5 / 19	♄ 6 / 25	♂ 5 / 30
CAPRICORN	♀ 6 / 6	☿ 6 / 12	♃ 7 / 19	♄ 6 / 25	♂ 5 / 30
AQUARIUS	♄ 6 / 6	☿ 6 / 12	♀ 8 / 20	♃ 5 / 25	♂ 5 / 30
PISCES	♀ 8 / 8	♃ 6 / 14	☿ 6 / 20	♂ 5 / 25	♄ 5 / 30

Table 12. The Governors of the Terms.

house = 5

exaltation = 4

term = 3

trine = 2

decan = 1

Each familiarity of the point in question is given points according to the above scheme. That planet with the most points then becomes the ruler. For example, let the point be 12 Libra. The house is that of Venus, the exaltation is that of Saturn, the term Mercury, the trine Saturn, and the decan is ruled by Saturn. Saturn has seven points to five points for Venus and three points for Mercury. Saturn is the ruler. But if the point were at 11 Libra the term would belong to Venus. Venus, then, would become the ruler (eight points to seven for Saturn). Modern astrology simplifies this whole process by making Venus (the ruler of Libra) the ruler of both 12 degrees and 11 degrees Libra.

In certain applications the sect is substituted for the decan in the above scheme. If the chart is that of the ruler of a nation, or of the nation itself, the weights for the house and the exaltation are reversed. If this were the case in the above example, Saturn would be the ruler even if the term belonged to Venus.

Theory of the Years of the Planets and Signs

The hypothesis that classical astrology in general, and the attributes of the planets in particular, is based on hard astronomical observations is nowhere better illustrated than in the years and the firdoria of the planets (defined below). But to demonstrate this fact, we must first consider the apparent geocentric motions of the planets as described by Ptolemy.

The Ptolemic theory of planetary motions assumed that the appearance of the heavens is the product of regular and circular motions, but as a consequence of this hypothesis of circular motion, certain deviations, or anomalies, from the regular circular motions must be explained[24]. The explanation is based on the theory of epicycles. The primary motion of the planet is circular around the Earth, but each planet has a small orbit superimposed over the primary one known as an epicycle. According to the Ptolemc theory, the Earth is not within the epicycle. Its orbit is entirely above as shown in Figure 9. The planet moves on the circumference of this epicycle when on the upper part toward the east, and when on the lower part toward the west.

The epicycle itself is also constantly moving eastward on the circumference of an orbit called the deferent. When the planet is on the upper part of its movement on the eipcycle, then its movement

[24]C. Ptolemy, Syntaxis Mathematica, iii:l.

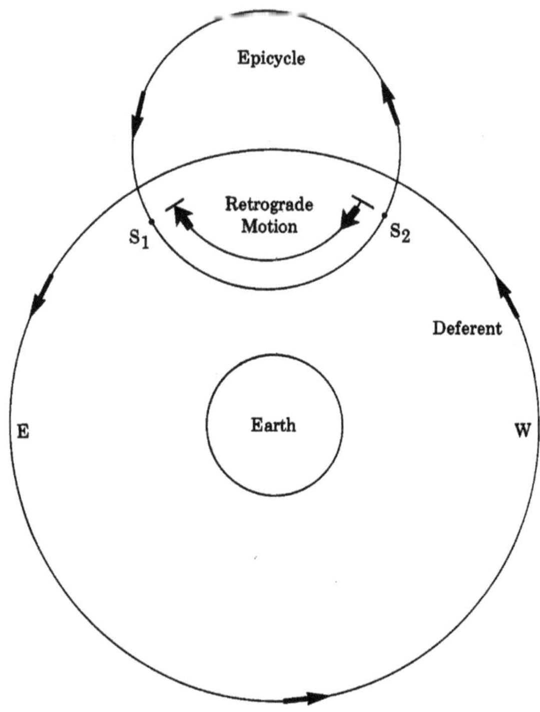

Figure 9. Ptolemic Concept of Planetary Motion.

coincides with the movement of the epicycle on the deferent. In this instance the planet appears to move quickly on a direct path. But when the planet is on the lower half of the epicycle, these two movements (that of the planet and of the epicycle) are contrary. The effect of this is a retrograde motion of the planet (as observed from the earth). This retrograde motion is preceded and followed by a period of apparent stationary motion: the points S_1 and S_2 m Figure 9. So rather than a simple circular motion, the Ptolemic theory envisioned a complex combination of motion. The difference between where the planet would be if its motion were a simple circle and its actual location is called the mean anomaly[25].

[25]Ibid.

All the planets, including the Sun, were presumed to have the motions as depicted in Figure 9 and described above. The regular motion of the planets is circular, and the anomalies are explained primarily by the epicycle. A period or periodic time is the least time required to collect all the differences in movement of the heavenly bodies into one complete cyclical restitution. For example, the anomalistic period of the Sun with respect to the stars is very nearly 19 years[26]. Now 19 years is also that period of time designated as the least years of the Sun, and it is also the number of years of the Sun's firdoria. The years of the planets is defined as the number of years of an individual's life indicated by that planet. The firdoria of the planet are those years in an individual's life governed by the planet. The years of a planet are used in timing an event, and the firdoria indicates that planet which has the greatest influence over a given period of life.

The least years and the firdoria of the planets, with the exception of the Moon and Mercury, are their anomalistic periods with respect to the Sun[27]. This period for Mercury is 20 years. However, as this planet has a dual nature only one-half the period, or 10 years, is used as the firdoria, but the full 20 years of its anomalistic period make up the least years of Mercury.

The basis for determining the years and the firdoria of the Moon is the synodic month. The synodic month has an anomalistic period with respect to the Sun of 25 years; and with respect to the stars of very nearly 432 years. Therefore, the least number of years of the Moon is assigned 25 years. Traditionally the Moon is said to rule the first four years of life. The Classicists reasoned that as 4 times 108 is equal to 432, the great number of years of the Moon should be indicated by 108.

The great number of years of the Sun is 120, or the longest period of life an individual could traditionally expect to attain. The great number of years of the other planets is the sum of their Ptolemic terms from Table 12. It is this correspondence between

[26]Years here are the Egyptian years of 365 days.

[27]*Syntaxis Mathematica*, iv.

the Ptolemic terms and the years of the planets that leads us to accept this scheme for the terms rather than one of the others.

To summarize, first for the firdoria. The age of infancy, from birth to the fourth year of life, is governed by the Moon which produces the suppleness and lack of fixity in the body, the changeability of the infant, and the imperfection and inarticulate state of its psyche. For the next 10 years, that of childhood, Mercury begins to articulate and fashion the intellect and logical part of the soul, to implant certain seeds and rudiments of learning, and to bring to light individual peculiarities of character. Youth and puberty is governed by Venus for a period of eight years, at which time (according to the Classicists) a kind of frenzy enters the soul along with intercourse, a desire for any chance sexual gratification, and a burning passion and the blindness of the impetuous lover.

The 19 years of the Sun is the young adulthood wherein finally there is mastery and direction in the individual's actions; and a desire for substance, glory, and position; and a change from playful, ingenuous error to an attitude of seriousness, decorum, and ambition. The 15 years from 41 to 56 introduces severity and misery to life. The cares and troubles of this period are governed by Mars who gives the individual some sense and notion of passing his prime and urges him, before he approaches his end, to labor harder so as to accomplish something worthy of note. The twelve years of the elderly age is governed by Jupiter. This planet brings about the renunciation of manual labor, toil, turmoil, and dangerous activity; and in their place it brings decorum, foresight, retirement, and consolation. Finally to Saturn falls the lot of old age. Now the movements of both the body and the soul are cooled. No longer does the individual go fast after enjoyment and desires; but he is worn down with age, and he is weak, easily offended and hard to please in all situations.

That the Classicists were able to correlate the apparent geocentric positions of the planets and their periodic movements with a logical division of a man's life (and the chronology of these divisions in the same order as the presumed distance of the planets from the earth) is quite indicative of the viability of astrology in their day. Indeed, ancient critics of astrology were set down by pointing to this remarkable correlation. If a planet could be shown to rule (read "relate") in a logical manner with a given division of a man's life, then it can be assumed that these same planets and their periods can be used to time events such as the length of life of an individual. And so each of the planets were given least years and great years as described above. Table 13 presents the years of the planets.

The derivation of the greatest years as given in Table 13 is presently unknown. Al-Bamni states that they ". . . are only used for marking certain time-cycles, although some people say that in ancient days the planets granted such long years of life.[28] The mean years are merely one-half the sum of the least years and the great years, except for the Sun and the Moon. For these later bodies the mean years are:

$$\text{mean} = \frac{\text{least} + \frac{1}{2}\,\text{great}}{2}$$

The years of the signs as presented in the last chapter are the least years of the planets whose domicile the sign is. So the years of the signs are also related to observational astronomical facts. It was well recognized by the Classicists that these numbers are not always to be interpreted literally as years; but also as months, weeks, days, and even hours. The table of years of the signs gives the interpretation of these times in terms of the smaller increments too. These smaller increments of time also apply to the planets whose house is the sign in question.

The years of the planet were computed on the basis of their periods in a geocentric solar system. In actuality, of course, all the planets, including Earth, revolve about the Sun in elliptical orbits with the Sun at one of the foci. Part of the reasoning justifying these years was also the apparent distance of the planets (including

[28] *The Book of Instruction in the Elements of the Art of Astrology*, p. 394.

Table 13. The Years of the Planets

Planet	*Least*	*Mean*	*Great*	*Greatest*
Saturn	30	43½	57	265
Jupiter	12	45½	79	427
Mars	15	40½	66	284
Sun	19	39½	120	1461 sothiac cycle
Venus	8	45	82	1151
Mercury	20	48	76	461
Moon	25	39½	108	520

the Sun and the Moon) from Earth. However, despite the truth of the heliocentric movements, and the error placing Mercury closer to Earth than Venus, the years of the planets still have a firm foundation in observational astronomy.

The anomalistic periods used by the Classicists were those that placed the planets in the same relative positions as regards the stars and the Sun as seen from Earth. Modern celestial mechanics using the simplifications introduced by Kepler's laws have redefined the term "anomalistic period" to mean the interval of time between successive passages through perihelion of the planet. But astrology is concerned with the relative positions of heavenly bodies as seen from Earth. Mercury, for example, seems "closer" to Earth than does Venus because its apparent speed relative to the Earth is faster. Hence, if "closeness" to Earth is defined in terms of relative apparent speed, then there are no inconsistencies between ancient and modern celestial mechanics on this point.

It is an error of today's astrologers to assume that what is inconsistent with modern celestial mechanics must be rejected out of hand. But mathematics allows perfect liberty to define its terms in any manner whatsoever, and to make any translation of coordinates desired that is consistent with the logic of mathematics. Which is not to say that modern astrologers should be so foolish as to compute planetary positions using the theories and mathematics of Ptolemy. But given the positions of the planets as computed using today's theories, these positions must then be translated to geocentric coordinates to astrologically viable. Once translated, the terms and relationships of the Classicists can then be validly used.

The Nodes

It has been said that the orbits of the planets are all in the same plane: the ecliptic. This is only approximately true. Actually the orbits are inclined to the ecliptic as shown in Figure 10. The point where the orbit of the planet crosses the ecliptic such that the planet's motion is carrying the planet above the ecliptical plane is called the ascending node. The opposite point, where the orbital and ecliptical planes meet such that the planet's motion is carrying it below the ecliptical plane is called the descending node. The angle, X, measured toward the east from the direction of the ascending node is called "the longitude of the ascending node." Due to precession and other orbital perturbations, the nodes are continually displaced westward about the ecliptic. For the five visible planets, this movement is very small, averaging less than one degree per century. The highly erratic movements of the Moon, however, cause a precession of its nodes in the amount of almost 19½° a year. This motion of the Moon's nodes did not go unnoticed by the classical astrologers, and they attempted to use the nodes in their scheme of prognostication.

Al-Biruni has this to say concerning the Moon's nodes: "Many astrologers attribute a definite nature to the ascending and descending nodes, saying that the former is warm and beneficient, and denotes an increase in all things; and that the latter is cold, maleficient, and accompanied by a dimutation of influences. It is related that the Babylonians held that the ascending node increases the effects of both beneficient and maleficient planets; but it is not everyone who will accept these statements, for the analogy seems to be rather far-fetched."[29]

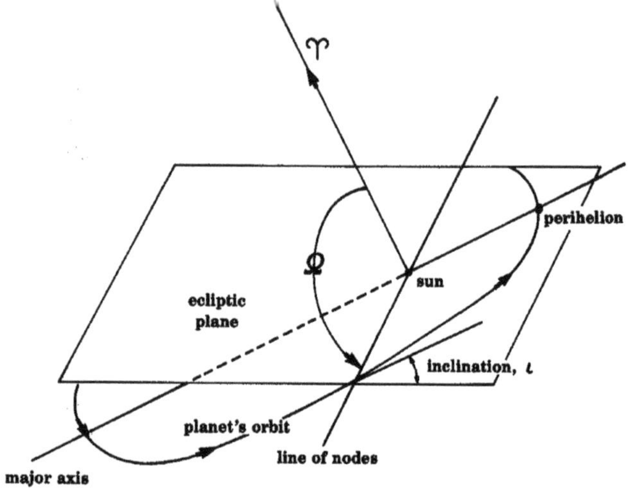

Figure 10. Space Orientation of Planetary Orbits.

The Trans-Saturnian Planets

In 1781, English astronomer Herschel discovered Uranus. Lacking knowledge of the astrology of the Classicists, modern astrologers immediately began to attempt to incorporate the new planet into their art. Each sign had a ruler, and so, therefore, must Uranus. Completely discarded was the concept of planetary houses, and the reasons for assigning the houses to the planets. Neglected also were many other attributes of the planets that have been discussed in this chapter. In particular the theory that a planet's efficacy increased with its apparent magnitude was completely repudiated; and along with this concept, the close connection of astrology with observational astronomy. This tendency has increased until today few astrologers have any knowledge of astronomy. Indeed there are today "astrologers" who believe in the existence of planets that apparently have no mass or gravitational attraction and whose orbits obey no known laws of physics. That

[29]Ibid.

space probes have gone right through the places where these planets are supposed to be has not seemed to bother them one bit.

But Uranus is a true planet. So are Neptune and Pluto. Because they cannot be seen by the naked eye, their efficacy would be so slight that it is doubtful that the Classicists would have used them even had they known that they existed. This is not to say that valid correlations of events on Earth with the positions of these planets is not possible. Quite the contrary. In the case of Uranus especially, modern astrologers seem to have come up with some very remarkable correlations. But still these planets must be considered outside the mainstream of classical astrology. Most of the attributes discussed previously concerning the other planets have no analog with the trans-Saturnian planets.

In modern astrology Uranus is associated with revolutionary and disruptive change. It is given rulership over Aquarius, and the 11th locus is said to be its natural place. (The "house of hopes and wishes" the natural place for the planet of violent change?) Character traits associated with Uranus include: autocratic, friendly, inventive, magnetic, outspoken, unconventional, strong-willed, perverse, rebellious, changeful, dangerous, and willful.

Neptune is characterized by the non-material. Its keywords according to M. Hone[30] are nebulousness and impressionability. The planet is said to rule Pisces, and its natural place is said to be the 12th locus. Character traits include: artistic, careless, subversive, dreamy, emotional, deceptive, idealistic, unstable, sensitive, subtle, hypersensitive, inspirational, and spiritual.

Pluto has these keywords: elimination, renewal and regeneration[31]. Modern astrologers assert that Pluto is an individual's subconscious and can be a new (or renewed) source of power for the native. It is given rulership over Scorpio, and is said to have an affinity for the 8th locus. Character traits include: violent, revealing, regenerative, and eruptive.

---

[30]M.E. Hone, *The Modern Textbook of Astrology*, Fowler, London, 1969, p.35.

[31]Ibid, p.35.

The trans-Saturnian planets move very slowly with respect to Earth. Uranus takes seven years to pass through a single sign, and Neptune and Pluto take 14 years and 21 years, respectively. As a result, their influence will be the same for many millions of individuals. Even in modern astrology the best astrologers consider these planets more an indication of the nature of a generation of people than as correlative of the nature of any single individual. Such considerations using the planet Uranus, for example, have led to accurate predictions concerning such events as the widespread unrest in the United States in the latter part of the 1960s.

Review Questions

1. What are the natures of the signs shown in Figure 5? How have they changed from the primary descriptions given in Chapter III.

2. List the familiarities of the planets (house, term, face, etc.) as posited in the chart in Figure 5.

3. From the list developed for the last question, which planet has the most influence? Which planet the least? Explain.

4. From the influences of the planets as determined above the loci in which they are posited in Figures 5 and 6 determine the probable consequences for the native. Explain your reasoning.

5. Which planet rules each of the loci in Figures 5 and 6.

6. Given that the planet that rules a locus has a primary affect on those things connected to that locus, extend your remarks of Question 4 to include all the loci.

7. What is the sex of the chart in Figure 5? Explain.

8. Which planet rules the horoscope (ASC), the MC, and the cusps of the loci in the charts of Figures 5 and 6?

9. What planet rules the hour and day of birth of the native whose chart is Figure 5?

Chapter V

The Aspects

The Classical Theory of Aspects

It has been stated previously that one of the major differences between modern and classical astrology is that the former considers that the natures of the signs are fixed, and that the natures of the planets are variable; while in classical astrology just the reverse is true. This is only partially correct. In actuality, both the signs and the planets have a variable nature; and in both cases their changing natures are due to the movements of the planets. As described in Chapter III, the movements of the planets into and out of the signs brings about a change in the natures of the signs by the addition and deletion of the four Aristotelian elements. Changes in the natures of the planets are caused by the relative geometrical relationships between them. The ancients explained these changes also by an intermingling of the constituent elements that are basic to the nature of all the planets. (Note that the location of a planet in one of the significant degrees of a sign [such as a pit, degree of exaltation, etc.] does not alter the nature of the planet, though such degrees do affect the strength of their influence.)

Geometrical relationships between heavenly bodies are called aspects. As mentioned in the last chapter, certain of these aspects are very important in astrology. When planets are in these aspects to one another, there is a co-mingling of their constituent elements (or so the ancients thought) with a resultant change in the natures of the planets involved. The reason these particular aspects, and not others, are important is because these same geometrical relationships between the signs are also important. For as always in classical astrology, we start with the zodiac and the ecliptic where the effects indicated have a major influence over large portions of mankind. Over a period of hundreds (or even thousands) of years, the Classicists observed that certain signs have an affinity of effects that are compatible with one another; while other signs had effects that were undesirable when mixed together. The relative geometry of these pairs of signs are the aspects: conjunction, sextile, quartile, trine, and opposition.

Ptolemy tells why only these relationships are aspects:[1]

> "The parts of the zodiac that have an affinity to one another are those that are in aspect. These are the ones which are in opposition, enclosing two right angles, six signs, and 180-degrees; and those which are in trine; enclosing one and one-third right angles, four signs, and 120-degrees; those which are said to be in quartile, enclosing one right angle, three signs, and 90-degrees; and finally those (signs) that occupy the sextile position, enclosing two-thirds of a right angle, two signs, and 60-degrees.
>
> "We may learn from the following why only these intervals have been taken into consideration. The explanation of opposition is obvious: because it causes the signs to meet in one straight line. For the other aspects, we consider the two fractions most important in music. First, if the fractions one-half and one-third be applied to the opposition, composed of two right angles, the half makes the quartile, and the third makes the sextile. Next, if of the superparticulars, the sesquialter and the sesquiterian is applied to the quartile aspect of one right

[1]C. Ptolemy, *Tetrabiblos*, i:13.

angle, the sesquialter makes the ratio of the quartile to the sextile and the sesquiterian makes the ratio of the trine to the quartile. Of these aspects, the trine and the sextile are harmonious because they are composed of signs of the same kind: either entirely of feminine or entirely of masculine signs. On the other hand, the quartile and the opposition are disharmonious because they are composed of signs of opposite kinds."

While Ptolemy does not classify the conjunction as an aspect, it is treated as one throughout the *Tetrabiblos*. Also called aspects by the Classicists are the nine types of rising, culminations, and settings described in the *Almagest*[2]. The latter type of relationships differ from the aspects of the signs and the planets, however, and will be discussed separately.

The four aspects mentioned in the *Tetrabiblos*, i:13, and the conjunction were all that were used in astrology until the beginning of the 17th century. Ptolemy explains the reason for using only these aspects. Other aspects are in use today (e.g., semi-sextile of 45 degrees, sesquiquadrate of 135 degrees, quincunx of 150 degrees, and semi-sextile of 30 degrees). However, the latter aspects were invented by Kepler, probably to force an interpretation. As Kepler "played with the foolish daughter only to be near the wise mother" these additional aspects must be considered artificial as regards conventional astrology. Astrologers today would do well to heed Ptolemy and discard all the aspects but those based on solid astrological principles.

The superparticular is an improper fraction with the numerator one larger than the denominator[3]. The fractions most important to music that Ptolemy writes about are 1/3 and ½; so that the superparticulars would be 3/2 (sesquialter) and 4/3 (sesquitertian). Ptolemy generated the aspects as follows: ½ of 180 degrees (opposition) is 90 degrees (quartile), and 1/3 of 180 degrees is 60 degrees (sextile). Also, 3/2 equals 90/60, or the ratio of the quartile to the

[2]C. Ptolemy, *Syntaxis Mathematica*, viii.4.

[3]Nicomachus, *An Introduction to Arithmetic*, i:19.

sextile; and 4/3 equals 120/90, or the ratio of the trine to the quartile.

The numbers used to generate the aspects are all even fractions of the circle (360 degrees). They are also made up of the numbers 1, 2, 3, and 4 which have a mystical connotation with the Pythagorians. In the form

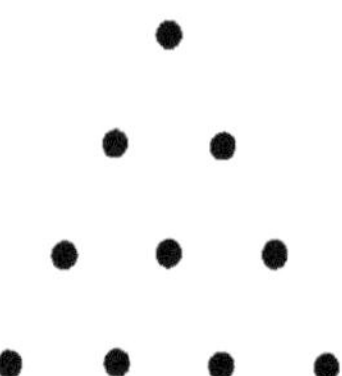

they are called the "tetractys"; and Pythagorian initiates were required to swear their allegiance by the "Oath of the Tetractys"[4]: "I swear by Him who reveals Himself to our minds in the Tetractys, which contains the source of everlasting nature."

In music Pythagoras discovered that the ratios mentioned by Ptolemy had a special significance. ½ is the ratio of a tone to its octave, 3/2 is the ratio of a tone to its fifth, and 4/3 to its fourth. This led Pythagoras to the theory that the musical scale and the planets were closely related. He maintained that the universe sings, and that the fast planets like Mercury sing in a higher voice than do the slow ones. Hence the ancient theory of the "Music of the Spheres" which related each of the planets to a note on the old diatonic scale. The faster planets closest to, the Earth are the ones with the higher note.

Even the lyre strings were associated with the planets. The middle string was associated with the Sun, which in its apparent yearly course travels along the center line of the zodiac. Each string was then associated with each of the planets in the order in

[4]In *Auction of Souls*, iv, by Lucian the following dialogue is found—Pythagoras: After this you must count. Agorastes: Oh, I know how to do that already. Pythagoras: How do you count? Agorastes: One, two, three, four. . . . Pythagoras: Do you see? What you think is four is ten, a perfect triangle and our oath.

Table 14. Relationship of Planets Distance from the Sun to the Frequency of Tone G.

Tone	*Frequency (Hertz)*	*Planet*	*Actual Mean Distance to Sun: Earth Equals 10*
G-4	1.5	Mercury	3.9
G-3	3.0	Venus	7.2
G-2	6.0	Earth	10.0
G-l	12.0	Mars	15.2
G_0	24.0	Asteroids	28.1
G_1	48.0	Jupiter	52.0
G_2	96.0	Saturn	95.4
G_3	192.0	Uranus	192.9
G_4	384.0	Neptune	300.7

which their distances appeared from the Earth: the highest note belonging to the closest (fastest) planet. The relationship is as follows:

E D B A G F E

That Pythagoras was correct in principle can be seen from Table 14, which relates the distances of the planets from the Sun to the frequency of the successive octaves of the musical tone G.

From the foregoing, it is evident that the importance Ptolemy gave to the two fractions and the superparticulars in music was based on the philosophy of Pythagoras. This philosophy, which anticipated modern science by assuming a solar system often planets (including the Sun and the Moon) moving in circular orbits, maintained that the whole universe was describable in term of even whole number fractions: the rational numbers of mathematics. Therefore, it is not surprising that Ptolemy had all the aspects be an integral number of signs and divide the circle evenly. The concept of aspects that are a fractional number of signs would have appalled the ancient astrologers.

It is to be emphasized that although the so-called aspects such as the semi-quartile and quincunx are completely artificial as aspects, they are quite valid as significant points. It will be seen that significant points and areas are very important in classical astrology. Indeed some of these points and areas are very important in classical astrology. Indeed some of these points and areas are far more indicative than are the aspects.

Ptolemy describes the aspects as being either harmonious or disharmonious. Most Classicists were more flowery in their language, and made use of analogy in describing their natures. For example, al-Biruni[5] describes planets or signs in sextile or trine aspect as being "friendly" to one another; those in quartile as being "unfriendly"; and those in opposition as being "hostile" to one another. These descriptions are all valid. As a matter of fact, they describe the subtle differences between quartile and opposition better than does the modern explanation (e.g., opposition: "tenseness"; and quartile: "difficulty of working").

The Power of the Aspects

In modern astrology the permissible aspects according to the Classicists are called major aspects. They are all considered to be of equal importance, or power (given equal importance of the planets in the chart of course). Classical astrology, however, distinguishes carefully the relative powers of the aspects. The most powerful is the conjunction, followed in order by the opposition, dexter quartile, sinister quartile, dexter trine, sinister trine, dexter sextile, and finally the sinister sextile. Also, if a planet has two aspects, the more powerful renders the weaker one incompetent and takes away most, or even all, of its power.

Dexter aspects are those contrary to the order of the signs, (see Figure 11), so that a planet in Aries casts a dexter quartile to one in Cancer, and a sinister quartile to one in Capricorn. For reasons to be developed presently the planet determining the aspect is normally Moon, Mercury, Venus, Sun, Mars, Jupiter, and Saturn in

[5]Al-Biruni, *The Book of Instruction in the Elements of the Art of Astrology*, p. 374.

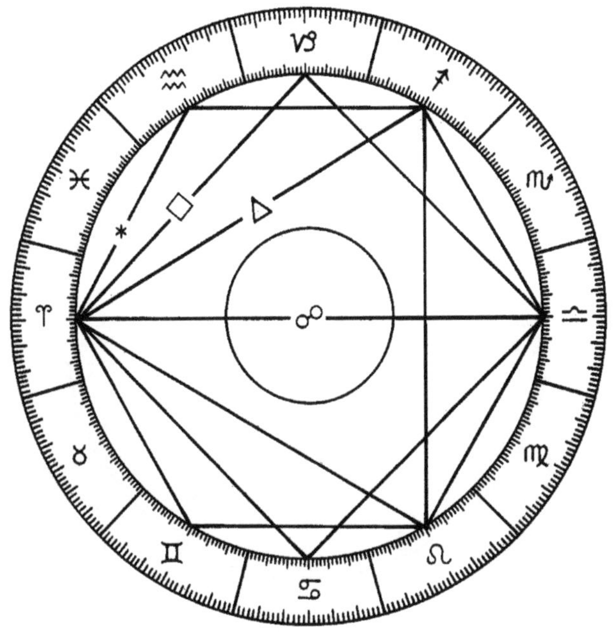

Figure 11. The Aspects.

that order. Therefore, in Figure 12 the Moon is conjunct the Sun, opposed Mars, trine sinister Mercury, and sextile sinister Jupiter; Mercury is trine dexter the Sun, sextile dexter to Jupiter, and sextile sinister to Mars; Venus is quartile sinister Jupiter; the Sun is opposed Mars, and sextile sinister Jupiter; and mars is trine dexter Jupiter. There is no aspect with Saturn in the classical sense.

Analysis of these aspects is complex. The conjunction of the Sun and Moon certainly dominate the aspects. Venus quartile sinister Jupiter is next in power, followed by Mercury sextile sinister Mars. The other aspects are all dominated by one of these. For example, the Moon or the Sun opposition Mars, which normally would take precedence of the aspect between Mercury and Mars, is ruled out because of the conjunction of the Sun and Moon. This is not to say that the other aspects have no effect. Quite the contrary!

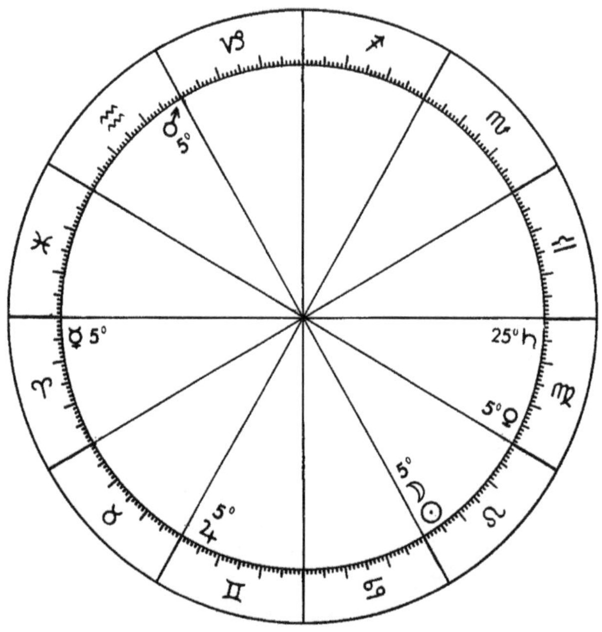

Figure 12. Aspectual Examples.

But their influence is markedly reduced due to their being dominated. For example, if Mars and/or Jupiter were related to the first locus and if (say) Venus were related to the fifth locus, then the following interpretation might be made: "the optimistic enthusiasm for the enjoyment of life that would be expected from Mars trine dexter Jupiter will lead to disappointments in love, and unhappiness in life, because of the dominance of the Venus-Jupiter aspect." Of course if the dominance had been the other way around (Venus-Jupiter aspect being dominated by the Mars-Jupiter aspect) the indication might be for a happy life despite some difficulties in love. Naturally these interpretations are oversimplified. The true interpretation requires a synthesis of the whole chart.

The distinction between dexter and sinister aspects has a much wider meaning than merely ordering the power of the aspects.

Whether the aspect is dexter or sinister affects the very meaning of the interpretation. A dexter aspect is much more powerful than a sinister one. A planet in dexter aspect is exercising its full influence, while a sinister can only be weakly benefic and a sextile sinister may even imply a bit of strain. Planets in quartile sinister are still unfriendly, but the potency of its force if diminished.

A few years ago Joyce Collin-Smith of the Astrological Association of England reported[6] that the Federation of Australian Astrologers completed a research project on the aspects in which ". . . the researchers obtained some unexpected results which do not always bear out the 'traditional' interpretation. . . ." This is not the first time such results have been observed. Many astrologers over the past 100 years or so have mentioned similar experiences. The most definitive modern book on the aspects is *The Astrological Aspects* by C.E.O. Carter. In the 1967 introduction to this book, Mr. Carter writes: ". . . I have studied two or three dozen examples of each aspectual contact; and I have often found that the text-book descriptions are not true in many of these cases. . . ."

Such observations are not at all surprising when considering the over-simplified manner in which modern astrology uses the aspects. The descriptions of dominance, and of the difference between dexter and sinister aspects given above, would account for many of the results by Carter et al. But modern astrology no longer uses these concepts that are so important in classical astrology. And, there are many other facets of the aspects as used by the Classicists that are unknown today and that quite probably have contributed to the misunderstanding reported by modern astrologers.

The Apparent Velocity and Acceleration of the Planets

Ptolemy mentions that a planet is at its maximum power when oriental and adding to its proper motion; and of minimum power when occidental and diminishing in speed[7]. The concepts of orien-

[6] *The Astrological Journal*, Winter 1972-73, p. 9.

[7] *Tetrabiblos*, i:24 and iii:3.

Table 15. Velocities and Accelerations of the Planets on March 1, 1973.

Planet	Moon	Mercury	Venus	Sun	Mars	Jupiter	Saturn
Velocity (deg/day)	12.5667	0.0067	0.0208	1.0033	0.0117	0.0033	0.0006
Acceleration (deg/day)	0.3275	-0.0028	0.0	-.0003	0.0	0.0003	0.0

tal and occidental are discussed below. It is now necessary to describe the effects of a planet's velocity and acceleration on the development of the aspects and their planetary influence.

Classical astrology is based on observational astronomy, and all astronomical parameters that could be measured or observed were used in correlations with phenomena on Earth. Of prime importance is the planet's velocity and acceleration as it appears on Earth. It was mentioned previously that the planet determining an aspect is normally Moon, Mercury, Venus, Sun, Mars, Jupiter, and Saturn in that order. The reason for this is that the relative velocity of the planets with respect to the Earth is greatest for the Moon, and decreases in the order given. However, the relative velocity of the planets changes with time. As a result, the order of the planets in determining the aspects also changes with time.

On March 1, 1973, the velocities and accelerations of the planets were as indicated in Table 15. From these data the order of the planets in determining the aspects are: Moon, Sun, Venus, Mars, Mercury, Jupiter, and Saturn in that order. Based on the artificial configuration depicted in Figure 12, the significant changes are Sun sextile sinister Mercury (from Mercury sextile dexter Sun), and Mars sextile dexter Mercury (from Mercury sextile sinister Mars). This change from sinister to dexter and vice versa is not trivial. Even with the sextile, the sinister Mercury-Mars aspect implies a tendency to some kind of mental illness if either of these planets are related to the sixth locus. But the dexter aspect can mean a keen, alert mind. hence it is seen once again that the dexter/sinister relationship must be taken into account when interpreting aspectual contacts. And it is the planetary velocities that determine this relationship. Also we note that the acceleration of the Moon and Jupiter are positive, so that these planets are increasing in influence. The accelerations of Mercury and the Sun, on the other hand, are negative, indicating the decreasing influence of these planets.

One example should suffice to illustrate the method of determining velocities and accelerations. The following table lists the Moon's position at noon GMT for successive dates:

Date	*Position*	△	$△^2$
March 1	28 ♑ 46' 00"		
March 2	11 ♒ 20' 14"	12° 34' 14"	
March 3	24 ♒ 14' 07"	12° 53' 53"	00° 19' 39"

The mean daily motion of the Moon, found by subtracting the successive positions, is the Moon's velocity. The velocities for March 1 and March 2 are found in the column labeled △ . The acceleration is found by subtracting the successive velocities. The acceleration for 1 March is found in the column labeled $△^2$. If the velocity is negative, the planet's motion is retrograde.

Applications and Separations of Aspects

In order to introduce certain preliminary concepts such as aspects, dexter, sinister, etc., we spoke in generalities concerning "the planet determining the aspect." We are now in a position to discuss this latter point in more detail. The theory of the determination and the completion of aspects takes us to a consideration of application, separation, and orbs.

The terms application and separation refer to the formation of aspects between planets and the withdrawal from such positions. These are dependent on the signs. When two signs are in aspect, the planets within them are in aspect also; and when the former are not in aspect, the planets within them are "inconjunct and concealed from each other." (This requirement for the signs to be in aspect has no counterpart in modern astrology, and will be discussed in more detail later). When two planets are in the same sign, or in two signs in aspect to each other, and the two planets are at the same degree, they are said to be in aspect in reality. And the planet whose velocity is greater is said to apply itself to the other whose velocity is slower. When two planets are in aspect, and the degree of the swifter one is less than that of the slower one, the faster planet is said to be applying in aspect. When the degree of the swifter is greater, the planets are separating in aspect.

The swifter planet, when it enters a sign where it comes into aspect with a slower one, begins to show the effects of its application when the difference in degrees between the planets is less than the orb of the swifter one. Separation begins when the faster planet's position is one minute of arc greater than that of the slower planet. The effects of separation continue until the distance between the planets is greater than the orb of the slower one. Modern astrology has dropped any consideration of planetary velocity. As a result, the aspectual orbs, or the nearness to an aspect in reality to be effective, are connected to the aspects rather than to the planets as in classical astrology. Hence, also in modern astrology, the orb is the same whether the planets are applying or separating. The orbs of the planets are as indicated in Table 16[8]. As described above, they act in the same manner as the aspectual orbs of modern astrology. However, the analysis is a bit more complex. Consider Saturn at 10 Taurus. Mars in Sagittarius is disjunct with respect to Saturn. That is, the two planets are "concealed" from one another, and their effects are completely independent. When Mars enters

[8]In modern astrology, the orbs are generally given as conjunction, 8°; opposition, 8°; trine, 8°; quartile, 8°; sextile, 4°; and the rest of the aspects 2°. Llewellyn George in *A to Z Horoscope Maker and Delineator* and Dal Lee in his *Dictionary of Astrology* use planetary orbs; but this is at variance with most of modern astrology which uses the aspectual orbs as given above. However, neither L. George nor D. Lee uses planetary velocities and so the influence of the aspects has the number of degrees whether applying or separating.

Table 16. The Orbs of the Planets.

Planet	*Orb*
Moon	12° 30'
Mercury	6° 30'
Venus	7° 30'
Sun	15° 00'
Mars	7° 30'
Jupiter	10° 30'
Saturn	9° 00'

Capricorn, it is trine dexter with Saturn. However, at the instant Mars enters Capricorn, there is a distance of at least ten degrees separating them. Hence, while the aspect exists, it has effect only in potentiality. The influence of the aspect does not begin to exert itself until Mars is within 7° 30' of Saturn (e.g., until Mars gets to about 2° 30' of Capricorn). This influence continues until Mars passes Saturn by nine degrees (e.g., until Mars reaches about 19° 00' of Capricorn). In terms of interpretation, the application phase promises what is to come; while the separation phase indicates the results of what has already happened.

Had Saturn been at 2 Taurus, there would have been no aspect until Mars entered Capricorn even though Saturn was within the orb of Mars from 24° 30' of Sagittarius! Also, the effects of separation from the trine aspect end when Mars leaves Capricorn even if the planet is still within the orb of Saturn! In classical astrology there can be no aspect unless the planets involved are within signs that are in aspect. Modern astrology differs in that the effect of the aspect is independent of the signs of the zodiac, and depends only on the orbs of influence of the aspect in question. In modern astrology, if two planets are within the aspectual orb, they are in aspect regardless of which signs they are in.

What has been said regarding application and separation is true when both planets are in direct motion. When one, or both planets, are in retrograde, other factors must be taken into consideration. Direct motion always takes precedence over retrograde motion, when the planet in direct motion is dexter to the one in retrograde. Hence a planet in direct motion dexter to one in retrograde is always the applying planet. When a planet in direct motion is sinister to one in retrograde, or when both planets are in retrograde, the planet with the largest absolute velocity is the one that is applying to aspect. Hence if, for example, Saturn is in direct motion at a velocity of one degree per day sinister to Mercury retrograde at a velocity of -3°/day, then Mercury would apply to any aspect between them. Care must be taken, however, when determining if the aspect is in the application or separation phase. Indeed, planets in retrograde tend to go into, and out of, these phases quite rapidly. Because of these consideration, it is sometimes necessary to know the velocity and acceleration of a planet at the instant that a chart is cast, rather than the mean of these values for the twenty-four hour period on the day for which the chart is cast. Methods for making this rather involved calculation are beyond the scope of this book[9].

Orientality and Occidentality of the Planets

It is now necessary to deal with the various positions of the planets in relation to the Sun. For it is the aspects with the Sun that the Classicists believed were responsible for most of the changes in planetary natures. Ptolemy, for example, states[10] that ". . . the Moon from its waxing from the new Moon to the first quarter Moon is more productive of moisture than of any other of the elements. From the first quarter Moon to the full Moon, the Moon is most productive of heat; from the full Moon to the last quarter of dryness; and from the last quarter to the occultation of the new Moon the element produced is cold." The other planets also change in the correlative element that is most active according to

[9]The interested student with the requisite mathematical sophistication is urged to consult texts on the calculus and numerical analysis for the solution of this problem.

[10]*Tetrabiblos*, i:8.

their position relative to the Sun: "... from rising to first station the element moisture is produced; from first station to evening rising the element is heat; from evening rising to second station the element is dryness; and from the second station to the setting of the planet, the planet is most productive of the element cold."[11]

In this modern age it is likely that many readers are just a bit confused as concerns some of the terms used in the preceding paragraph. These terms are based on what an observer on Earth would see, and are coached in the language of geocentric astronomy. Consider first the inferior planets: those planets (in heliocentric astronomy) between the Earth and the Sun—Mercury and Venus.

The inferior planets are never far from the Sun. The angle between the lines Earth-to-planet and Earth-to-sun is called the elongation (see Figure 13). The elongation is never greater than 28° for Mercury, nor 48° for Venus. Now as viewed from the Earth, when the inferior planets are east of the Sun (the Classicists would say precede the Sun) they become visible after sunset in the evening. Their visibility increases with the angular distance from the Sun until the greatest eastern elongation is reached. Thereafter, that apparent velocity of these planets as seen from the Earth becomes slower, and the elongation decreases (the Classicists would say that the planet approaches the Sun). Finally the planet's apparent motion appears to stop. At this point the planet has reached its first station before appearing to move backward in the sky (e.g., before retrograde motion). The planet now begins to pick up speed until, at inferior conjunction, the planet becomes invisible to an observer on Earth. Inferior conjunction is also called vespertine (evening) occultation. After inferior conjunction, the planet appears to emerge from the other side of the Sun, moving now more slowly in retrograde motion. The planet is now rising in the east before the Sun: a condition called matutine (morning) apparition or rising (the Classicists would say that the planet has escaped from the rays of the Sun). The apparent movement of the planet now slows and finally stops at the point of the second station before preceding

[11]Ibid.

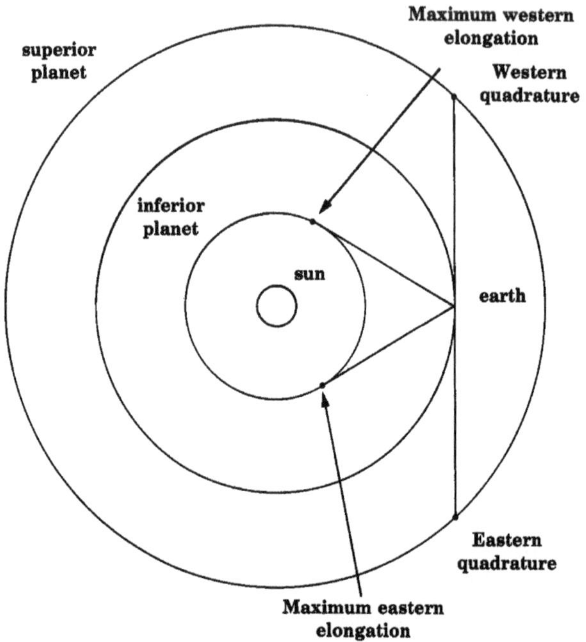

Figure 13. Planetary Configurations.

again on a direct course. The planet begins to pick up speed on its direct course and soon reaches its greatest distance from the Sun—the western elongation (see Figure 13). The planet proceeds on its direct path until it reaches the point of superior conjunction—the matutine occultation. Emerging from the other side of the Sun, again as an evening star, the sequence just described is repeated.

The superior planets Mars, Jupiter, and Saturn are not restricted in the angles they can make with the Sun. Let us start at a superior planet's conjunction with the Sun. The apparent speed of the Sun is generally greater than that of the superior planets, and so after conjunction it appears as though the Sun moves away from the planet. The planet is then visible in the east in the morning. Every day the distance between the planet and the Sun increases until the planet reaches its first station before retrograde where it appears to be stationary in the sky. The distance between the Sun and the planet continues to increase, but now the planet appears to move backward through the background of the stars. At the midpoint of this retrograde movement, the planet and the Sun come in opposition to one another. After opposition, the planet, still in retrograde motion, begins to rise in the east at sunset; it is now an evening star. The planet's retrograde motion slows to a stop at its second station, after which the planet moves in a direct motion and the angle between the Sun and the planet becomes smaller. Finally, just before conjunction, the planet "comes under the rays of the Sun" and becomes invisible in the west.

What has just been described must now be interpreted astrologically. But some further definition of terms will be necessary to fully understand all the relationships used by the Classicists. As it was the Arabs who were most detailed in their descriptions of the various relations between the Sun and the planets, the Islamic terminology will be used.

A planet is at the height of its power (all else equal) if oriental with respect to the Sun if a superior planet, or if it is occidental as regards the elongation Sun if it is an inferior planet. Figures 14 and 15 depict the orientality and occidentality of the planets with respect to the Sun in heliocentric coordinates. From what has been said previously, and with a comparison of Figures 14 and 15, it can be seen that in regard to orientality, the inferior planets in the middle of their retrograde course resemble the superior planets in the middle of their direct course. This led the classical astrologers to interpret an inferior conjunction of an inferior planet in the same manner as that of a conjunction of a superior planet, and to interpret a superior conjunction of an inferior planet in the same manner as an opposition[12]. Note, however, the opposition of the superior planet is more malefic than is the superior conjunction of the inferior planet. This practice differs from that of modern astrology which does not distinguish between the inferior and superior con-

[12]Al-Biruni, p. 481.

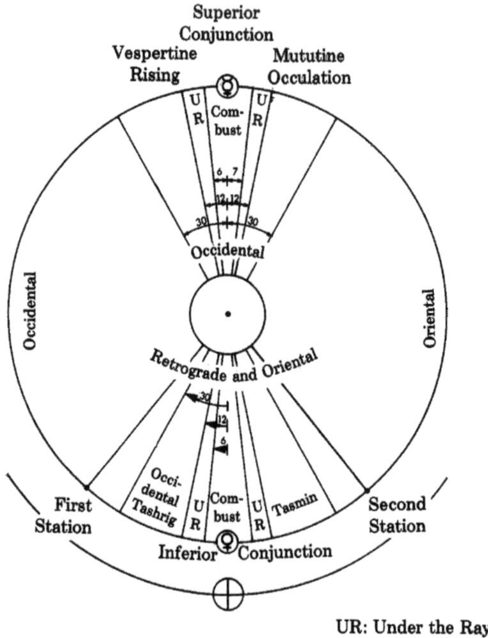

Figure 14. Positions of Inferior Planets Heliocentric Coordinates.

junctions of the inferior planets with the Sun.

To fix more firmly the concept of orientality and occidentality of the planets as regards the Sun, let us review their apparent motions with this in mind. If a planet should be within 16 degrees of a conjunction with the Sun (plus or minus) it is designated at samin[13]. A planet within 6 degrees of the Sun is said to be combust. When a planet is farther from the Sun than 6 degrees, but still samin, it is said to be under the rays (of the Sun). In this position, the Islamic astrologers asserted that the planets ". . . remain like prisoners in confinement." This condition of being "under the rays" of the Sun differs a bit from samin due to the magnitude of the planets. Mercury and Venus are under the rays only within 12 degrees of the Sun, Saturn and Jupiter within 15 degrees, and Mars

[13]Samin, literally in the middle of the sun.

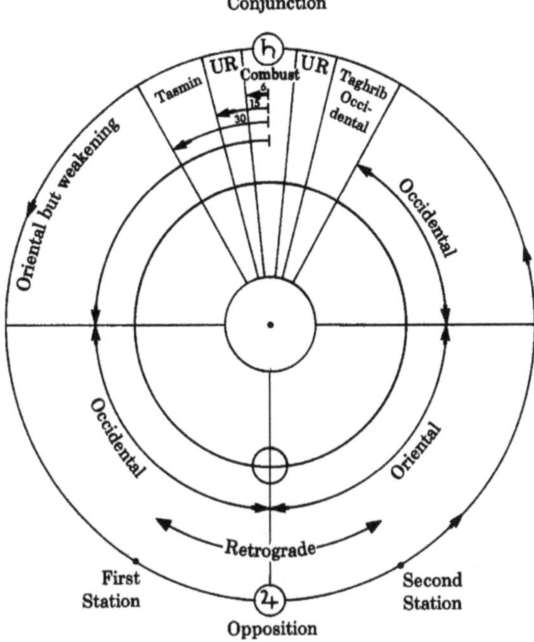

Figure 15. Position of Superior Planets Heliocentric Coordinates.

is still said to be under the rays as far away as 18-degrees. So that samin is a general condition that must be made particular with the individual planets. These conditions must be used with care as regards the planet Venus (and Pluto). The inclination of the orbit of Venus is greater than that of the other planets. When the latitude of Venus is farther from the ecliptic than 6-degrees (plus or minus), the terms "combust" and "under the rays" do not apply. In such a situation when samin Venus is said to be merely "accompanying the Sun." When a superior planet after conjunction (and an inferior planet after inferior conjunction) emerge from "under the rays," they are tashrig oriental and enter into a condition the Arabs call tasmin. When a planet is tashrig, it is west (to the right) of the Sun, rises before the Sun in the east (heliacal rising), and becomes a morning star.

First we shall discuss the orientality and occidentality of the superior planets (Figure 15). The condition of tasmin persists until the planets are 30 degrees from the Sun. From the end of tasmin until 90 degrees from the Sun a superior planet is said to be "weakly oriental." Thereafter, the term tashrig ceases to apply and the planet becomes occidental with respect to the Sun. After the second station, the planet is again oriental until the angle between the planet and the Sun is less than 90 degrees, at which time it becomes occidental. When the planet gets to within 30 degrees of conjunction, the planet is said to be taghrib occidental. It remains taghrib until the planet comes under the rays.

An inferior planet remains oriental after tasmin until it reaches its second station (Figure 14), or until it gets to within 30 degrees of the Sun. From this point through superior conjunction to the planet's first station, it is occidental. Taghrib occurs when the planet comes out from under the rays after superior conjunction.

The position of the Moon with regard to the Sun as to tasmin and combustion is similar to that of the superior planets. Combustion occurs within six degrees of the Sun; and the Moon is under the rays to within 12 degrees of the Sun. Thereafter, the description of the Moon's position with respect to the Sun is given by the Moon's phases.

Classical astrologers are all agreed that a planet is at its maximum influence at tasmin, and that during this period the indications are of happiness and good news. They are also agreed that a planet's influence is at a minimum during combustion. However, distinctions are made in accordance with the concord and discord of the nature of the planets: as, e.g., heat may become increased and moisture diminished, and vice versa. Hence the injurious influence of combustion is less with some planets and is greater with others. We are using the colorful terminology of the classical period in describing the indications of the planets; so, therefore, the maximum and minimum influence is to be interpreted as the ability of a planet to presage that which is favorable.

After conjunction, the planet, when under the rays, is "like a sick person advancing to convalescence." When the planet is oriental in tasmin, it attains its full strength and "is in the position to bestow all its benefits." Al-Biruni mentions that the Persians wait until their planet is tasmin before doing any good works[14]. When a superior planet is at a 30 degrees aspect with respect to the sun after combustion, it leaves tasmin and its beneficial action begins to stop; and "the indications of happiness becomes moderate." This 30 degree point is called "the minor unlucky point." Although still oriental, when a planet reaches a 75 degree aspect with the Sun after combustion its action begins to change from "lucky" to "unlucky." This 75 degree point is called "the middle unlucky point." Later we shall meet these aspects again when we discuss the minor aspects of modern astrology.

In the language of the Classicists, a planet at its first station appears "strangled" and "hopeless." The planet then moves into the first section of its retrograde motion where it is described as "sluggish" and "depressed." After opposition or conjunction the planet is in its second course of its retrograde motion where there is "hope of succour," which is confirmed at the second station where "delivery is near at hand." A planet in direct motion indicates, of course, prosperity and power. Similarly, the natures of the planets in terms of their correlative (Aristotelian) elements alters in their orbit. A planet tends to be dry at rising and moist at setting, without, however, the basic nature of their action being affected. Also, in their oriental phase until their first station, the planets are moist, then to the middle of retrograde they are hot; and from the middle of retrograde to the second station, the planets tend to be dry; and finally after the second station, they are cold. In each instance, of course, these elements add to those of the planet's basic nature.

The orientality of the superior planets occur on the direct course after combustion. On this account they are then more powerful because, as it were, they "are escaping from distress and calamity." Comparable to this is the orientality of the inferior planets after an inferior conjunction (see Figure 14). The occidentality of

[14]Al-Biruni, p. 486.

Table 17. Orientality and Occidentality of the Planets.

Planet	Indications When Oriental	Indications When Occidental
Saturn	Beginning of old age, happy in farming and art of irrigation, profound and effective judgement, sharp and authoritative dispatch of all business matters.	Advanced old age, miserable standard of living, business mean and samll in extant, work in conjunction with irrigation and wells, poor food, fraud.
Jupiter	Beginning of manhood and maturity, good conduct, beauty, elegance, desirous of office as vizar so as to insure justice; many possessions; good reputation, joy in children.	Advanced middle age; occupations of moderate importance, position as prefect or law agent, and all things connected with religion such as copying books of traditions; immoral acts, pilgrimage, sufficient wealth.
Mars	Leading in battle, commanding armies, reputation for courage, eagerness for conquest; quickness in business, success in mining.	Mean positions in the army such as butcher, cook, smith, farrier, surgeon; theft; work to do with fire and iron.
Sun	Oriental and occidental positions relative to the sun are not applicable to the sun itself.	
Venus	Actions when oriental are less effective than when occidental.	Beauty, hatred, love, joy, gladness, pleasure, marriage, gifts; forbidden pleasures; as to crafts: work with colors, pictures, brocades, and embroidery.
Mercury	Intelligence, reasoning power, long consideration, wise decisions, poetry, eloquence, clerk of taxes, surveyor, orderliness, affability, medicine, astrology.	Same as oriental but less efficient; occidentality occasions little harm to it and Venus.
Moon	From the middle of the month to the 22nd denotes mature manhood, thereafter to conjunction, old age.	From conjunction to the 7th day, childhood; from there to opposition youth; when the moon in under the rays it points to things secret and concealed, and especially it points to the ill condition of creatures resembling the light at that stage.

the superior planets occur likewise on their direct course as they precede toward combustion. This is comparable to the matutine occultation of the inferior planets also on their direct course. The orientality of the inferior planets resembles that of the superior ones in as much as in both cases it takes place after combustion. But the occidentality of the inferior planets, when their movements become slow, is a much more "injurious" and weakening influence than is the occidentality of the superior ones. The Classicists asserted that this is because the former have now "turned their faces towards the retrograde course" and combustion. It is for these reasons that the Classicists considered the occidental phases of the superior "safer" than that of the inferior planets.

Table 17 presents the different indications of the planets when oriental and occidental with respect to the Sun as set down by Ishaq al-Kindi (see Chapter I).

Planets' Power as Regards the Loci

In addition to positions with respect to the Sun, a planet's efficacy varies as regards its position in relation to the loci and to the signs. Planets posited at one of the poles have an increase in power, especially if the sign is a fixed one. Calamity and adversity are also intensified in a fixed sign, especially if cadent to the poles; while these factors are weakened in a tropical sign, especially if not cadent. The Classicists used the term prosperity in associating planets with the poles, as these loci "indicate a happy mean"; and they used the term adversity for planets located at the wanes. Planets in loci which are the supports are considered to be beyond the half-way line to prosperity, for the "supports are the paths leading there from adversity." Also prosperity and adversity are not to be considered equal in all the loci. For example, the wanes are not alike in their destructive influences, because although the 3rd and the 9th loci are wanes, the 6th and the 12 locie are not only wanes, but are also inconjunct to the horoscope (ASC)[15].

Modern astrology has nothing comparable to the descriptions we have given of the effects of orientality and occidentality. Neither do modern astrologers distinguish the efficacy of the planets posited in the various loci, although they do recognize the impor-

[15]Ibid, p. 499.

tance of planetary aspects to the angles themselves. Another area where the simplification of modern astrology is evident is the theory of conjunctions. Here the modern theory is so different from the classical that it can be questioned whether the former ever emerged from the latter at all.

In classical astrology there are two other aspects not yet mentioned that have the force of a conjunction: conjunction in latitude and conjunction in nature. A conjunction in latitude occurs when the latitude of the two planets is the same, either both north or both south, and the degrees of latitude are equal. Then the two planets are said to be "conjoint by latitude." If the degrees are not equal, one must look whether that of the lower latitude is rising in the quarter in question, and whether the latitude of the higher planet is setting in the same quarter. If so, they are said to be moving toward conjunction. If the latitude of the setting planet is lower than that of the rising one, they are separating. If both are rising, one must see whether the extreme latitude of the lower one is higher than the (potential) maximum latitude of the higher planet. If this is so, they .are moving toward conjunction; if not, a conjunction cannot occur. Finally, if both planets are setting (in latitude) and the higher planet is setting faster than the lower one, a conjunction will occur unless the lower planet crosses the ecliptic before the higher one overtakes it. What has been said is true of conjunctions in north latitude. The corresponding rules for a conjunction in south latitude are obvious.

The Classicists believed that a conjunction by latitude is superior to that by longitude because of the fact that a conjunction by latitude cannot occur unless the planets are in signs that aspect one another. There is another advantage that can be explained thus: suppose a planet (say Mars) is applying itself to another (say Saturn) to a conjunction by longitude. Also suppose that Mars is applying to a third planet (say Jupiter) to a conjunction by latitude. Now if Jupiter and Saturn are inconjunct, then the Mars-Jupiter conjunction by latitude dominates the Mars-Saturn conjunction by longitude. The Mars-Saturn conjunction is completely negated in such an instance.

Modern astrology does not use the conjunction by latitude that the Classicists thought so important. Instead there has been substituted the parallel. The parallel occurs when both planets have the same declination, either north or south. But a planet the same distance south of the equator as another is north of it is also said to be parallel by modern astrologers. The orb of influence of this aspect has been variously put at five degrees by Dal Lee[16] and at one degree by Llewellyn George[17]. In classical astrology, as no orb is mentioned exactitude is meant (less than one minute of arc). But note the rules for determining when a conjunction is applying. For the latitude-longitude conjunctions applying will dominate separating; and, of course, exactitude dominates all.

Before preceding to describe a conjunction in nature, it is necessary to define equipollent signs, and signs that are corresponding in course (Figure 16). Two signs equidistant from an equinoctial point are said to be equipollent because the days, hours of each are equal to the night hours of the other. Equipollent signs are Aries and Pisces, Taurus and Aquarius, etc. The correspondence is by inverse degrees: the first degree of Aries being equipollent to the 29th of Pisces, the 10th degrees of Aries to the 20th of Pisces, etc.

Two signs revolving in the same parallel, equidistant from a solstice, are described as corresponding in course, the day hours of one is equal to the day hours of the other, and the same is true of the night hours. Such pairs of signs as Gemini and Cancer, Taurus and Leo, etc., are said to be corresponding in course, this correspondence is also by inverse degrees: the beginning of Cancer corresponding to the end of Gemini etc.

Conjunction in nature occurs when two planets are in equipollent signs, and it becomes exact when they arrive at corresponding inverse degrees. This conjunction becomes fortified if

[16]D. Lee, *Dictionary of Astrology*, Constellation International, New York, 1968.

[17]L. George, *A to Z Horoscope Maker and Delineator*, Llewellyn Publications, St. Paul, 1972.

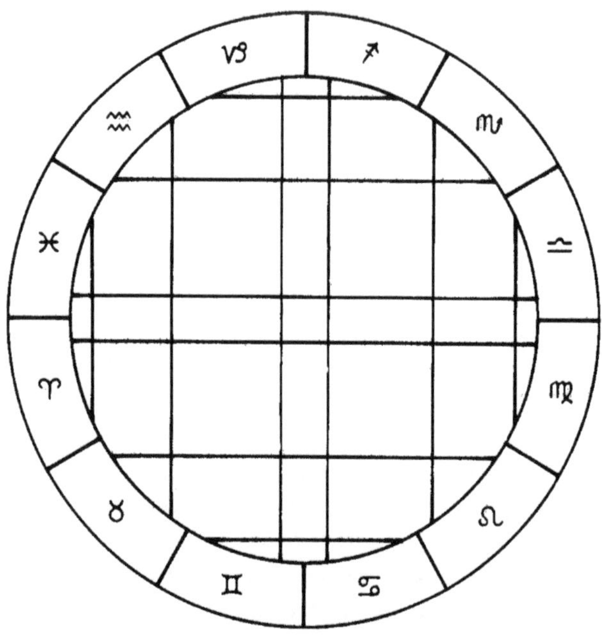

Figure 16. Equipollent Signs and Signs Corresponding in Course.

the planets are also in signs that are in aspect to one another. A weaker form of conjunction by nature occurs when two planets are at corresponding inverse degrees of signs that are corresponding in course. This conjunction too becomes fortified if the planets are also in signs that are in aspect to one another.

There are a number of other relationships between the planets, or between the planets and the signs, that the Classicists used to describe the condition of a chart. Most of these are all but unknown to modern astrologers. They will be discussed below.

Other Significant Planetary Relationships

When a diurnal planet is above the horizon in a daytime chart, or a ' nocturnal planet is below the horizon in a nighttime chart, the planet is said to be in its halb. If a male planet is in a male sign, or a female planet is in a female sign, in addition to the planet being in its halb the condition is called hayyiz, and a planet is said to be or not to be in its hayyiz. It is evident that a hayyiz is more comprehensive than a halb, because every hayyiz is a halb, but not every halb is a hayyiz.

Contention (manakarah) is nearly the reverse of a hayyiz and occurs when a diurnal planet is in the domicile of a nocturnal planet, and the latter is in the domicile of a diurnal planet, and vice versa. For example, if Saturn is in Aries and Mars is in Pisces, a condition of contention occurs.

A planet is said to be besieged when situated between two others, as when a planet is sign one is surrounded by other planets in signs two and twelve. It also occurs when three planets are in the same sign and the middle one's degree is less than the one and higher than the other. It is said to be corporally besieged. Again, a planet is said to be besieged by the rays when in front of it is a planet in sextile or quartile, and another behind it in like aspect. When besieged by two unfortunates, the influences are extremely bad; while if between two fortunates, they are extremely good.

A planet on which a number of unfavorable conditions is heaped in an "evil" situation on account of being combust or retrograde, in its detriment or fall, in a wane, inconjunct, "antagonized" by infortunates, or whose aspects are inimical) is said to be suspect in its significance; that is, if the planet shows any promise, it is unable to carry it out.

If a planet is in its fall or in a pit, it is (as it were) "in a tight place or cave." If now one of the friendly planets (see Table 9, Chapter IV) comes in aspect to it, the friendly planet is said to "give a helping hand to deliver its friend from its calamitous situation." The friendly planet is then described as conferring a favor on the first planet, and is the latter planet's benefactor. If the benefactor arrives at a similar disadvantageous situation, and is applied by the first planet, this is called a requital.

Note that in classical times the concept of a benefactor conferring favors was quite prevalent. The situation just described in a natives chart should be interpreted in a like manner, with the type of favor being received determined by the loci involved.

If during the whole time a planet is within a sign, no other planet enters the sign, the former is said to be void of course. This name is given to it because the field is empty and the planet moves without any "companion." In classical astrology, a planet may be void of course even if in aspect with planets not in the sign it is in.

When a planet is in a sign and no other planet has been in aspect with it from the time of its entry to that of its exit from a sign it is said to be feral in its course. This is practically impossible with the superior planets and the Sun, and can rarely occur with them. But with the Moon it occurs frequently. In modern astrology a planet not in aspect from any point in a sign until its exit is said to be "void of course." With the proliferation of aspects in modern astrology (see below), feral in the classical sense could hardly occur, even with the Moon.

The latter part of Libra and the first part of Scorpio is called the "combust way" by classical astrologers. These two signs are not congenial to the Sun and Moon on account of the obscurity and ill-luck connected with them, and because each of them is the fall of one of the luminaries. They are also familiar with the two malefics: the one by exaltation (Libra-Saturn), and the other by house (Scorpio-Mars).

Completion of the Aspect

The importance of the aspects in both classical and in modern astrology has been previously stressed. In modern astrology the concept of the completion of the aspect is minimized. Completion, of course, occurs if, and only if, the aspect becomes exact. In classical astrology completion is very important, and if completion does not occur the reason for the non-completion is of equal importance. The Classicists distinguished six ways in which completion might be inhibited: return, evasion, intervention, refranation, abscission of light, and prevention. Each of these will be discussed below. The terms "inferior" and "superior" planets will be used in this discussion, but here an inferior planet is any planet whose orbit in Ptolemic astronomy is closer to the Earth than that of the superior planet. In general the inferior planet is the one that is applying to the aspect.

Return happens to a superior planet when retrograde or under the rays, for "from weakness it is unable to hold what is offered to it, and so therefore returns and does not accept it." In this instance the aspect first becomes exact, but then through a retrograde motion the planets "return" to the previous condition of no aspect. If the situation is such that the aspect had been completed, but the inferior planet is at an angle, or both planets are at angles or supports, the end result of the return is satisfactory. If, however, it is the inferior planet that is retrograde or under the rays, and the superior planet is at an angle or at a support, the result is destruction even if at first hope was indicated. If both planets are in a weak situation to the end, there is nothing but "destruction and ruin". Note that it is assumed that a planet "under the rays" cannot complete an effective aspect with any other planet. This is at complete variance with modern astrology which does not consider this factor at all in assessing aspects.

Evasion occurs when an inferior planet is about to complete an aspect with a superior planet; but before the aspect is exact the latter planet moves out of the sign (it. becomes inconjunct by signs), and the inferior planet applies itself to another planet, the first aspect never having been completed. Modern astrology would not recognize the evasion either, as the aspects used today are quite independent of sign.

Intervention occurs when an inferior planet is about to complete an aspect with a superior planet, but in the latter part of the sign in which is posited the superior planet there is a third planet. Before the completion of the first aspect, the third planet retrogrades towards the superior planet, passes it by, and comes into aspect with the inferior planet. This aspect takes on much of the nature of the first. That is the aspect not completed by intervention still holds forth in the aspect between the third planet and the inferior planet.

If the third planet is not in the same sign as the superior planet, but is in the sign next to it, and the intervention occurs as before, it is said that the aspect between the inferior and superior planets is frustrated by the abscission of light. Abscission of light also occurs when an inferior planet is about to complete an aspect with a superior planet, in the latter part of whose sign is a third planet. But before the completion of the first aspect the superior planet conjuncts with the third: both the superior planet and the third planet being in direct motion.

If an inferior planet tend to an aspect with a superior one, but before completion becomes retrograde, the familiarity is said to be frustrated by refranation.

When a third planet is so located that an inferior planet must aspect it before aspecting a superior planet, the aspect between the inferior and superior planet is said to be denied by prevention.

When a retrograde inferior planet overtakes a retrograde superior planet, the situation is called muradafah. Here there is no return on account of the similarity of their situations, but if the aspect is completed the indication is for the successful completion of the business which was threatened with ruin. However, the Classicists taught that this aspect is not equal to one in direct course, but is far inferior in significance.

Modern Aspects

Very few of the relationships just mentioned are used by modern astrologers. Indeed, by comparison the theory of aspects in modern astrology is a gross simplification of that of its classical counterpart. In addition, over the years since astrology has become a less than a respectable science, many errors and perversions have crept into this noble art.

Many of these have been pointed out above; but it is the proliferation of permissible aspectual relationships that distinguish modern and classical astrology. Two of these, semi-sextile (30 degrees) and quincunx (150 degrees), were proposed by Kepler. They extend the idea of significant points presented under the discourse on orientality and occidentality to the planets in general. They also have the advantage of being whole numbers of signs, and so preserve at least some of the theory as given by Ptolemy. However, it is because of these aspects that the concept of aspect by sign, as described above, has been lost.

But then modern astrology goes from the ridiculous to the completely absurd by adding at least eight more aspects: vigintile (18 degrees), quindecile (24 degrees), decile (36 degrees), semiquartile (45 degrees), quintile (72 degrees, not 75 degrees which would have been reasonable), tredecile (108 degrees), sesquiquadrate (135 degrees), and biquintile (144 degrees). The better modern astrologers use only two os these in addition to the ones proposed by Kepler: semi-quartile and sesquiquadrate. But "astrologers" such as Llewellyn George use them all and even propose more[18]. As mentioned previously, there may indeed be valid correlations with these "aspects." But, as is well known in statistics, it is generally possible to find "correlations" almost anywhere if one is not too particular. The very fact of their number and recent introduction to astrology leads these additional aspects to be suspect. The burden of proof is on their users to demonstrate their viability.

In interpretation of these additional aspects, modern astrology asserts the following: vigintile, slightly good; quindecile, slightly good; semi-sextile, difficulty (but L. George asserts that this aspect is slightly good); decile, slightly good; quintile, slightly good (the middle unlucky point?); tredecile, slightly good; sesquiquadrate, difficulty; bi-quintile, slightly good; and quincunx, strain. The orbs are usually one degree; but some astrologers assert two degrees for the semi-sextile, semi-quartile, sesquiquadrate, and quincunx.

[18]George even reversed the meaning of dexter-sinister (cited above, p .102) and propounds many other errors in his book.

Review of the Theory of Planetary Power

To review the strengths and weaknesses of the planets in their orbits, in relation to each other, and to the signs we will append a short assessment. A planet is at the height of its power when the following conditions are present:

- Motion direct, rapid, and accelerating.
- Far from the sun's rays.
- Oriental if superior, occidental if inferior.
- In aspect to both the Sun and Moon, and these in a fortunate state.
- Besieged by fortunates, or in aspect to them.
- Relieved of infortunates.
- Associated with fixed stars of the same character.
- Rising.
- Passing above the infortunates (i.e., above the horizon while the malefics are below).
- Passing below the fortunates.
- North latitude increasing.
- In domiciles of the fortunates.
- In its own hayyiz.
- At a pole or support.

A planet is week and unfortunate for the native when:

- Slow.
- Retrograde.
- Occidental if superior.
- Moving westward toward retrograde if inferior.
- Inconjunct to Sun and Moon, or in adverse aspect to them.
- Associated with fixed stars of contrary nature.
- Setting.
- Decreasing in south latitude.
- In unlucky loci.
- In parts of the sign foreign to them.
- At the nadir of their joys (see Chapter II).

In regard to the foregoing there is a considerable difference between the Sun and the Moon on the one hand, and the rest of the planets on the other. When both of the luminaries are in aspect to each other, or to the benefics, and are in sections of the signs of the benefics (terms, decans, etc.) both of them are strong. But if they are in situations unsuitable to them, such as the malefics being higher in the sky and the benefics lower, or if they are eclipsed, or near the ascending or descending nodes (especially within 12 degrees of the latter), then both of them are weak and detrimental to the native.

The Moon is especially weak when in conjunction with the Sun, or on the wane, or below the horizon, or in the combust way. Many classical astrologers also asserted that the Moon was weak when in the 9th locus; but al-Biruni states that this is true of the planets also[19].

Review Questions

1. Table 18 gives the ephemeris entries for the chart depicted in Figure 5. Compute all the aspectual relationships.

2. Comment on the meaning of all the aspectual relationships determined above.

3. Discuss the changes and the meanings of the planets and the signs as regards the various aspectual relations determined above.

4. The reasons for the non-completion of aspects was given using the colorful terms of classical astrology. Describe the effects of each of these conditions in modern terms.

---

[19]Al-Biruni, p. 513.

Appendix A

Time

The basis of all astrological (and astronomical) calculations is time. The rotation of Earth on its axis provides the basis for the measurement of time. It is assumed that this rotation is uniform. It is true that the angular rotation rate of Earth changes appreciable. But this happens only over the course of centuries. Two units of time will be of interest: sidereal time and solar[1] time. As these names imply, these units of time depend upon a star or upon the sun being used as a clock.

The sidereal day (24 sidereal hours) is defined as the interval of time between two successive passages of the vernal equinox across the observer's meridian. To an observer on Earth's surface, the entire celestial sphere appears to rotate once every 24 sidereal hours. But because the motion of the vernal equinox with respect to the stars is not uniform, the sidereal day varies in length. Zero hours local sidereal time is the instant at which the vernal equinox crosses the upper meridian. Most astrological ephemerae list the sidereal time for noon at the Greenwich Observatory in England. However for astronomical work, midnight, or zero hours, at Greenwich is used instead.

---

[1]No distinction is made in this text between the apparent and mean solar day.

The mean sidereal time at zero hours, Greenwich, θ_G, can also be computed from:

$$\theta_G = 6^h38^m45^s835 + 8640184^S542\ T + 0.^S0929\ T^2$$

T in this equation is the number of Julian centuries from January 0.5, 1900 (e.g., from midnight between 31 December and 1 January). A Julian century is 36525 days. The number of Julian centuries for any date in the 20th century can readily be determined by use of the table of Julian Day numbers (Table Al). For example, from Table Al, the Julian Day Number for June 0,1973 is 2441834. On June 10, therefore, the Julian Day Number is 2441844. The Julian Day Number for January 0, 1900 is 2415020. Subtracting, we note that there are 26824 Julian days from noon January 0, 1900 until noon June 10, 1973. Since T is measured from January 0.5, we subtract one-half day and compute:

$$T = 26823.5/36525 = 0.734378$$

Substituting into the equation we have:

$$\theta_G = 6^h38^m45^s836 + 634242^S762$$
$$= 6^h38^m45^s836 + 73^d10^h34^m02^2762$$
$$= 6^h38^m45^s836 + 73^d10^h34^m02^s762$$
$$= 17^h12^m48^s598$$

which is the mean sidereal time at Greenwich for zero hours June 10, 1973.

Had the sidereal time for 19 December 1973 been desired, then 19 days would have been added to the Julian Day Number for 0 December, 1973 (2442017 + 19) and the procedure continued as before.

$$\theta_G = 6^h38^m45^s836 + 23^h11^m01^s392$$
$$= 29^h49^m47^s228$$

Since the mean sidereal time is greater than 24 hours, we subtract this amount:

$$\theta_G = 5^h49^m47^s228.$$

The solar day is defined as the interval of time between two successive transits of the Sun's center over the lower meridian of the observer. As this time is local, an observer moving on the surface of Earth would require clocks that would have to be continuously adjusted. Therefore, four convenience standard time zones have been established. In the United States these are centered on the 75th, 90th, 105th, and 120th meridian of longitude.

It is no accident that these time zones are 15 degrees apart. The local time at any two positions on the surface of Earth differ according to their longitudes: 15 degrees of longitude is equivalent to a one hour difference in local time. Hence, the clocks on the 75th meridian west of Greenwich would read five hours less than at Greenwich; while the clocks on the 75th meridian east of Greenwich would read five hours more than those at Greenwich. Tables A2 and A3 are convenient for converting time into arc, and vice versa. These tables are based on the relationships: one hour of time equals 15 degrees of arc; one minute of time equals 15 minutes of arc; and one second of time equals 15 seconds of arc.

Consider an observer at 0, Figure Al, and let the Sun be crossing the lower (northern) meridian at the same time as the vernal equinox is transiting the upper (southern) meridian. The observer's time (solar clock) is exactly zero hours. One sidereal day later the vernal equinox is again on the upper meridian. In this interval of time the Sun has moved eastward from M^1 to M^2. Hence the observer's clock reads 23^h56^m rather than 0^h00^m as on the previous day. At the end of another sidereal day the Sun is at M^3 when the vernal equinox is on the upper meridian. Now the observer's clock reads 23^h52^m. Thus the sidereal clock appears to gain on the solar clock approximately four minutes a day. In the course of a month the loss in solar time as compared to sidereal time is approximately two hours; and in the course of a year, a whole day is lost More precisely, the difference between solar and sidereal time increases by 9^s8565 for each hour of solar time.

In astrological work the local mean (solar) time, T_m, the local sidereal time, θ_L, and the solar time at Greenwich, T_g, are all required. Let L be the geographical longitude at the place in ques-

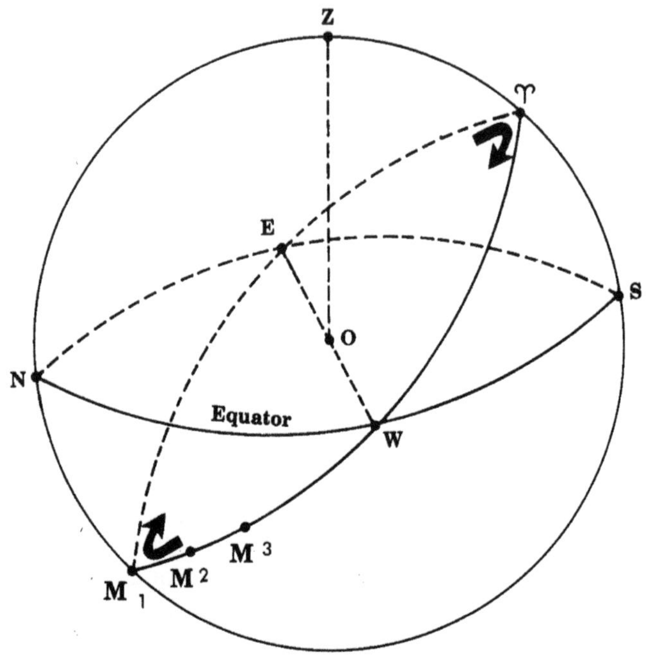

Figure A1. Gain in Sidereal Time with Reference to Solar Time.

tion; and let T_s be the local standard time. Then if the longitude is measured in time[2]:

$$T_m = Ts + (L^*\text{-}L)$$

Note that if daylight savings time is in effect, then appropriate corrections must be made to the time as noted by the local clocks and watches.

Also

$$T_g = T_m + L$$

where L is considered positive if west longitude, and negative

[2]In the equation, L* is the reference longitude. Every 16-degrees from the Greenwich meridian there is a reference longitude, plus (+) if west, and minus (-) if east. For the Pacific Coast of the United States L* = 120°; and for New York L* = 75°.

if east longitude.

Finally the local sidereal time can be computed from

$$\theta_L = \theta_G + 9^s8565\,(L + T_m) + T_m$$

where again the longitude is converted to time (Table A3) and is considered positive if west Greenwich and negative if east of Greenwich.

Appendix B

Classical Loci Division

To understand the theory of the Classicists as it concerns the division of the various loci, it is first necessary to have knowledge of the various astronomical coordinate systems. These are described in appropriate textbooks[1] together with the mathematics of the transformations between them. However, continuity of exposition of the concepts in this appendix dictate that they be repeated here. It is recommended that those who have forgotten their elementary trigonometry first read a text on the subject, and then return to this appendix.

There are two systems of astronomical coordinates that are directly related to the Earth: the horizon system and the equator system. To understand the manner in which the classical scientist related the positions of the planets directly to Earth, an understanding of these coordinate systems and their relationship to the celestial system of coordinates is a requisite. Ptolemic astronomy leads to very difficult and messy mathematics. So as astrology is not wedded to Ptolemy's astronomy, we shall use the modem notation is discussing the various coordinate systems and their relationships.

[1]For example W.M. Smart, *Textbook on. Spherical Astronomy*, Cambridge University Press, Cambridge, England, 1971.

The plane of the apparent movement of the planets and the Sun is the ecliptic. The plane of rotation of Earth (and hence the apparent diumal movement of the stars) is the equator. Classical astronomers did not believe that Earth rotates. However, they did admit[2] that a rotating Earth would also explain the diumal movements. In either event, it is evident that the equator is to the apparent diumal motion of the celestial sphere as the ecliptic is to the apparent sidereal motion. Therefore, the reference frame for relating the positions of heavenly bodies directly to Earth is the equator.

An observer on Earth does not generally “see” the equator. The observer’s horizon must also be taken into account. These effects are the heliacal risings and settings of the stars and their culminations. Therefore, the Classicists reasoned that if sidereal phenomena of the seasons are used to measure the effects of the planets and stars and so divide the ecliptic, then also the diurnal phenomena must be the basis for dividing the equator. That is correlations of widespread phenomena that affect many people are made by use of measurements on the ecliptic and are based on the sidereal movements of celestial bodies; while the correlations of phenomena that affect only single individuals are made by use of measurements on the equator, and are based on the apparent diurnal movements of the celestial bodies. As man is ever a slave to his total environment, these latter measurements must be transformed back to the ecliptic so that judgements can be made.

At the risk of boring the more sophisticated reader, it is well to digress a bit so as to instruct those who have but a hazy knowledge of these various coordinate systems. Imagine, then, an observer on the surface of Earth. The sky overhead appears to be a spherical dome centered on the observer. Where a plumb line at the observer’s position, extended upward to the sky, would pierce the dome is the observer’s zenith. The position on the celestial sphere directly opposite the zenith is the nadir.

The plane perpendicular to the zenith-nadir line at the ob-

[2]Abu’l-Rayhan Muhammed ibn al-Biruni, *The Book of Instruction in the Elements of the Art of Astrology*, R. Ramsey, trans., Luzac, London, 1934.

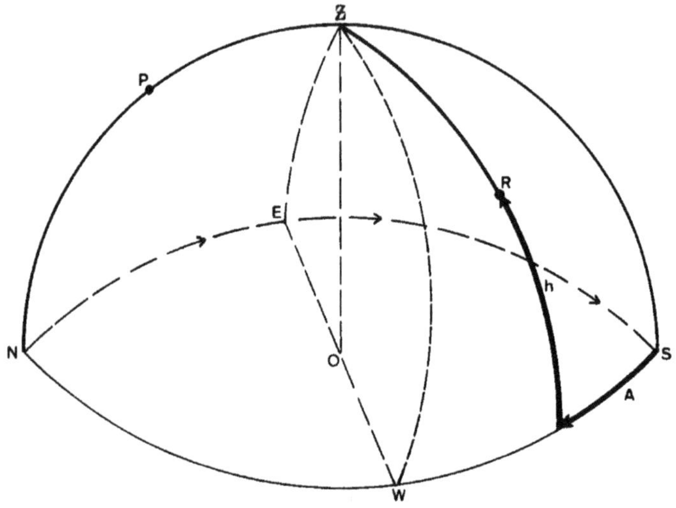

Figure A2. The Horizon System of Coordinates.

server's position intersects the celestial sphere in a great circle: the horizon. Figure A2 shows the horizon circle NWSE. In the Figure, Z is the zenith, R a star, 0 the observer, and P is a point where the northward projection of the Earth's axis of rotation appears to pierce the sky. This point is called the north celestial pole. It is marked today by the star Polaris.

A great circle through the zenith and north celestial pole intersects the horizon at the points N and S: the observer's north and south points. This great circle is the observer's meridian.

The position of a star, R, at any instant is given by its altitude, h, and its azimuth, A. The altitude is measured along a circle perpendicular to the horizon that passes through the star and zenith. The altitude is the number of degrees above or below the horizon. The azimuth is the number of degrees from north in an easterly direction along the horizon to the foot of the vertical circle passing through the star. The altitude of a star varies from zero degrees at the horizon to ninety-degrees at the zenith or nadir. It is positive

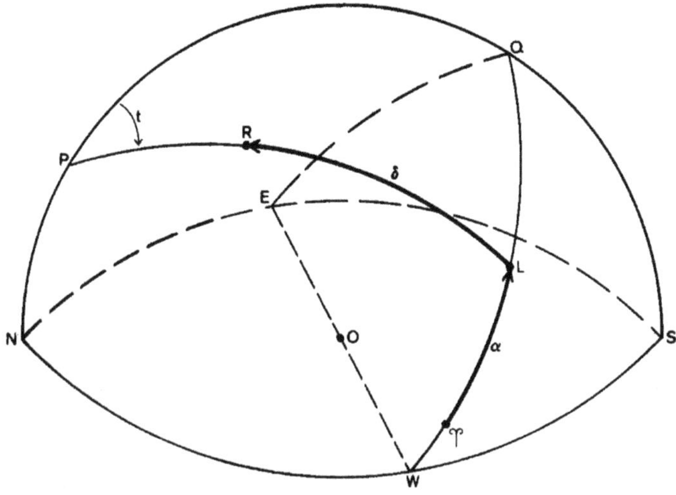

Figure A3. The Equator System of Coordinates.

when the star is above the horizon, and negative when the star is below the horizon. The zenith distance is 90° - h. The azimuth varies from 0° to 360°, and is zero-degrees when the star is directly north of the observer, 90° when east, 180° when south, and 270° when west of the observer.

These coordinates are purely local. As the observer moves on Earth's surface, his zenith and horizon change. Furthermore, the celestial sphere and the stars on it appear to rotate for any observer. Hence the altitude and azimuth of any star changes with time.

The local nature and time dependence of the coordinates of a celestial object m the horizon system is eliminated by choosing the celestial equator as the fundamental circle of reference. In Figure A3, let EQLW be the celestial equator. The observer is at 0, and the north celestial pole is at P. As in Figure A2, NWSE is the observer's horizon. The great circle which passes through P and the star, R, and is perpendicular to the equator is called an hour circle. Let δ be the angular distance in degrees from the equator along the hour circle to the star, R. δ is the declination R; and is positive when R is north of the equator, and negative when R is south of this circle. The right ascension α or R.A.) of R is the angular distance in degrees measured from the vernal equinox (0° Aries) along the celestial equator toward the east to the foot of the hour circle through R. The right ascension, α, varies from 0° to 360°.

Included in the equator system is a semi-local system of coordinates consisting of the declination and the local hour angle, t. The local hour angle is the angular distance in degrees measured along the equator from the observer's meridian toward the west to the foot of the hour circle through the star. From the definition of sidereal time (see Appendix A):

$$T = \theta_L - \alpha$$

where θ_L is the local apparent sidereal time. When a star crosses an observer's meridian, it is culminating. At this time $t = 0$, and therefore $\alpha = \theta_L$, or the local sidereal time is equivalent to the right ascension of the observer's mid-heaven.

The equator system of coordinates is one that is presently used by astronomers for al observational work from the Earth. However, the celestial system of latitude and longitude is more familiar to astrologers. The celestial longitude, λ, is the angular distance to the circle that passes through the celestial object at right angles to the ecliptic. The celestial latitude, /3, is the angular distance of the object from the ecliptic, measured northward or southward along the perpendicular circle.

In scientific work celestial longitude, λ, varies from 0° to 360°. To aid those more familiar with the astrological notation, the following Table Al is appended:

Table A1. Astrological Notation.

Astrological Notation	*Celestial Longitude*
0° Aries	0°
0° Taurus	30°

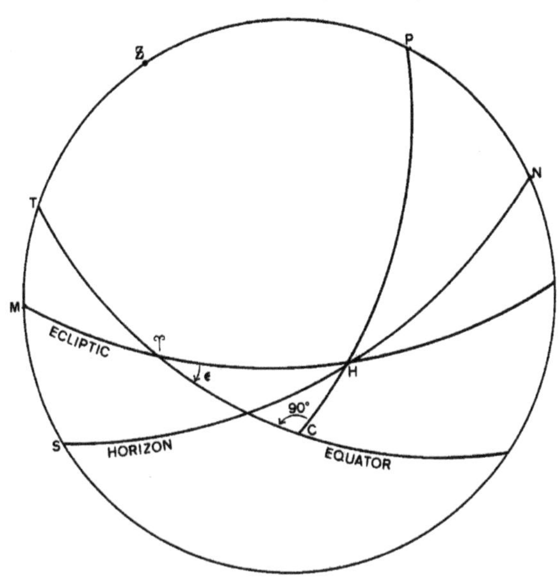

Figure A4. Relationships between the Coordinate Systems.

0° Gemini	60°
0° Cancer	90°
0° Leo	120°
0° Virgo	150°
0° Libra	180°
0° Scorpio	210°
0° Sagittarius	240°
0° Capricorn	270°
0° Aquarius	300°
0° Pisces	330°

That is, 13° of Virgo is equivalent to a celestial longitude of 163°: 150° + 13°.

Figure A4 presents the relationships between the three coordinate systems just described. SMTZPN is the observer's meridian.

The point M is the midheaven, or MC, found in astrological ephemerae. The point H is the horoscope, or ascendent.

As the equinoxes and solstices were the first to be identified for the division of the ecliptic, the horoscope (ASC) and the midheaven, and their opposites, were the first to divide the equator. As they were already on the ecliptic, they could immediately be related to the more general indications of zodiacal astrology. The results were remarkable: life and the length of life, parents and (perhaps) what happens after death, marriage (whether for good or evil), and career and honors could all now be correlated with the positions of heavenly bodies[3].

The Classicists called these divisions "loci," or "places," where particular events of an individual's life might be indicated. The term "domicile" or "house" meant that division of the ecliptic that had a correlative nature similar to that of the planets: as Leo is the House of the Sun, or Pisces is the lunar House of Jupiter. The modern misnomer of "ruler" was borrowed from the superstitions of the Middle Ages. Indeed, it is absurd to suppose that a planet could ever be considered to "rule" a whole constellation of suns as is imagined today.

Other points of division of the loci are only alluded to in classical astrological works such as the *Tetrabiblos*[4] and al-Biruni's treatise cited above. The cusps of the loci are determined from the principles set forth in such works as the *Almagest* by Ptolemy. A knowledge of texts such as the *Almagest* was considered a prerequisite to any study of astrology; and so the classical astrological treatises generally assume knowledge of the reader not presently available today. But a recent translation of fragments of the works of a 6th-century astrologer, Rhetorius, "describes explicitly how to determine the cusps of the loci[5].

---

[3]ibid.

[4]C. Ptolemy, *Tetrabiblos*, F.E. Robbins, trans. The Loeb Classical Library, Harvard University Press, 1940.

[5]*Catalogus coduim astrologorum Graecorum*, Brussels, Lamertin, 12 vols., 1953.

We read in the *Tetrabiblos* (iii:10) that the cusp of the first locus is determined by subtracting five degrees from the horoscope (ASC). Al-Biruni[6] also states that planets in these degrees are in the first locus. The reason for this is given in the Almagest (viii:4-6). One of the primary diurnal effects that must be accounted for is the heliacal risings of the stars and planets. But due to the refraction of the atmosphere and the large apparent size of the sun with respect to the stars, a star may be obscured in its heliacal rising. Only by subtracting five degrees from the horoscope (ASC) will all heliacal risings be included within the first locus as is necessary. Again, remember that classical astrology uses observational astronomy as a tool.

As each sign of the zodiac represents one-twelfth of the apparent sidereal movement of the celestial sphere (e.g., one-twelfth of a year), each locus represents one-twelfth of the apparent diurnal movement (e.g., one-twelfth of a day). Now the word "day" has two meanings. In the first instance it is a period between two successive transits of the upper meridian by the Sun. In the second instance it is the period of time between sunrise and sunset. The first definition is called a "tropical" or "equinoctial" day; and the latter definition if a "seasonal" or "civil" or "ordinary" day. Both of these definitions are combined in the divisions of the loci.

The 360 degrees containing the circle of the twelve loci represent one tropical day, just as the 12 signs of the zodiac represent one year. But each locus represents two civil or seasonal hours. Seasonal hours vary with the time of year and location (geographic latitude) on the surface of the Earth. The time of daylight is .longer in the summer than in winter; but if it is assumed that there are always exactly twelve hours of daylight, then each summer hour is longer than each winter hour.

For example, on July 4, 1973 at 40 degrees north latitude (just south of New York City), sunrise occurs at 0436 and sunset at 1932 hours. Therefore, there are 14 hours and 56 minutes of daylight

---

[6]Al-Biruni, p. 491.

(using tropical hours). But this time interval is 12 seasonal hours; and so each seasonal hour of daylight equals $1^h14^m40^s$ tropical hours. As there are 24 tropical hours in a day, there must be 24 - $14^h56^m = 9^h04^m$ of nighttime on July 4 at this latitude. Or each seasonal hour of nighttime equals 45^m20^s tropical hours. From this it is evident that always one seasonal hour of daytime plus one seasonal hour of nighttime on any given day is equal to two tropical hours (120 minutes).

Again, on February 4, 1973, at 40 degrees north latitude, sunrise occurs at 0706 and sunset at 1723 hours. From which there are 10h17m of daylight; and each seasonal hour of daylight is 51^m25^s, and each seasonal hour of nighttime is $1^h08^m35^s$.

Now the distance on the equator from the right ascension of the horoscope to the right ascension of the upper meridian, (arc C♈T of Figure A4), can be shown to be equal to six seasonal hours of daylight for the day on which the Sun rises at H. So if we find the day for which the sun is rising at the cusp of the first locus, we also know the length of the seasonal hours from the right ascension of the first cusp to the right ascension of the corresponding meridian. If this distance is trisected, we have the right ascensions of the 10th,11lth, and 12th loci.

Going in the other direction, the direction on the equator from the right ascension of the cusp of the first locus to the right ascension of the lower meridian is equal to six seasonal hours of nighttime. So by trisecting this distance we have the right ascension of the cusps of the 2nd and 3rd loci.

Transform these points from the equator to the ecliptic and the job is done. The planets and stars are referenced directly to the Earth's diurnal movement in a manner consistent with their reference to the sidereal movements.

So closely tied are these two reference systems, the signs of the zodiac and the 12 loci, that if one is in error, then so must be the other! In other words, we have here a perfectly logical and consistent scientific system—the beauty of classical astrology.

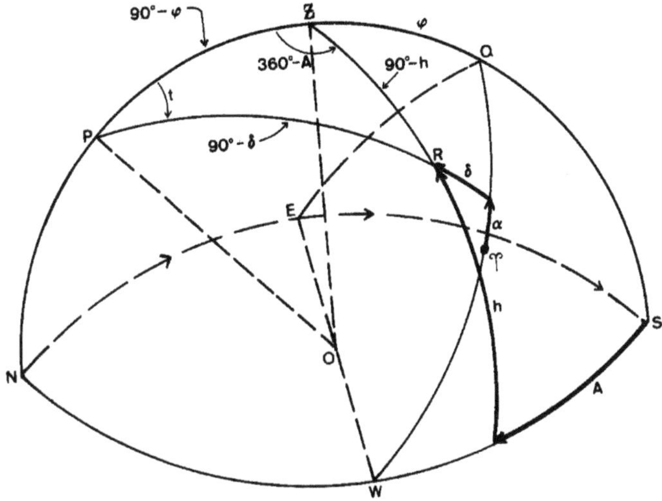

Figure A5. Geometry of Transformation Horizon to Equator Systems.

There is, of course, no tables of houses for this method of loci division. Fortunately, they are not needed because calculators with trigonometric functions are available. To show how these loci can be easily computed, let us see how, by elementary spherical trigonometry, the coordinates of a celestial object in one system can be transformed into another system.

The geometry for transformation between the horizon and the equator is given in Figure A5. In the figure, φ is the geographic latitude of the observer. Now suppose that the altitude, h, and the Azimuth, A, of a star are to be determined given its right ascension, α , and declination, σ , together with the time and place of the observation. Then by the cosine law for the spherical triangle PZR:

$$\sin h = \sin \varphi \sin \delta + \cos \varphi \cos \delta \cos t \quad (2)$$

where t is the hour angle of the star. Since the local apparent time is known, the local apparent sidereal time, θ_L, can be determined. t can then be determined from (1). Hence all quantities on the right hand side of (2) are known, and h can be determined.

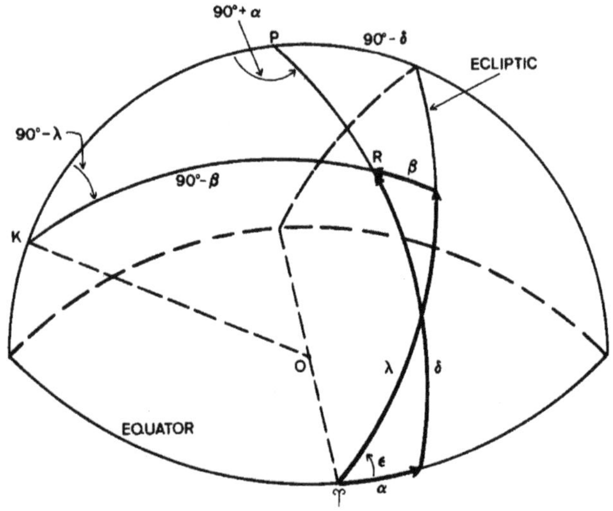

Figure A6. Geometry of Transformation Equator to Celestial Systems.

Also we have

$$[\sin(2\Pi\text{-}A)/\sin(\Pi/2\text{-}\delta)] = [\sin t/\sin(\Pi/2 - h)] \ (3)$$

from which

$$\sin A = \cos \quad \sec h \sin t \ (4)$$

Of course α and δ can also be determined in the same manner as α and δ are given.

The geometry for transformation between the equator and the ecliptic is given in Figure A6. The observer on Earth is at 0. The obliquity of the ecliptic is ε, or the arc KP. The pole of the ecliptic is K; and that of the equator is P. In the spherical triangle KPR, the angle 90° + α and the sides 90° - δ and ε are given. Therefore, if α and δ are known:

$$\sin \beta = \sin \delta \cos \varepsilon - \cos \delta \sin \ \varepsilon \sin \alpha \ \ (5)$$

$$\sin \lambda \cos \beta = \sin \delta \cos \varepsilon + \cos \delta \sin \ \varepsilon \sin \alpha \ (6)$$

$$\cos \lambda \sin \beta = \sin \delta \cos \alpha \ (7)$$

And if λ and β are known

$$\sin \delta = \cos \varepsilon - \cos \sin \beta \sin \varepsilon \cos \beta \sin \lambda \ (8)$$

$$\sin \alpha \cos \delta = - \sin \varepsilon \sin \beta + \cos \varepsilon - \cos \beta \sin \lambda \ (9)$$

$$\cos \alpha \cos \delta = \cos \beta \cos \lambda \ (10)$$

With these relationships, we can now derive the equations that will enable us to compute all the points on the chart. Let the local sidereal time, θ_L, be determined in the normal way (see Appendix A). Let also the geographic latitude, φ, be given. Then the right ascension of the MC, α_{m}, is

$$\alpha_{m}, = \theta_L \ (11)$$

To determine λ_m, the longitude of the MC, we note that on the ecliptic $\beta = 0$ so it becomes

$$\sin \delta \cos \varepsilon - \cos \delta \sin \ = 0 \ (12)$$

and dividing by $\cos \delta \cos \varepsilon$, we have

$$\tan \delta - \tan \varepsilon \sin \alpha = 0 \ (13)$$

or

$$\tan \delta = \tan \varepsilon \sin \alpha \ (14)$$

Now on dividing (6) by (7) we have

$$\tan \lambda = (\sin \varepsilon \tan \delta \ / \cos \alpha) + \cos \varepsilon \tan \alpha \ (15)$$

and on substituting (14) into (15)

$$\tan \lambda = (\sin^2 \varepsilon \tan \alpha \ / \cos \varepsilon \ ) + \cos \varepsilon \tan \alpha \ (16)$$

$$= \tan \alpha \ / \cos \varepsilon \ (17)$$

or

$$\lambda_m = \tan^{-1}(\tan \alpha_m / \cos \varepsilon) \ (18)$$

To determine λ_H, the longitude of the horoscope, we note from Figure A4 that the altitude, h, must be zero. Therefore (2) becomes, after dividing by $\cos \varphi \cos \delta$ and substituting for t from (1):

$$\tan \varphi \tan \delta + \cos(\varphi_L \ - \alpha) = 0 \ (19)$$

Now also from Figure A4, $\beta = 0$, and equation (14) can be substituted in (19). Therefore, after expanding $\cos(\varphi_L, -\alpha)$, we have

$$\tan\varphi \tan\varepsilon \sin\alpha + \cos\varphi_L, \cos\alpha + \sin\varphi_L \sin\alpha = 0 \quad (20)$$

Dividing by $\sin\alpha$ and solving we then obtain

$$\cot\alpha = -(\tan\varphi \tan\varepsilon / \cos\varphi_L) - \tan\varphi_L \quad (21)$$

But since $\beta = 0$ we can divide (9) by (10)

$$\tan\alpha = \cos\varepsilon \tan\lambda \, (22)$$

from which

$$\cot\lambda = -(\tan\varphi \sin\varepsilon + \sin\theta \cos\varepsilon)/\cos\theta_L \quad (23)$$

$$\lambda_H = \cot^{-1}[-(\tan\varphi \sin\varepsilon + \sin\theta_L \cos\varepsilon)/\cos\theta_L] \quad (24)$$

and, finally, the right ascension of the horoscope is from (22)

$$\alpha_H = \tan^{-1}(\cos\varepsilon \tan\lambda_H) \, (25)$$

Given the longitude of the horoscope, λ_H, the longitude of the corresponding MC can be found as follows:

Since $h = 0$

$$\cos t = -\tan\varphi \tan\delta \, (26)$$

From (14)

$$\tan\delta = \tan\varepsilon \tan\alpha \quad (27)$$

where

$$\alpha = \tan^{-1}(\cos\varepsilon \tan\lambda_H) \quad (28)$$

therefore

$$t = \cos\text{-}1(-\tan\varphi \tan\varepsilon \sin\alpha_H) \, (29)$$

But t is the distance from the right ascension of the horoscope (ASC) to the right ascension of the meridian. Therefore

$$\alpha_m = \alpha_H - t \, (30)$$

The equations (11), (18), (24), (25), and (29) are all that are required to find the horoscope (ASC), the MC, and the cusps of the twelve loci. An example should make clear all of these concepts.

Suppose it is desired to erect a chart for an individual born 15^h 15^m local apparent sidereal time at 40° north latitude. Then we have

$$\theta_L = 15^h 15^m$$

Remembering that one hour of time is equivalent to 15 degrees of arc. So

$$\theta_L = \alpha_M = 228°45'$$

From the *American Ephemeris and Nautical Almanac* it is noted that the mean obliquity of the ecliptic for 1973 is 23° 26' 34".

So, therefore, applying (18), we have

$$\lambda_M = 231° \ 10' \ 48''$$

or the MC of the chart is at 21♏10'48".

To find the horoscope (ASC) apply (24).

$$\lambda_H = \cot^{-1}(-0.53987)$$
$$= 298° \ 21'48''$$

or the horoscope (ASC) is 28♑21'48".

The longitude of the cusp of the first locus, λ_{L1}, is λ_H -5°, or 293° 21' 48". The right ascension is (applying (25)):

$$\alpha_{L1} = 295° \ 12' \ 47''$$

Using (29) we find:

$$t = \cos^{-1} (0.32919)$$
$$= 70° \ 46'48''$$

then from (30)

$$\alpha_{L10} = \alpha_H - t$$
$$= 224° \ 25' \ 59''$$

To find the right ascension of the cusps of the 11th and 12th loci, divide t by 3 and add α_{L10} to the 11th cusp.

That is

$$t/3 = 23° \ 35' \ 36''$$

Adding to α_{L10} $\alpha_{L11} = \alpha_{L10} + t/3 = 248° \ 01' \ 35''$

Adding again to α_{L11} $\alpha_{L12} = \alpha_{L11} + t/3 = 271° 37' 11''$

Now α_{L14} is, of course, α_{L10} - 180°, or α_{L4}= 44° 25' 59"

Therefore, if we subtract t from 180 degrees and divide by three we have the right ascension of the 2nd and 3rd cusps.

$$(180° - t)/3 = 36° 24' 24''$$

$$= + (180° - t)/3$$

$$° 331° 37'11''$$

$$= + (180° - t)/3$$

$$= 8° 01' 35''$$

Successive applications of (18) transform these points to the ecliptic. Table A2 presents these results.

Table A2. Results of Loci Computations.

	Right Ascension	*Longitude*	*Astrological Notation*
Horoscope (ASC)	300° 29'	298° 22'	28 ♑ 22
MC	228° 45'	231° 11'	21 ♏ 11
10th locus	224° 26'	226° 54'	16 ♏ 54
11th locus	248° 02'	249° 41'	09 ♐ 41
12th locus	271° 37'	271° 29'	01 ♑ 29
1st locus	295° 13'	293° 22'	23 ♑ 22
3rd locus	8° 02'	8° 44'	08 ♈ 44

With these data, the chart can now be set up in the ordinary manner. Note that all the points, including the horoscope (ASC) and MC, were accurately determined without reference to a tables of houses. Indeed, no astrologer prior to the 18th century ever bothered with a tables of houses.

But as sophisticated as were the Renaissance astrologers in the tools of their trade, astronomy and mathematics, without the aid of the fragments of papyri cited above, they were all unable to correctly reconstruct the true method of loci division. Regiomontanus correctly assessed the importance of the equator, but used spatial rather than time arcs. Placidus correctly uses time arcs; but not based on a reasonable division of the day. Campanus divided the prime vertical, pseudo-Porphy the ecliptic between the horoscope (ASC) and the MC; and, finally, the equal house system divided the ecliptic equally from the horoscope (ASC) etc.

The problem was that Western Europe had lost the knowledge of the Greeks after the fall of the Roman Empire. It was the Arabic world that kept the flame of scholarship alight during the Dark Ages. When knowledge finally returned to Europe, astrology was rediscovered also, but it was Ptolemy as interpreted by astrologers such as ibn Ezra. Of course this led to large doses of Jewish mysticism. This mysticism suited the superstitions of the day, but the result was that those astrologers who were serious scientists did not have the whole story.

This complete misunderstanding of the loci persists down to this very day. The full story is related in Chapter I. Suffice to state that fortunately most methods of loci division are sufficiently close to the "scientific" one that they all "work" a fair percentage of the time. Table A3 illustrates this point. It was computed for 50° north latitude, sidereal time equals 0800 hours, and tends to maximize the differences.

Table A3: Comparison of Loci Division Systems

Locus	Placidus	Regiomontanus	Campanus	Porphyry	Equal House	Classical
X	27♋55	27♋55	25♋55	25♋55	21♋31	21♋17
XI	2♍20	4♍09	23♌48	25♌47	21♌31	17♌58
XII	0♎00	0♎00	20♍37	23♍39	21♍31	16♍45
I	21♎31	21♎31	21♎31	21♎31	21♎31	16♎31
II	18♏01	14♏53	26♏10	23♏59	21♏31	20♏15
III	20♐38	16♐40	29♐20	25♐47	21♐31	21♐11

The extremely close approximation to the classical method of loci division that is given by the equal house system shows why this latter has gained so in popularity over the past few years. The Faculty of Astrological Studies in London teaches that the Equal House system is superior to all others (with exception, of course, to the classical method, which has not as yet been formally evaluated by modem astrologers). Carl Jung, who was also an astrologer, used this system exclusively. However, Margaret Hone of the Faculty of Astrological Studies admits that the equal house system does not always "work"[7]. But this is a typical result of a theory with a fundamental scientific flaw; for example, Newtonian mechanics is only an approximation of the reality it is supposed to describe, and hence Relativistic physics has superceded the Newtonian.

[7]Margaret E. Hone, *The Modern Textbook of Astrology*, Fowler, London, 1951.

Bibliography

Aristotle. *De Caelo*, W. Guthris, trans., Harvard University Press, Cambridge, Mass., 1960.

____*De Generatone Et Corruptione,* E. Forester, trans., Harvard University Press, Cambridge, Mass., 1965.

____*De Mundo,* D. Furley, trans., Harvard University Press, Cambridge, Mass., 1965.

____*Meteorologica,* H. Lee, trans., Harvard University Press, Cambridge, Mass., 1962.

____*Physicia, 2* vols., P. Wickstead and F. Comford, trans., Harvard University Press, Cambridge, Mass., 1963.

al-Biruni, Abu'l-Rayhan Muhammed ibn. *The Book of Instruction in the Elements of the Art of Astrology,* R. Ramsey, trans., Luzac, London, 1934.

Carter, C. *The Astrological Aspects,* Fowler, London, 1930.

____*Encyclopedia of Psychological Astrology,* Theosophical Publishing House, London, 1972.

Lee, Dal. *Dictionary of Astrology,* Coronet, New York, 1968.

Ezra, Abraham ibn. *The Beginning of Wisdom,* F. Cantera, trans., Universidad de Madrid, Madrid, Spain, 1939.

Hone, Margaret E. *The Modern Textbook of Astrology,* Fowler, London, 1951.

____*Applied Astrology,* Fowler, London, 1953.

Kennedy, E.S. and Pingree, D. *The Astrological History of Masha'allah,* Harvard University Press, Cambridge, Mass., 1971.

George, Llewellyn. *A to Z Horoscope Maker and Delineator,* Llewellyn, St. Paul, 1972.

Matemus, Firmicus. *Mathesis libri VIII,* J. Bram, trans., Noyes Press, Park Ridge, N.J., 1975.

Parker, D.J. *The Compleat Astrologer,* Bantam Books, New York, 1975.

Plato, *Timaeus.* B. Bury, trans., Harvard University Press, Cambridge, Mass., 1955.

____*Epinomis,* W. Lamb, trans., Harvard university Press, Cambridge, Mass., 1956.

Pingree, David. *The Thousands of Abu-Mashar,* The Warburg Institute, London, 1968.

Ptolemy, C. *Tetrabiblos,* F.E. Robbins, trans., Harvard University Press, Cambridge, Mass., 1952.

____*Almagest,* Great Books of the Western World, Encyclopedia Britannica, Chicago, 1953.

Smart W. M. *Textbook on Spherical Astronomy,* Cambridge University Press, Cambridge, England, 1971.

Table 18.

D M	D W	Sidereal Time H. M. S.	☉ Long.	☉ Dec.	☽ Long.	☽ Lat.	☽ Dec.	Midnight ☽ Long.	Midnight ☽ Dec.	☽ Node	♆ Long.	♆ Lat.	♆ Dec.	♅ Long.	♅ Lat.	♅ Dec.
JULY		(FOWLER'S EPHEMERIS)								1957						
1	M	6 37 6	9♋21	23N 7	29♌ 8	4S59	7N 1	6♍28	4N37	17♏ 6	29♎52	1N46	9S46	5♌32	0N35	19N29
2	TU	6 41 3	10 18	23 3	13 42	4 36	2 8	20 56	0S22	17 3	29R52	1 46	9 46	5 36	0 35	19 28
3	W	6 45 0	11 16	22 58	28 2	3 55	2S49	5♎ 9	5 16	17 0	29 52	1 46	9 46	5 39	0 35	19 27
4	TH	6 48 56	12 13	22 53	12♎ 7	3 0	7 31	19 5	9 47	16 57	29 51	1 46	9 46	5 43	0 35	19 26
5	F	6 52 52	13 10	22 47	25 54	1 56	11 45	2♏44	13 43	16 54	29 51	1 46	9 46	5 46	0 35	19 26
6	SA	6 56 49	14 7	22 41	9♏25	0 47	15 17	16 7	16 51	16 51	29 51	1 46	9 46	5 50	0 35	19 25
7	SU	7 0 45	15 4	22 35	22 42	0N23	17 57	29 17	19 3	16 47	29 51	1 46	9 46	5 53	0 35	19 24
8	M	7 4 42	16 2	22 29	5♐45	1 31	19 35	12♐13	20 12	16 44	29 51	1 46	9 46	5 57	0 35	19 23
9	TU	7 8 39	17 0	22 22	18 35	2 34	20 15	24 58	20 18	16 41	29 50	1 46	9 46	6 0	0 35	19 22
10	W	7 12 35	17 57	22 15	1♑14	3 27	19 51	7♑32	19 23	16 38	29 50	1 46	9 46	6 4	0 35	19 21
11	TH	7 16 32	18 54	22 7	13 39	4 10	18 28	19 56	17 32	16 35	29 50	1 46	9 46	6 8	0 35	19 20
12	F	7 20 28	19 51	21 59	26 3	4 40	16 14	2♒11	14 56	16 32	29D50	1 46	9 46	6 11	0 35	19 19
13	SA	7 24 25	20 48	21 51	8♒14	4 57	13 20	14 17	11 43	16 28	29 50	1 46	9 46	6 15	0 35	19 18
14	SU	7 28 21	21 45	21 42	20 17	5 1	9 54	26 16	8 4	16 25	29 50	1 46	9 46	6 18	0 35	19 17
15	M	7 32 18	22 42	21 32	2♓13	4 51	6 6	8♓ 9	4 8	16 22	29 50	1 46	9 46	6 22	0 35	19 16
16	TU	7 36 14	23 39	21 22	14 5	4 29	2 6	20 0	0 3	16 19	29 50	1 46	9 46	6 26	0 35	19 15
17	W	7 40 11	24 37	21 12	25 56	3 55	2N 0	1♈52	4N 2	16 16	29 50	1 46	9 46	6 29	0 35	19 14
18	TH	7 44 8	25 34	21 2	7♈51	3 11	6 1	13 49	8 0	16 13	29 50	1 45	9 47	6 33	0 35	19 13
19	F	7 48 4	26 32	20 52	19 52	2 18	9 51	25 56	11 42	16 9	29 51	1 45	9 47	6 36	0 35	19 12
20	SA	7 52 1	27 29	20 41	2♉ 7	1 17	13 21	8♉18	15 0	16 6	29 51	1 45	9 47	6 40	0 35	19 11
21	SU	7 55 57	28 26	20 29	14 39	0 12	16 20	21 0	17 40	16 3	29 51	1 45	9 47	6 44	0 35	19 10
22	M	7 59 54	29 23	20 17	27 33	0S56	18 35	4♊ 7	19 30	16 0	29 51	1 45	9 47	6 47	0 35	19 9
23	TU	8 3 50	0♌20	20 5	10♊54	2 3	19 54	17 41	20 18	15 57	29 52	1 45	9 47	6 51	0 35	19 8
24	W	8 7 47	1 18	19 53	24 42	3 5	20 5	1♋44	19 52	15 54	29 52	1 45	9 47	6 54	0 35	19 7
25	TH	8 11 43	2 15	19 40	8♋58	3 57	19 1	16 13	18 9	15 50	29 53	1 45	9 47	6 58	0 35	19 6
26	F	8 15 40	3 13	19 27	23 39	4 35	16 41	1♌ 5	15 12	15 47	29 53	1 45	9 47	7 2	0 35	19 5
27	SA	8 19 37	4 10	19 14	8♌37	4 55	13 12	16 9	11 12	15 44	29 54	1 45	9 47	7 5	0 35	19 4
28	SU	8 23 33	5 7	19 0	23 42	4 56	8 51	1♍16	6 30	15 41	29 54	1 45	9 47	7 9	0 35	19 3
29	M	8 27 30	6 4	18 46	8♍46	4 36	3 58	16 16	1 25	15 38	29 55	1 45	9 47	7 13	0 35	19 2
30	TU	8 31 26	7 2	18 32	23 38	3 57	1S 7	1♎ 1	3S40	15 35	29 55	1 45	9 48	7 17	0 35	19 1
31	W	8 35 23	8 0	18 17	8♎13	3 3	6 2	15 25	8 25	15 31	29 56	1 45	9 48	7 21	0 35	19 0

D M	♄ Long.	♄ Lat.	♄ Dec.	♃ Long.	♃ Lat.	♃ Dec.	♂ Long.	♂ Lat.	♂ Dec.	♀ Long.	♀ Lat.	♀ Dec.	☿ Long.	☿ Lat.	☿ Dec.	♇ Long.	♇ Lat.	♇ Dec.
1	9♐ 0	1N49	20S 1	24♍30	1N16	3N21	6♌17	1N14	19N53	0♌ 4	1N29	21N36	6♋ 1	0N59	24N16	28♌38	11N29	22N28
2	8R56	1 49	20 1	24 38	1 16	3 18	6 54	1 14	19 43	1 17	1 30	21 21	8 11	1 7	24 15	28 39	11 29	22 28
3	8 53	1 48	20 0	24 45	1 15	3 15	7 32	1 14	19 33	2 30	1 31	21 5	10 22	1 14	24 13	28 40	11 29	22 27
4	8 49	1 48	20 0	24 53	1 15	3 12	8 9	1 13	19 24	3 43	1 31	20 49	12 33	1 21	24 11	28 42	11 29	22 27
5	8 46	1 48	20 0	25 0	1 15	3 9	8 47	1 13	19 14	4 56	1 32	20 32	14 43	1 27	24 4	28 43	11 28	22 26
6	8 43	1 48	19 59	25 8	1 15	3 6	9 25	1 13	19 4	6 9	1 33	20 15	16 52	1 33	23 54	28 44	11 28	22 26
7	8 40	1 48	19 59	25 15	1 15	3 3	10 2	1 13	18 53	7 22	1 34	19 57	19 1	1 38	23 42	28 46	11 28	22 25
8	8 36	1 48	19 59	25 23	1 15	3 0	10 40	1 13	18 43	8 35	1 34	19 39	21 8	1 41	23 28	28 47	11 28	22 24
9	8 33	1 47	19 58	25 31	1 14	2 56	11 17	1 13	18 33	9 48	1 35	19 21	23 13	1 44	23 12	28 48	11 28	22 24
10	8 30	1 47	19 58	25 39	1 14	2 52	11 55	1 12	18 22	11 1	1 35	19 1	25 18	1 46	22 55	28 50	11 27	22 23
11	8 27	1 47	19 58	25 47	1 14	2 49	12 33	1 12	18 11	12 14	1 35	18 40	27 21	1 48	22 34	28 51	11 27	22 23
12	8 24	1 47	19 58	25 55	1 14	2 45	13 10	1 12	18 0	13 27	1 36	18 19	29 22	1 49	22 6	28 53	11 27	22 23
13	8 21	1 47	19 57	26 4	1 14	2 42	13 48	1 12	17 49	14 40	1 36	17 57	1♌22	1 50	21 38	28 54	11 27	22 22
14	8 18	1 46	19 57	26 12	1 13	2 38	14 25	1 12	17 38	15 53	1 36	17 35	3 19	1 49	21 10	28 56	11 27	22 22
15	8 16	1 46	19 57	26 21	1 13	2 35	15 3	1 11	17 27	17 6	1 36	17 13	5 15	1 48	20 41	28 57	11 26	22 21
16	8 13	1 46	19 57	26 29	1 13	2 31	15 41	1 11	17 15	18 19	1 36	16 51	7 9	1 47	20 12	28 59	11 26	22 21
17	8 11	1 46	19 57	26 38	1 13	2 27	16 19	1 11	17 3	19 32	1 36	16 28	9 1	1 45	19 41	29 0	11 26	22 20
18	8 9	1 46	19 56	26 47	1 13	2 24	16 56	1 11	16 52	20 45	1 35	16 5	10 52	1 42	19 8	29 2	11 26	22 20
19	8 6	1 45	19 56	26 56	1 12	2 20	17 34	1 10	16 40	21 57	1 35	15 41	12 41	1 38	18 33	29 3	11 26	22 19
20	8 4	1 45	19 56	27 5	1 12	2 16	18 12	1 10	16 28	23 10	1 35	15 17	14 29	1 34	17 58	29 5	11 25	22 19
21	8 2	1 45	19 56	27 14	1 12	2 13	18 50	1 10	16 17	24 23	1 35	14 53	16 14	1 29	17 23	29 7	11 25	22 18
22	8 0	1 45	19 56	27 24	1 12	2 9	19 28	1 10	16 5	25 36	1 34	14 28	17 57	1 24	16 47	29 8	11 25	22 18
23	7 58	1 45	19 56	27 33	1 12	2 5	20 6	1 10	15 53	26 48	1 34	14 3	19 38	1 19	16 10	29 10	11 25	22 17
24	7 57	1 44	19 55	27 43	1 11	2 1	20 43	1 9	15 41	28 1	1 34	13 37	21 18	1 13	15 33	29 12	11 25	22 17
25	7 55	1 44	19 55	27 52	1 11	1 57	21 21	1 9	15 28	29 13	1 33	13 11	22 55	1 7	14 56	29 13	11 24	22 16
26	7 54	1 44	19 55	28 2	1 11	1 53	21 59	1 9	15 16	0♍26	1 32	12 45	24 32	1 0	14 18	29 15	11 24	22 16
27	7 52	1 44	19 55	28 12	1 11	1 49	22 37	1 9	15 4	1 39	1 31	12 18	26 5	0 53	13 40	29 17	11 24	22 15
28	7 51	1 44	19 55	28 22	1 11	1 45	23 14	1 9	14 51	2 51	1 30	11 51	27 38	0 45	13 1	29 19	11 24	22 14
29	7 49	1 44	19 55	28 32	1 11	1 41	23 52	1 9	14 39	4 4	1 29	11 24	29 9	0 37	12 22	29 20	11 24	22 14
30	7 48	1 43	19 55	28 42	1 11	1 37	24 30	1 8	14 26	5 16	1 28	10 56	0♍38	0 29	11 43	29 22	11 23	22 13
31	7 47	1 43	19 55	28 52	1 11	1 33	25 8	1 8	14 15	6 29	1 27	10 28	2 5	0 21	11 3	29 24	11 23	22 13

Table 18 continued.

AUGUST							(FOWLER'S EPHEMERIS)					1957				
D M	D W	Sidereal Time	☉ Long.	☉ Dec.	☽ Long.	☽ Lat.	☽ Dec.	Midnight ☽ Long.	Midnight ☽ Dec.	☽ Node.	♆ Long.	♆ Lat.	♆ Dec.	♅ Long.	♅ Lat.	♅ Dec.
		H. M. S.	° ′	° ′	° ′	° ′	° ′	° ′	° ′	° ′	° ′	° ′	° ′	° ′	° ′	° ′
1	TH	8 39 19	8♌57	18N 2	22♎25	1S59	10S30	29♎25	12S36	15♎28	29♎57	1N45	9S48	7♌24	0N35	18N59
2	F	8 43 16	9 54	17 47	6♏14	0 50	14 17	13♏ 3	15 59	15 25	29 57	1 45	9 48	7 28	0 35	18 58
3	SA	8 47 12	10 52	17 31	19 41	0N21	17 12	26 19	18 26	15 22	29 58	1 45	9 49	7 32	0 35	18 57
4	SU	8 51 9	11 49	17 15	2♐47	1 28	19 8	9♐16	19 51	15 18	29 59	1 45	9 49	7 36	0 35	18 56
5	M	8 55 6	12 46	16 59	15 37	2 30	20 2	21 58	20 14	15 15	0♏ 0	1 45	9 49	7 40	0 35	18 55
6	TU	8 59 2	13 44	16 42	28 13	3 23	19 55	4♑28	19 35	15 12	0 1	1 44	9 49	7 43	0 36	18 54
7	W	9 2 59	14 41	16 25	10♑38	4 5	18 49	16 48	18 2	15 9	0 1	1 44	9 50	7 46	0 36	18 53
8	TH	9 6 55	15 39	16 8	22 53	4 36	16 51	28 59	15 40	15 6	0 2	1 44	9 50	7 50	0 36	18 52
9	F	9 10 52	16 36	15 51	5♒ 1	4 53	14 10	11♒ 3	12 40	15 3	0 3	1 44	9 50	7 54	0 36	18 52
10	SA	9 14 48	17 34	15 34	17 3	4 58	10 55	23 2	9 10	14 59	0 4	1 44	9 51	7 58	0 36	18 51
11	M	9 18 45	18 32	15 16	29 0	4 49	7 15	4♓57	5 20	14 56	0 5	1 44	9 51	8 1	0 36	18 50
12	TU	9 22 41	19 29	14 58	10♓53	4 28	3 20	16 48	1 19	14 53	0 6	1 44	9 52	8 5	0 36	18 49
13	W	9 26 38	20 27	14 40	22 43	3 55	0N43	28 38	2N45	14 50	0 7	1 44	9 52	8 8	0 36	18 48
14	TH	9 30 35	21 25	14 22	4♈34	3 11	4 44	10♈30	6 43	14 47	0 8	1 44	9 53	8 12	0 36	18 47
15	F	9 34 31	22 22	14 4	16 29	2 19	8 36	22 27	10 28	14 44	0 9	1 44	9 53	8 16	0 36	18 46
16	SA	9 38 28	23 20	13 45	28 30	1 21	12 8	4♉34	13 49	14 40	0 10	1 44	9 54	8 19	0 36	18 45
17	SU	9 42 24	24 17	13 25	10♉44	0 17	15 13	16 54	16 38	14 37	0 11	1 44	9 54	8 23	0 36	18 44
18	SU	9 46 21	25 15	13 6	23 13	0S49	17 41	29 33	18 44	14 34	0 12	1 44	9 55	8 26	0 36	18 44
19	M	9 50 17	26 13	12 47	6♊ 4	1 53	19 19	12♊35	19 54	14 31	0 13	1 44	9 55	8 30	0 36	18 43
20	TU	9 54 14	27 10	12 27	19 20	2 54	19 57	26 5	20 0	14 28	0 14	1 44	9 56	8 34	0 36	18 42
21	W	9 58 10	28 8	12 7	3♋ 5	3 47	18 57	10♋ 4	18 53	14 25	0 16	1 44	9 56	8 37	0 36	18 41
22	TH	10 2 7	29 6	11 47	17 18	4 28	17 43	24 33	16 32	14 21	0 17	1 44	9 57	8 41	0 36	18 40
23	F	10 6 3	0♍ 4	11 26	2♌ 0	4 53	14 48	9♌27	13 3	14 18	0 18	1 44	9 57	8 44	0 36	18 39
24	SA	10 10 0	1 2	11 6	17 2	4 59	10 51	24 38	8 39	14 15	0 20	1 44	9 58	8 48	0 36	18 38
25	SU	10 13 57	2 0	10 46	2♍17	4 43	6 10	9♍56	3 40	14 12	0 21	1 44	9 58	8 51	0 36	18 38
26	M	10 17 53	2 58	10 25	17 33	4 8	1 5	25 10	1S31	14 9	0 23	1 44	9 59	8 55	0 36	18 37
27	TU	10 21 50	3 56	10 4	2♎39	3 15	4S 2	10♎ 9	6 33	14 6	0 24	1 43	9 59	8 58	0 36	18 36
28	W	10 25 46	4 54	9 43	17 28	2 10	8 48	24 47	11 4	14 2	0 26	1 43	10 0	9 2	0 36	18 35
29	TH	10 29 43	5 52	9 22	1♏52	0 58	12 56	8♏57	14 49	13 59	0 27	1 43	10 0	9 5	0 36	18 34
30	F	10 33 39	6 50	9 0	15 49	0N15	16 12	22 41	17 36	13 56	0 29	1 43	10 1	9 8	0 36	18 33
31	SA	10 37 36	7 48	8 38	29 20	1 26	18 28	5♐59	19 20	13 53	0 30	1 43	10 2	9 11	0 36	18 33

D M	♄ Long.	♄ Lat.	♄ Dec.	♃ Long.	♃ Lat.	♃ Dec.	♂ Long.	♂ Lat.	♂ Dec.	♀ Long.	♀ Lat.	♀ Dec.	☿ Long.	☿ Lat.	☿ Dec.	♇ Long.	♇ Lat.	♇ Dec.
	° ′	° ′	° ′	° ′	° ′	° ′	° ′	° ′	° ′	° ′	° ′	° ′	° ′	° ′	° ′	° ′	° ′	° ′
1	7♐46	1N43	19S55	29♍ 3	1N11	1N29	25♌46	1N 8	14N 0	7♍41	1N26	10N 0	3♍30	0N13	10N24	29♌26	11N23	22N12
2	7R45	1 43	19 55	29 13	1 11	1 25	26 23	1 8	13 47	8 54	1 24	9 32	4 53	0 3	9 46	29 28	11 23	22 12
3	7 44	1 42	19 56	29 23	1 10	1 20	27 1	1 8	13 34	10 6	1 22	9 4	6 15	0S 7	9 8	29 30	11 23	22 12
4	7 44	1 42	19 56	29 34	1 10	1 16	27 39	1 7	13 21	11 19	1 21	8 35	7 34	0 16	8 30	29 31	11 22	22 11
5	7 43	1 42	19 56	29 44	1 10	1 12	28 17	1 7	13 8	12 31	1 19	8 6	8 51	0 26	7 52	29 33	11 22	22 11
6	7 43	1 41	19 56	29 55	1 10	1 7	28 55	1 7	12 54	13 43	1 17	7 37	10 6	0 36	7 15	29 35	11 22	22 11
7	7 42	1 41	19 56	0♎ 5	1 10	1 3	29 33	1 7	12 40	14 56	1 16	7 7	11 17	0 45	6 38	29 37	11 22	22 10
8	7 42	1 41	19 56	0 16	1 10	0 59	0♍11	1 7	12 27	16 8	1 14	6 37	12 30	0 55	6 2	29 38	11 22	22 10
9	7 41	1 40	19 57	0 26	1 10	0 54	0 49	1 6	12 13	17 19	1 12	6 7	13 39	1 5	5 26	29 40	11 21	22 10
10	7 41	1 40	19 57	0 37	1 10	0 50	1 27	1 6	11 59	18 33	1 11	5 37	14 45	1 16	4 50	29 42	11 21	22 9
11	7 41	1 40	19 57	0 48	1 10	0 45	2 5	1 6	11 45	19 45	1 9	5 7	15 49	1 26	4 16	29 44	11 21	22 9
12	7D41	1 39	19 57	1 0	1 9	0 40	2 43	1 6	11 31	20 57	1 7	4 36	16 51	1 37	3 43	29 45	11 21	22 9
13	7 41	1 39	19 58	1 11	1 9	0 36	3 21	1 5	11 17	22 10	1 5	4 5	17 50	1 48	3 10	29 47	11 21	22 8
14	7 41	1 39	19 58	1 22	1 9	0 31	3 59	1 5	11 3	23 22	1 3	3 35	18 46	1 58	2 38	29 49	11 20	22 8
15	7 41	1 39	19 58	1 33	1 9	0 26	4 37	1 5	10 49	24 34	1 1	3 4	19 39	2 9	2 7	29 51	11 20	22 7
16	7 42	1 39	19 58	1 45	1 9	0 22	5 15	1 5	10 35	25 46	0 59	2 33	20 29	2 20	1 38	29 53	11 20	22 7
17	7 42	1 39	19 59	1 56	1 9	0 17	5 53	1 5	10 21	26 58	0 57	2 3	21 15	2 30	1 11	29 55	11 20	22 7
18	7 43	1 38	19 59	2 8	1 9	0 13	6 31	1 4	10 7	28 11	0 54	1 32	21 58	2 41	0 44	29 56	11 20	22 6
19	7 43	1 38	19 59	2 19	1 9	0 9	7 9	1 4	9 52	29 23	0 51	1 1	22 37	2 51	0 18	29 58	11 19	22 6
20	7 44	1 38	19 59	2 31	1 9	0 4	7 47	1 4	9 38	0♎35	0 49	0 31	23 13	3 1	0S 4	0♍ 0	11 19	22 6
21	7 45	1 38	20 0	2 43	1 9	0S 1	8 25	1 4	9 23	1 47	0 46	0S 1	23 44	3 12	0 25	0 1	11 19	22 5
22	7 46	1 38	20 0	2 54	1 9	0 6	9 3	1 4	9 9	2 58	0 43	0 32	24 11	3 22	0 46	0 3	11 19	22 5
23	7 47	1 38	20 0	3 6	1 9	0 10	9 42	1 3	8 54	4 10	0 41	1 3	24 34	3 31	1 3	0 5	11 19	22 5
24	7 48	1 37	20 1	3 18	1 8	0 15	10 20	1 3	8 40	5 22	0 38	1 34	24 52	3 40	1 18	0 6	11 18	22 4
25	7 50	1 37	20 1	3 30	1 8	0 20	10 58	1 3	8 25	6 34	0 36	2 5	25 5	3 49	1 31	0 8	11 18	22 4
26	7 51	1 37	20 1	3 42	1 8	0 24	11 36	1 3	8 10	7 45	0 33	2 35	25 12	3 57	1 41	0 10	11 18	22 4
27	7 53	1 37	20 2	3 54	1 8	0 29	12 14	1 2	7 55	8 57	0 30	3 6	25 14	4 4	1 48	0 12	11 18	22 3
28	7 54	1 36	20 2	4 6	1 8	0 34	12 53	1 2	7 40	10 8	0 27	3 37	25R10	4 10	1 54	0 13	11 18	22 3
29	7 56	1 36	20 3	4 18	1 8	0 39	13 31	1 2	7 25	11 20	0 24	4 7	25 0	4 15	1 53	0 15	11 17	22 3
30	7 58	1 36	20 3	4 30	1 8	0 44	14 9	1 2	7 10	12 31	0 21	4 38	24 45	4 20	1 52	0 17	11 17	22 2
31	8 0	1 36	20 4	4 42	1 8	0 49	14 47	1 1	6 55	13 43	0 18	5 9	24 23	4 24	1 51	0 18	11 17	22 2

Table A1.

JULIAN DAY NUMBER

DAYS ELAPSED AT GREENWICH NOON, A. D. 1900–1950

Year	Jan. 0	Feb. 0	Mar. 0	Apr. 0	May 0	June 0	July 0	Aug. 0	Sept. 0	Oct. 0	Nov. 0	Dec. 0
1900	241 5020	5051	5079	5110	5140	5171	5201	5232	5263	5293	5324	5354
1901	5385	5416	5444	5475	5505	5536	5566	5597	5628	5658	5689	5719
1902	5750	5781	5809	5840	5870	5901	5931	5962	5993	6023	6054	6084
1903	6115	6146	6174	6205	6235	6266	6296	6327	6358	6388	6419	6449
1904	6480	6511	6540	6571	6601	6632	6662	6693	6724	6754	6785	6815
1905	241 6846	6877	6905	6936	6966	6997	7027	7058	7089	7119	7150	7180
1906	7211	7242	7270	7301	7331	7362	7392	7423	7454	7484	7515	7545
1907	7576	7607	7635	7666	7696	7727	7757	7788	7819	7849	7880	7910
1908	7941	7972	8001	8032	8062	8093	8123	8154	8185	8215	8246	8276
1909	8307	8338	8366	8397	8427	8458	8488	8519	8550	8580	8611	8641
1910	241 8672	8703	8731	8762	8792	8823	8853	8884	8915	8945	8976	9006
1911	9037	9068	9096	9127	9157	9188	9218	9249	9280	9310	9341	9371
1912	9402	9433	9462	9493	9523	9554	9584	9615	9646	9676	9707	9737
1913	9768	9799	9827	9858	9888	9919	9949	9980	*0011	*0041	*0072	*0102
1914	242 0133	0164	0192	0223	0253	0284	0314	0345	0376	0406	0437	0467
1915	242 0498	0529	0557	0588	0618	0649	0679	0710	0741	0771	0802	0832
1916	0863	0894	0923	0954	0984	1015	1045	1076	1107	1137	1168	1198
1917	1229	1260	1288	1319	1349	1380	1410	1441	1472	1502	1533	1563
1918	1594	1625	1653	1684	1714	1745	1775	1806	1837	1867	1898	1928
1919	1959	1990	2018	2049	2079	2110	2140	2171	2202	2232	2263	2293
1920	242 2324	2355	2384	2415	2445	2476	2506	2537	2568	2598	2629	2659
1921	2690	2721	2749	2780	2810	2841	2871	2902	2933	2963	2994	3024
1922	3055	3086	3114	3145	3175	3206	3236	3267	3298	3328	3359	3389
1923	3420	3451	3479	3510	3540	3571	3601	3632	3663	3693	3724	3754
1924	3785	3816	3845	3876	3906	3937	3967	3998	4029	4059	4090	4120
1925	242 4151	4182	4210	4241	4271	4302	4332	4363	4394	4424	4455	4485
1926	4516	4547	4575	4606	4636	4667	4697	4728	4759	4789	4820	4850
1927	4881	4912	4940	4971	5001	5032	5062	5093	5124	5154	5185	5215
1928	5246	5277	5306	5337	5367	5398	5428	5459	5490	5520	5551	5581
1929	5612	5643	5671	5702	5732	5763	5793	5824	5855	5885	5916	5946
1930	242 5977	6008	6036	6067	6097	6128	6158	6189	6220	6250	6281	6311
1931	6342	6373	6401	6432	6462	6493	6523	6554	6585	6615	6646	6676
1932	6707	6738	6767	6798	6828	6859	6889	6920	6951	6981	7012	7042
1933	7073	7104	7132	7163	7193	7224	7254	7285	7316	7346	7377	7407
1934	7438	7469	7497	7528	7558	7589	7619	7650	7681	7711	7742	7772
1935	242 7803	7834	7862	7893	7923	7954	7984	8015	8046	8076	8107	8137
1936	8168	8199	8228	8259	8289	8320	8350	8381	8412	8442	8473	8503
1937	8534	8565	8593	8624	8654	8685	8715	8746	8777	8807	8838	8868
1938	8899	8930	8958	8989	9019	9050	9080	9111	9142	9172	9203	9233
1939	9264	9295	9323	9354	9384	9415	9445	9476	9507	9537	9568	9598
1940	242 9629	9660	9689	9720	9750	9781	9811	9842	9873	9903	9934	9964
1941	9995	*0026	*0054	*0085	*0115	*0146	*0176	*0207	*0238	*0268	*0299	*0329
1942	243 0360	0391	0419	0450	0480	0511	0541	0572	0603	0633	0664	0694
1943	0725	0756	0784	0815	0845	0876	0906	0937	0968	0998	1029	1059
1944	1090	1121	1150	1181	1211	1242	1272	1303	1334	1364	1395	1425
1945	243 1456	1487	1515	1546	1576	1607	1637	1668	1699	1729	1760	1790
1946	1821	1852	1880	1911	1941	1972	2002	2033	2064	2094	2125	2155
1947	2186	2217	2245	2276	2306	2337	2367	2398	2429	2459	2490	2520
1948	2551	2582	2611	2642	2672	2703	2733	2764	2795	2825	2856	2886
1949	2917	2948	2976	3007	3037	3068	3098	3129	3160	3190	3221	3251
1950	243 3282	3313	3341	3372	3402	3433	3463	3494	3525	3555	3586	3616

Table A1 continued.

JULIAN DAY NUMBER

DAYS ELAPSED AT GREENWICH NOON, A. D. 1950–2000

Year	Jan. 0	Feb. 0	Mar. 0	Apr. 0	May 0	June 0	July 0	Aug. 0	Sept. 0	Oct. 0	Nov. 0	Dec. 0
1950	243 3282	3313	3341	3372	3402	3433	3463	3494	3525	3555	3586	3616
1951	3647	3678	3706	3737	3767	3798	3828	3859	3890	3920	3951	3981
1952	4012	4043	4072	4103	4133	4164	4194	4225	4256	4286	4317	4347
1953	4378	4409	4437	4468	4498	4529	4559	4590	4621	4651	4682	4712
1954	4743	4774	4802	4833	4863	4894	4924	4955	4986	5016	5047	5077
1955	243 5108	5139	5167	5198	5228	5259	5289	5320	5351	5381	5412	5442
1956	5473	5504	5533	5564	5594	5625	5655	5686	5717	5747	5778	5808
1957	5839	5870	5898	5929	5959	5990	6020	6051	6082	6112	6143	6173
1958	6204	6235	6263	6294	6324	6355	6385	6416	6447	6477	6508	6538
1959	6569	6600	6628	6659	6689	6720	6750	6781	6812	6842	6873	6903
1960	243 6934	6965	6994	7025	7055	7086	7116	7147	7178	7208	7239	7269
1961	7300	7331	7359	7390	7420	7451	7481	7512	7543	7573	7604	7634
1962	7665	7696	7724	7755	7785	7816	7846	7877	7908	7938	7969	7999
1963	8030	8061	8089	8120	8150	8181	8211	8242	8273	8303	8334	8364
1964	8395	8426	8455	8486	8516	8547	8577	8608	8639	8669	8700	8730
1965	243 8761	8792	8820	8851	8881	8912	8942	8973	9004	9034	9065	9095
1966	9126	9157	9185	9216	9246	9277	9307	9338	9369	9399	9430	9460
1967	9491	9522	9550	9581	9611	9642	9672	9703	9734	9764	9795	9825
1968	9856	9887	9916	9947	9977	*0008	*0038	*0069	*0100	*0130	*0161	*0191
1969	244 0222	0253	0281	0312	0342	0373	0403	0434	0465	0495	0526	0556
1970	244 0587	0618	0646	0677	0707	0738	0768	0799	0830	0860	0891	0921
1971	0952	0983	1011	1042	1072	1103	1133	1164	1195	1225	1256	1286
1972	1317	1348	1377	1408	1438	1469	1499	1530	1561	1591	1622	1652
1973	1683	1714	1742	1773	1803	1834	1864	1895	1926	1956	1987	2017
1974	2048	2079	2107	2138	2168	2199	2229	2260	2291	2321	2352	2382
1975	244 2413	2444	2472	2503	2533	2564	2594	2625	2656	2686	2717	2747
1976	2778	2809	2838	2869	2899	2930	2960	2991	3022	3052	3083	3113
1977	3144	3175	3203	3234	3264	3295	3325	3356	3387	3417	3448	3478
1978	3509	3540	3568	3599	3629	3660	3690	3721	3752	3782	3813	3843
1979	3874	3905	3933	3964	3994	4025	4055	4086	4117	4147	4178	4208
1980	244 4239	4270	4299	4330	4360	4391	4421	4452	4483	4513	4544	4574
1981	4605	4636	4664	4695	4725	4756	4786	4817	4848	4878	4909	4939
1982	4970	5001	5029	5060	5090	5121	5151	5182	5213	5243	5274	5304
1983	5335	5366	5394	5425	5455	5486	5516	5547	5578	5608	5639	5669
1984	5700	5731	5760	5791	5821	5852	5882	5913	5944	5974	6005	6035
1985	244 6066	6097	6125	6156	6186	6217	6247	6278	6309	6339	6370	6400
1986	6431	6462	6490	6521	6551	6582	6612	6643	6674	6704	6735	6765
1987	6796	6827	6855	6886	6916	6947	6977	7008	7039	7069	7100	7130
1988	7161	7192	7221	7252	7282	7313	7343	7374	7405	7435	7466	7496
1989	7527	7558	7586	7617	7647	7678	7708	7739	7770	7800	7831	7861
1990	244 7892	7923	7951	7982	8012	8043	8073	8104	8135	8165	8196	8226
1991	8257	8288	8316	8347	8377	8408	8438	8469	8500	8530	8561	8591
1992	8622	8653	8682	8713	8743	8774	8804	8835	8866	8896	8927	8957
1993	8988	9019	9047	9078	9108	9139	9169	9200	9231	9261	9292	9322
1994	9353	9384	9412	9443	9473	9504	9534	9565	9596	9626	9657	9687
1995	244 9718	9749	9777	9808	9838	9869	9899	9930	9961	9991	*0022	*0052
1996	245 0083	0114	0143	0174	0204	0235	0265	0296	0327	0357	0388	0418
1997	0449	0480	0508	0539	0569	0600	0630	0661	0692	0722	0753	0783
1998	0814	0845	0873	0904	0934	0965	0995	1026	1057	1087	1118	1148
1999	1179	1210	1238	1269	1299	1330	1360	1391	1422	1452	1483	1513
2000	245 1544	1575	1604	1635	1665	1696	1726	1757	1788	1818	1849	1879

Table A2.
CONVERSION OF TIME TO ARC

m	0^h	1^h	2^h	3^h	4^h	5^h	SECONDS					
	° '	° '	° '	° '	° '	° '	s	' "	s	"	s	"
0	0 00	15 00	30 00	45 00	60 00	75 00	0	0 00	0.00	0.00	0.50	7.50
1	0 15	15 15	30 15	45 15	60 15	75 15	1	0 15	.01	0.15	.51	7.65
2	0 30	15 30	30 30	45 30	60 30	75 30	2	0 30	.02	0.30	.52	7.80
3	0 45	15 45	30 45	45 45	60 45	75 45	3	0 45	.03	0.45	.53	7.95
4	1 00	16 00	31 00	46 00	61 00	76 00	4	1 00	.04	0.60	.54	8.10
5	1 15	16 15	31 15	46 15	61 15	76 15	5	1 15	0.05	0.75	0.55	8.25
6	1 30	16 30	31 30	46 30	61 30	76 30	6	1 30	.06	0.90	.56	8.40
7	1 45	16 45	31 45	46 45	61 45	76 45	7	1 45	.07	1.05	.57	8.55
8	2 00	17 00	32 00	47 00	62 00	77 00	8	2 00	.08	1.20	.58	8.70
9	2 15	17 15	32 15	47 15	62 15	77 15	9	2 15	.09	1.35	.59	8.85
10	2 30	17 30	32 30	47 30	62 30	77 30	10	2 30	0.10	1.50	0.60	9.00
11	2 45	17 45	32 45	47 45	62 45	77 45	11	2 45	.11	1.65	.61	9.15
12	3 00	18 00	33 00	48 00	63 00	78 00	12	3 00	.12	1.80	.62	9.30
13	3 15	18 15	33 15	48 15	63 15	78 15	13	3 15	.13	1.95	.63	9.45
14	3 30	18 30	33 30	48 30	63 30	78 30	14	3 30	.14	2.10	.64	9.60
15	3 45	18 45	33 45	48 45	63 45	78 45	15	3 45	0.15	2.25	0.65	9.75
16	4 00	19 00	34 00	49 00	64 00	79 00	16	4 00	.16	2.40	.66	9.90
17	4 15	19 15	34 15	49 15	64 15	79 15	17	4 15	.17	2.55	.67	10.05
18	4 30	19 30	34 30	49 30	64 30	79 30	18	4 30	.18	2.70	.68	10.20
19	4 45	19 45	34 45	49 45	64 45	79 45	19	4 45	.19	2.85	.69	10.35
20	5 00	20 00	35 00	50 00	65 00	80 00	20	5 00	0.20	3.00	0.70	10.50
21	5 15	20 15	35 15	50 15	65 15	80 15	21	5 15	.21	3.15	.71	10.65
22	5 30	20 30	35 30	50 30	65 30	80 30	22	5 30	.22	3.30	.72	10.80
23	5 45	20 45	35 45	50 45	65 45	80 45	23	5 45	.23	3.45	.73	10.95
24	6 00	21 00	36 00	51 00	66 00	81 00	24	6 00	.24	3.60	.74	11.10
25	6 15	21 15	36 15	51 15	66 15	81 15	25	6 15	0.25	3.75	0.75	11.25
26	6 30	21 30	36 30	51 30	66 30	81 30	26	6 30	.26	3.90	.76	11.40
27	6 45	21 45	36 45	51 45	66 45	81 45	27	6 45	.27	4.05	.77	11.55
28	7 00	22 00	37 00	52 00	67 00	82 00	28	7 00	.28	4.20	.78	11.70
29	7 15	22 15	37 15	52 15	67 15	82 15	29	7 15	.29	4.35	.79	11.85
30	7 30	22 30	37 30	52 30	67 30	82 30	30	7 30	0.30	4.50	0.80	12.00
31	7 45	22 45	37 45	52 45	67 45	82 45	31	7 45	.31	4.65	.81	12.15
32	8 00	23 00	38 00	53 00	68 00	83 00	32	8 00	.32	4.80	.82	12.30
33	8 15	23 15	38 15	53 15	68 15	83 15	33	8 15	.33	4.95	.83	12.45
34	8 30	23 30	38 30	53 30	68 30	83 30	34	8 30	.34	5.10	.84	12.60
35	8 45	23 45	38 45	53 45	68 45	83 45	35	8 45	0.35	5.25	0.85	12.75
36	9 00	24 00	39 00	54 00	69 00	84 00	36	9 00	.36	5.40	.86	12.90
37	9 15	24 15	39 15	54 15	69 15	84 15	37	9 15	.37	5.55	.87	13.05
38	9 30	24 30	39 30	54 30	69 30	84 30	38	9 30	.38	5.70	.88	13.20
39	9 45	24 45	39 45	54 45	69 45	84 45	39	9 45	.39	5.85	.89	13.35
40	10 00	25 00	40 00	55 00	70 00	85 00	40	10 00	0.40	6.00	0.90	13.50
41	10 15	25 15	40 15	55 15	70 15	85 15	41	10 15	.41	6.15	.91	13.65
42	10 30	25 30	40 30	55 30	70 30	85 30	42	10 30	.42	6.30	.92	13.80
43	10 45	25 45	40 45	55 45	70 45	85 45	43	10 45	.43	6.45	.93	13.95
44	11 00	26 00	41 00	56 00	71 00	86 00	44	11 00	.44	6.60	.94	14.10
45	11 15	26 15	41 15	56 15	71 15	86 15	45	11 15	0.45	6.75	0.95	14.25
46	11 30	26 30	41 30	56 30	71 30	86 30	46	11 30	.46	6.90	.96	14.40
47	11 45	26 45	41 45	56 45	71 45	86 45	47	11 45	.47	7.05	.97	14.55
48	12 00	27 00	42 00	57 00	72 00	87 00	48	12 00	.48	7.20	.98	14.70
49	12 15	27 15	42 15	57 15	72 15	87 15	49	12 15	.49	7.35	0.99	14.85
50	12 30	27 30	42 30	57 30	72 30	87 30	50	12 30	0.50	7.50	1.00	15.00
51	12 45	27 45	42 45	57 45	72 45	87 45	51	12 45				
52	13 00	28 00	43 00	58 00	73 00	88 00	52	13 00				
53	13 15	28 15	43 15	58 15	73 15	88 15	53	13 15				
54	13 30	28 30	43 30	58 30	73 30	88 30	54	13 30				
55	13 45	28 45	43 45	58 45	73 45	88 45	55	13 45				
56	14 00	29 00	44 00	59 00	74 00	89 00	56	14 00				
57	14 15	29 15	44 15	59 15	74 15	89 15	57	14 15				
58	14 30	29 30	44 30	59 30	74 30	89 30	58	14 30				
59	14 45	29 45	44 45	59 45	74 45	89 45	59	14 45				

$6^h = 90°$

$12^h = 180°$

$18^h = 270°$

Table A3.

CONVERSION OF ARC TO TIME

DEGREES						MINUTES		SECONDS					
°	h m	°	h m	°	h m	′	m s	″	s	″	s	″	s
0	0 00	60	4 00	120	8 00	0	0 00	0	0.000	0.00	0.000	0.50	0.033
1	0 04	61	4 04	121	8 04	1	0 04	1	0.067	.01	.001	.51	.034
2	0 08	62	4 08	122	8 08	2	0 08	2	0.133	.02	.001	.52	.035
3	0 12	63	4 12	123	8 12	3	0 12	3	0.200	.03	.002	.53	.035
4	0 16	64	4 16	124	8 16	4	0 16	4	0.267	.04	.003	.54	.036
5	0 20	65	4 20	125	8 20	5	0 20	5	0.333	0.05	0.003	0.55	0.037
6	0 24	66	4 24	126	8 24	6	0 24	6	0.400	.06	.004	.56	.037
7	0 28	67	4 28	127	8 28	7	0 28	7	0.467	.07	.005	.57	.038
8	0 32	68	4 32	128	8 32	8	0 32	8	0.533	.08	.005	.58	.039
9	0 36	69	4 36	129	8 36	9	0 36	9	0.600	.09	.006	.59	.039
10	0 40	70	4 40	130	8 40	10	0 40	10	0.667	0.10	0.007	0.60	0.040
11	0 44	71	4 44	131	8 44	11	0 44	11	0.733	.11	.007	.61	.041
12	0 48	72	4 48	132	8 48	12	0 48	12	0.800	.12	.008	.62	.041
13	0 52	73	4 52	133	8 52	13	0 52	13	0.867	.13	.009	.63	.042
14	0 56	74	4 56	134	8 56	14	0 56	14	0.933	.14	.009	.64	.043
15	1 00	75	5 00	135	9 00	15	1 00	15	1.000	0.15	0.010	0.65	0.043
16	1 04	76	5 04	136	9 04	16	1 04	16	1.067	.16	.011	.66	.044
17	1 08	77	5 08	137	9 08	17	1 08	17	1.133	.17	.011	.67	.045
18	1 12	78	5 12	138	9 12	18	1 12	18	1.200	.18	.012	.68	.045
19	1 16	79	5 16	139	9 16	19	1 16	19	1.267	.19	.013	.69	.046
20	1 20	80	5 20	140	9 20	20	1 20	20	1.333	0.20	0.013	0.70	0.047
21	1 24	81	5 24	141	9 24	21	1 24	21	1.400	.21	.014	.71	.047
22	1 28	82	5 28	142	9 28	22	1 28	22	1.467	.22	.015	.72	.048
23	1 32	83	5 32	143	9 32	23	1 32	23	1.533	.23	.015	.73	.049
24	1 36	84	5 36	144	9 36	24	1 36	24	1.600	.24	.016	.74	.049
25	1 40	85	5 40	145	9 40	25	1 40	25	1.667	0.25	0.017	0.75	0.050
26	1 44	86	5 44	146	9 44	26	1 44	26	1.733	.26	.017	.76	.051
27	1 48	87	5 48	147	9 48	27	1 48	27	1.800	.27	.018	.77	.051
28	1 52	88	5 52	148	9 52	28	1 52	28	1.867	.28	.019	.78	.052
29	1 56	89	5 56	149	9 56	29	1 56	29	1.933	.29	.019	.79	.053
30	2 00	90	6 00	150	10 00	30	2 00	30	2.000	0.30	0.020	0.80	0.053
31	2 04	91	6 04	151	10 04	31	2 04	31	2.067	.31	.021	.81	.054
32	2 08	92	6 08	152	10 08	32	2 08	32	2.133	.32	.021	.82	.055
33	2 12	93	6 12	153	10 12	33	2 12	33	2.200	.33	.022	.83	.055
34	2 16	94	6 16	154	10 16	34	2 16	34	2.267	.34	.023	.84	.056
35	2 20	95	6 20	155	10 20	35	2 20	35	2.333	0.35	0.023	0.85	0.057
36	2 24	96	6 24	156	10 24	36	2 24	36	2.400	.36	.024	.86	.057
37	2 28	97	6 28	157	10 28	37	2 28	37	2.467	.37	.025	.87	.058
38	2 32	98	6 32	158	10 32	38	2 32	38	2.533	.38	.025	.88	.059
39	2 36	99	6 36	159	10 36	39	2 36	39	2.600	.39	.026	.89	.059
40	2 40	100	6 40	160	10 40	40	2 40	40	2.667	0.40	0.027	0.90	0.060
41	2 44	101	6 44	161	10 44	41	2 44	41	2.733	.41	.027	.91	.061
42	2 48	102	6 48	162	10 48	42	2 48	42	2.800	.42	.028	.92	.061
43	2 52	103	6 52	163	10 52	43	2 52	43	2.867	.43	.029	.93	.062
44	2 56	104	6 56	164	10 56	44	2 56	44	2.933	.44	.029	.94	.063
45	3 00	105	7 00	165	11 00	45	3 00	45	3.000	0.45	0.030	0.95	0.063
46	3 04	106	7 04	166	11 04	46	3 04	46	3.067	.46	.031	.96	.064
47	3 08	107	7 08	167	11 08	47	3 08	47	3.133	.47	.031	.97	.065
48	3 12	108	7 12	168	11 12	48	3 12	48	3.200	.48	.032	.98	.065
49	3 16	109	7 16	169	11 16	49	3 16	49	3.267	.49	.033	0.99	.066
50	3 20	110	7 20	170	11 20	50	3 20	50	3.333	0.50	0.033	1.00	0.067
51	3 24	111	7 24	171	11 24	51	3 24	51	3.400				
52	3 28	112	7 28	172	11 28	52	3 28	52	3.467				
53	3 32	113	7 32	173	11 32	53	3 32	53	3.533				
54	3 36	114	7 36	174	11 36	54	3 36	54	3.600				
55	3 40	115	7 40	175	11 40	55	3 40	55	3.667				
56	3 44	116	7 44	176	11 44	56	3 44	56	3.733				
57	3 48	117	7 48	177	11 48	57	3 48	57	3.800				
58	3 52	118	7 52	178	11 52	58	3 52	58	3.867				
59	3 56	119	7 56	179	11 56	59	3 56	59	3.933				

$90° = 6^h$

$180° = 12^h$

$270° = 18^h$

www.ingramcontent.com/pod-product-compliance
Ingram Content Group UK Ltd.
Pitfield, Milton Keynes, MK11 3LW, UK
UKHW041422180426
11947UKWH00007B/243

9 780866 900492